# Chef Infrastructure Automation Cookbook
## Second Edition

Over 80 recipes to automate your cloud and server infrastructure with Chef and its associated toolset

**Matthias Marschall**

PUBLISHING

BIRMINGHAM - MUMBAI

# Chef Infrastructure Automation Cookbook
## Second Edition

First published: August 2013

Second edition: May 2015

Production reference: 1260515

Published by Packt Publishing Ltd.
Livery Place
35 Livery Street
Birmingham B3 2PB, UK.

ISBN 978-1-78528-794-7

www.packtpub.com

# Credits

**Author**

Matthias Marschall

**Reviewers**

Robert Curth

Kristian Hoffmann

Max Manders

Greg Swallow

Earl Waud

**Commissioning Editor**

Ashwin Nair

**Acquisition Editor**

Vinay Argekar

**Content Development Editor**

Rohit Kumar Singh

**Technical Editor**

Naveenkumar Jain

**Copy Editor**

Adithi Shetty

**Project Coordinator**

Izzat Contractor

**Proofreaders**

Stephen Copestake

Safis Editing

**Indexer**

Priya Sane

**Production Coordinator**

Komal Ramchandani

**Cover Work**

Komal Ramchandani

# About the Author

**Matthias Marschall** is a software engineer "Made in Germany" and the author of the *Chef Infrastructure Automation Cookbook* by Packt Publishing. His four children make sure that he feels comfortable and stays in control of chaotic situations. A lean and Agile engineering lead, he's passionate about continuous delivery, infrastructure automation, and all things DevOps.

In recent years, Matthias has helped build several web-based businesses, first with Java and then with Ruby on Rails. He quickly moved into system administration, writing his own configuration management tool before moving his whole infrastructure to Chef in its early days.

In 2008, he started a blog (http://www.agileweboperations.com) with Dan Ackerson. There, they shared their ideas about DevOps since the early days of the continually emerging movement. You can fid him on Twitter at @mmarschall.

Matthias is the CTO of www.gutefrage.net GmbH that helps run Germany's biggest Q&A site among other high traffic sites. He holds a master's degree in computer science [Dipl.-Inf. (FH)] and teaches courses on Agile software development at the University of Augsburg.

When not writing or coding, Matthias enjoys drawing cartoons and playing Go. He lives near Munich, Germany.

Thanks go to my colleagues at gutefrage.net for all those valuable discussions.

I would also like to thank Adam Jacob, Joshua Timberman, and all the other great people at Chef, Inc. for your help with this book.

Special thanks go to my reviewers, Earl Waud, Greg Swallow, Max Manders, and Robert Curth, who made this book so much better.

# About the Reviewers

**Robert Curth** is an engineer at gutefrage gruppe. In his current project, HELPSTER, Chef is used to automate the server setup. When Robert is not programming, he organizes company events and talks about how to live a good life on his blog at `http://rocu.de`.

> I want to thank all the amazing authors of Chef cookbooks and tools. Chef has come a long way since the first edition of this book!
>
> Thanks, Matthias, for updating this book. I love how elegant many of these recipes are. I hope you, dear reader, enjoy them as much as I did!

**Kristian Hoffmann** is the sort of twisted individual who likes hacking code (in Perl, if possible) and cars (the smaller and faster, the better) and solving problems that would lead other people to throw their hands up in despair. After some early experimentation with Linux (circa Slackware 3.0), his tech career started as a lowly tech at a local ISP. He went on to complete his bachelor's in computer science, marry a fellow technophile, and rise to the ranks of the president/CTO in his adolescent ISP hacking grounds. He now enjoys the most significant challenge of raising two hopelessly tech-bound children.

**Max Manders** is a recovering PHP developer and former sysadmin, who currently works as a systems developer and ops engineer helping to run the Operations Centre for Cloudreach, an Amazon Web Services Premier Consulting Partner. Max has put his past experiences and skills to good use to evangelize all things DevOps, working to master Ruby and advocating infrastructure-as-code as a Chef practitioner.

Max is a cofounder and organizer of Whisky Web, a Scottish conference for the web development and ops community. When he's not writing code or tinkering with the latest and greatest monitoring and operations tools, Max enjoys the odd whisky and playing jazz and funk trombone. He lives in Edinburgh with his wife, Jo, and their cats, Ziggy and Maggie.

It's been an absolute pleasure to have the opportunity to provide a technical review of this book. I hope you enjoy reading it as much as I did! Thank you, Jo, for putting up with my mutterings and ignorance while I tinkered with the code in this book. And thank you, Shona, for sharing the load at work, affording me time to get this done!

**Greg Swallow** has been wrangling with all sorts of computers in the Indianapolis area for 20 years now, for folks like IN.gov, Expedient Data Centers, Salesforce, and Indigo BioAutomation. When he's not playing digital plumber, you can catch him on the roads and trails of Indiana, either on his bike or in his running shoes.

He has also reviewed *VMware vSphere 5.x Datacenter Design Cookbook* by *Hersey Cartwright, Packt Publishing*.

I would also like to thank Packt Publishing for offering me the opportunity to review this and other books. It's been fun!

**Earl Waud** is a Virtualization Development Professional with more than 9 years of focused industry experience creating innovative solutions for hypervisor provisioning, management, and automation. He is an expert in aligning engineering strategy with organizational vision and goals and delivering highly scalable and user-friendly virtualization environments.

With more than 20 years of experience developing customer-facing and corporate IT software solutions, Earl has a proven track record of delivering high-caliber and on-time technology solutions that significantly impact business results.

Earl lives in San Diego, California. He is blessed with a beautiful wife, Patti, and three amazing daughters, Madison, Daniella, and Alexis.

---

Thank you, my wonderful family, for allowing me to spend some of our precious family time to review this book. I love you and appreciate you, and I know I am truly blessed that you are my family.

---

Currently, Earl is a senior systems engineer with Intuit Inc., a company that creates business and financial management solutions that simplify the business of life for small businesses, consumers, and accounting professionals.

Earl can be reached online at `http://sandiegoearl.com`.

# www.PacktPub.com

## Support files, eBooks, discount offers, and more

For support files and downloads related to your book, please visit www.PacktPub.com.

Did you know that Packt offers eBook versions of every book published, with PDF and ePub files available? You can upgrade to the eBook version at www.PacktPub.com and as a print book customer, you are entitled to a discount on the eBook copy. Get in touch with us at service@packtpub.com for more details.

At www.PacktPub.com, you can also read a collection of free technical articles, sign up for a range of free newsletters and receive exclusive discounts and offers on Packt books and eBooks.

https://www2.packtpub.com/books/subscription/packtlib

Do you need instant solutions to your IT questions? PacktLib is Packt's online digital book library. Here, you can search, access, and read Packt's entire library of books.

## Why subscribe?

- Fully searchable across every book published by Packt
- Copy and paste, print, and bookmark content
- On demand and accessible via a web browser

## Free access for Packt account holders

If you have an account with Packt at www.PacktPub.com, you can use this to access PacktLib today and view 9 entirely free books. Simply use your login credentials for immediate access.

# Table of Contents

# Preface

Irrespective of whether you're a systems administrator or developer, if you're sick and tired of repetitive manual work and don't know whether you may dare to reboot your server, it's time for you to get your infrastructure automated.

This book has all the required recipes to configure, deploy, and scale your servers and applications, irrespective of whether you manage five servers, 5,000 servers, or 500,000 servers.

It is a collection of easy-to-follow, step-by-step recipes showing you how to solve real-world automation challenges. Learn techniques from the pros and make sure you get your infrastructure automation project right the first time.

This book takes you on a journey through the many facets of Chef. It teaches you simple techniques as well as full-fledged real-world solutions. By looking at easily digestible examples, you'll be able to grasp the main concepts of Chef, which you'll need to automate your own infrastructure. Instead of wasting time trying to get the existing community cookbooks running in your environment, you'll get ready-made code examples to get you started.

After describing how to use the basic Chef tools, the book shows you how to troubleshoot your work and explains the Chef language. Then, it shows you how to manage users, applications, and your whole Cloud infrastructure. The book concludes by providing you with additional, indispensable tools, and giving you an in-depth look into the Chef ecosystem.

Learn the techniques of the pros by walking through a host of step-by-step guides to solve your real-world infrastructure automation challenges.

## What this book covers

*Chapter 1*, *Chef Infrastructure*, helps you to get started with Chef. It explains some key concepts, such as cookbooks, roles, and environments, and shows you how to use some basic tools like the Chef development kit (ChefDK), such as Git, knife, chef shell, Vagrant, and Berkshelf.

*Chapter 2, Evaluating and Troubleshooting Cookbooks and Chef Runs*, is all about getting your cookbooks right. It covers logging and debugging as well as the why run mode, and shows you how to develop your cookbooks totally test driven.

*Chapter 3, Chef Language and Style*, covers additional Chef concepts, such as attributes, templates, libraries, and even Light Weight Resource Providers. It shows you how to use plain old Ruby inside your recipes and ends with writing your own Ohai and knife plugins.

*Chapter 4, Writing Better Cookbooks*, shows you how to make your cookbooks more flexible. It covers ways to override attributes, use data bags and search, and to make your cookbooks idempotent. Writing cross-platform cookbooks is covered as well.

*Chapter 5, Working with Files and Packages*, covers powerful techniques to manage configuration files, and install and manage software packages. It shows you how to install software from source and how to manage whole directory trees.

*Chapter 6, Users and Applications*, shows you how to manage user accounts, securing SSH and configuring sudo. Then, it walks you through installing complete applications, such as nginx, MySQL, WordPress, Ruby on Rails, and Varnish. It ends by showing you how to manage your own OS X workstation with Chef.

*Chapter 7, Servers and Cloud Infrastructure*, deals with networking and applications spanning multiple servers. You'll learn how to create your whole infrastructure using Chef provisioning. Then it shows you how to set up high-availability services and load-balancers, and how to monitor your whole infrastructure with Nagios. Finally, it'll show you how to manage your Amazon EC2 Cloud with Chef.

# What you need for this book

To run the examples in this book, you'll need a computer running OS X or Ubuntu Linux 14.04. The examples will use Sublime Text (http://www.sublimetext.com/) as the editor. Make sure you configured Sublime text command-line tool subl to follow along smoothly.

It helps if you have Ruby 2.1.0 with bundler (http://bundler.io/) installed on your system as well.

# Who this book is for

This book is for system engineers and administrators who have a fundamental understanding of information management systems and infrastructure. It helps if you've already played around with Chef; however, this book covers all the important topics you will need to know. If you don't want to dig through a whole book before you can get started, this book is for you, as it features a set of independent recipes you can try out immediately.

# Sections

In this book, you will find several headings that appear frequently (Getting ready, How to do it..., How it works..., There's more..., and See also).

To give clear instructions on how to complete a recipe, we use these sections as follows:

## Getting ready

This section tells you what to expect in the recipe and describes how to set up any software or preliminary settings required for the recipe.

## How to do it...

This section contains the steps required to follow the recipe.

## How it works...

This section usually consists of a detailed explanation of what happened in the previous section.

## There's more...

This section consists of additional information about the recipe in order to make the reader more knowledgeable about the recipe.

## See also

This section provides helpful links to other useful information for the recipe.

# Conventions

In this book, you will find a number of text styles that distinguish between different kinds of information. Here are some examples of these styles and an explanation of their meaning.

Code words in text, database table names, folder names, filenames, file extensions, pathnames, dummy URLs, user input, and Twitter handles are shown as follows: "The omnibus installer will download Ruby and all required Ruby gems into `/opt/chef/embedded`."

A block of code is set as follows:

```
name "web_servers"
description "This role contains nodes, which act as web servers"
run_list "recipe[ntp]"
default_attributes 'ntp' => {
  'ntpdate' => {
    'disable' => true
  }
}
```

When we wish to draw your attention to a particular part of a code block, the relevant lines or items are set in bold:

```
name "web_servers"
description "This role contains nodes, which act as web servers"
run_list "recipe[ntp]"
default_attributes 'ntp' => {
  'ntpdate' => {
    'disable' => true
  }
}
```

Any command-line input or output is written as follows:

**mma@laptop:~/chef-repo $ knife role from file web_servers.rb**

**New terms** and **important words** are shown in bold. Words that you see on the screen, for example, in menus or dialog boxes, appear in the text like this: "Open http://requestb.in in your browser and click on **Create a RequestBin**."

 Warnings or important notes appear in a box like this.

 Tips and tricks appear like this.

# Reader feedback

Feedback from our readers is always welcome. Let us know what you think about this book—what you liked or disliked. Reader feedback is important for us as it helps us develop titles that you will really get the most out of.

To send us general feedback, simply e-mail `feedback@packtpub.com`, and mention the book's title in the subject of your message.

If there is a topic that you have expertise in and you are interested in either writing or contributing to a book, see our author guide at `www.packtpub.com/authors`.

# Customer support

Now that you are the proud owner of a Packt book, we have a number of things to help you to get the most from your purchase.

## Errata

Although we have taken every care to ensure the accuracy of our content, mistakes do happen. If you find a mistake in one of our books—maybe a mistake in the text or the code—we would be grateful if you could report this to us. By doing so, you can save other readers from frustration and help us improve subsequent versions of this book. If you find any errata, please report them by visiting `http://www.packtpub.com/submit-errata`, selecting your book, clicking on the **Errata Submission Form** link, and entering the details of your errata. Once your errata are verified, your submission will be accepted and the errata will be uploaded to our website or added to any list of existing errata under the Errata section of that title.

To view the previously submitted errata, go to `https://www.packtpub.com/books/content/support` and enter the name of the book in the search field. The required information will appear under the **Errata** section.

## Piracy

Piracy of copyrighted material on the Internet is an ongoing problem across all media. At Packt, we take the protection of our copyright and licenses very seriously. If you come across any illegal copies of our works in any form on the Internet, please provide us with the location address or website name immediately so that we can pursue a remedy.

Please contact us at `copyright@packtpub.com` with a link to the suspected pirated material.

We appreciate your help in protecting our authors and our ability to bring you valuable content.

## Questions

If you have a problem with any aspect of this book, you can contact us at `questions@packtpub.com`, and we will do our best to address the problem.

# 1

# Chef Infrastructure

*"What made Manhattan Manhattan was the underground infrastructure, that engineering marvel."*

*Andrew Cuomo*

A well-engineered infrastructure builds the basis for successful companies. In this chapter, we will see how to set up the infrastructure around Chef as the basis of your infrastructure as code. We'll cover the following recipes in this chapter:

- ▸ Using version control
- ▸ Installing the Chef development kit on your workstation
- ▸ Using the hosted Chef platform
- ▸ Managing virtual machines with Vagrant
- ▸ Creating and using cookbooks
- ▸ Inspecting files on your Chef server with knife
- ▸ Defining cookbook dependencies
- ▸ Managing cookbook dependencies with Berkshelf
- ▸ Downloading and integrating cookbooks as vendor branches into your Git repository
- ▸ Using custom knife plugins
- ▸ Deleting a node from the Chef server
- ▸ Developing recipes with local mode
- ▸ Using roles
- ▸ Using environments
- ▸ Freezing cookbooks
- ▸ Running Chef client as a daemon
- ▸ Using chef-shell

# Introduction

This chapter will cover the basics of Chef, including common terminology, workflow practices, and various tools that work in accordance with Chef. We will explore version control using Git, walk through working with community cookbooks, and running those cookbooks on your own servers, so that you can configure them in the way you need them.

First, let's talk about some important terms used in the Chef universe.

A cookbook is a collection of all the components needed to change something on a server, such as installing MySQL, the most important one being recipes, which tell Chef which resources you want to configure on your host.

You need to deploy cookbooks to the nodes that you want to change. Chef offers multiple ways for this task. Most probably, you'll use a central **Chef server**. You can either run your own server or sign up for **hosted Chef**.

The Chef server is the central registry, where each node needs to be registered. The Chef server distributes the cookbooks you uploaded to it, to your nodes.

**Knife** is Chef's command-line tool to interact with the Chef server. You run it on your local workstation and use it to upload cookbooks and manage other aspects of Chef.

On your nodes, you need to install **Chef client**—the part that retrieves the cookbooks from the Chef server and executes them on the node.

In this chapter, we'll see the basic infrastructure components of your Chef setup at work and learn how to use the basic tools. Let's get started by taking a look at how to use Git as a version control system for your cookbooks.

# Using version control

Do you manually back up every file before you change it? And do you invent creative file name extensions such as _me and _you when you try to collaborate a file? If you answer yes to any of these, it's time to rethink your processes.

A **version control system** (**VCS**) helps you stay sane when dealing with important files and collaborating with them.

Using version control is a fundamental part of any infrastructure automation. There are multiple solutions (some free, some paid) to manage source version control, including Git, SVN, Mercurial, and Perforce. Due to its popularity among the Chef community, we will be using Git. However, you could easily use any other version control system with Chef.

Don't even think about building your infrastructure as code without using a version control system to manage it!

## Getting ready

You'll need Git installed on your local workstation. Either use your operating system's package manager (such as Apt on Ubuntu or Homebrew on OS X), or simply download the installer from www.git-scm.org.

Git is a distributed version control system. This means that you don't necessarily need a central host to store your repositories. However, in practice, using GitHub as your central repository has proven to be very helpful. In this book, I'll assume that you're using GitHub. Therefore, you need to go to www.github.com and create an (free) account to follow the instructions given in this book. Make sure that you upload your Secure Shell (SSH) key by following the instructions at https://help.github.com/articles/generating-ssh-keys, so that you're able to use the SSH protocol to interact with your GitHub account.

As soon as you have created your GitHub account, you should create your repository by visiting https://github.com/new while you're still logged in and using chef-repo as the repository name.

Make sure you have wget installed on your local workstation, in order to be able to download the required files from public servers.

## How to do it...

Before you can write any cookbooks, you need to set up your initial Git repository on your development box. Chef Software, Inc. provides an empty Chef repository to get you started. Let's see how you can set up your own Chef repository with Git, using Chef's skeleton.

1. Download Chef's skeleton repository as a tarball:

   ```
   mma@laptop $ wget http://github.com/chef/chef-repo/tarball/master
   ...TRUNCATED OUTPUT...
   2014-11-30 22:00:43 (1.30 MB/s) - 'master' saved [9309/9309]
   ```

2. Extract the downloaded tarball:

   ```
   mma@laptop $ tar xzvf master
   ```

3. Rename the directory:

   ```
   mma@laptop:~ $ mv opscode-chef-repo-* chef-repo
   ```

4. Change to your newly created Chef repository:

   ```
   mma@laptop:~ $ cd chef-repo/
   ```

5. Initialize a fresh Git repository:

   ```
   mma@laptop:~/chef-repo $ git init .
   Initialized empty Git repository in /Users/mma/work/chef-repo/.
   git/
   ```

6. Connect your local repository to your remote repository on github.com. Make sure to replace mmarschall with your own GitHub username:

   ```
   mma@laptop:~/chef-repo $ git remote add origin git@github.
   com:mmarschall/chef-repo.git
   ```

7. Configure Git with your user name and e-mail address:

   ```
   mma@laptop:~/chef-repo $ git config --global user.email "you@
   example.com"

   mma@laptop:~/chef-repo $ git config --global user.name "Your Name"
   ```

8. Add and commit Chef's default directory structure:

   ```
   mma@laptop:~/chef-repo $ git add .

   mma@laptop:~/chef-repo $ git commit -m "initial commit"

   [master (root-commit) 6148b20] initial commit
    11 files changed, 545 insertions(+), 0 deletions(-)
    create mode 100644 .gitignore
   ...TRUNCATED OUTPUT...
   create mode 100644 roles/README.md
   ```

9. Push your initialized repository to GitHub. This makes it available to all your co-workers to collaborate on:

   ```
   mma@laptop:~/chef-repo $ git push -u origin master

   ...TRUNCATED OUTPUT...
   To git@github.com:mmarschall/chef-repo.git
    * [new branch]      master -> master
   ```

## How it works...

You have downloaded a tarball containing Chef's skeleton repository. Then, you initialized chef-repo and connected it to your own repository on GitHub.

After that, you added all the files from the tarball to your repository and committed them. This makes Git track your files and the changes you make later.

Finally, you pushed your repository to GitHub, so that your co-workers can use your code too.

## There's more...

Let's assume you're working on the same `chef-repo` repository, together with your co-workers. They cloned your repository, added a new cookbook called `other_cookbook`, committed their changes locally, and pushed their changes back to GitHub. Now, it's time for you to get the new cookbook downloaded on to your own laptop.

Pull your co-workers' changes from GitHub. This will merge their changes into your local copy of the repository. Use the `pull` subcommand:

**mma@laptop:~/chef-repo $ git pull --rebase**

```
From github.com:mmarschall/chef-repo
 * branch            master      -> FETCH_HEAD
...TRUNCATED OUTPUT...
create mode 100644 cookbooks/other_cookbook/recipes/default.rb
```

In case of any conflicting changes, Git will help you merge and resolve them.

## See also

- Learn about Git basics at `http://git-scm.com/videos`
- Walk through the basic steps using GitHub at `https://help.github.com/categories/54/articles`
- You'll use more Git features in the *Downloading and integrating cookbooks as vendor branches into your Git repository* recipe in this chapter

# Installing the Chef development kit on your workstation

If you want to use Chef, you'll need to install the **Chef development kit (DK)** on your local workstation first. You'll have to develop your configurations locally and use Chef to distribute them to your Chef server.

Chef provides a fully packaged version, which does not have any external prerequisites. This fully packaged Chef is called the **omnibus installer**. We'll see how to use it in this section.

## How to do it...

Let's see how to install the Chef DK on your local workstation using Chef's omnibus installer:

1. Download the Chef DK for your specific workstation platform from `https://downloads.chef.io/chef-dk/` and run the installer.

2. Verify that Chef installed all the required components:

```
mma@laptop:~ $ chef verify
...TRUNCATED OUTPUT...
Verification of component 'rubocop' succeeded.
Verification of component 'kitchen-vagrant' succeeded.
Verification of component 'chefspec' succeeded.
Verification of component 'berkshelf' succeeded.
Verification of component 'fauxhai' succeeded.
Verification of component 'test-kitchen' succeeded.
Verification of component 'package installation' succeeded.
Verification of component 'chef-dk' succeeded.
Verification of component 'knife-spork' succeeded.
Verification of component 'chef-client' succeeded.
```

3. Add the newly installed Ruby to your path:

```
mma@laptop:~ $ echo 'export PATH="/opt/chefdk/embedded/bin:$PATH"'
>> ~/.bash_profile && source ~/.bash_profile
```

> You may not want to use (and don't have to use) ChefDK's Ruby, especially if you are a Rails Developer.
>
> If you're happily using your Ruby `rvm`, or `rbenv` environment, you can continue to do so. Just ensure that the ChefDK-provided applications appear first in your `PATH`, before any gem-installed versions, and you're good to go.

## How it works...

The omnibus installer will download Ruby and all required Ruby gems into `/opt/chefdk`.

## See also

- Find detailed instructions for OS X, Linux, and Windows at `https://learn.chef.io`
- Find ChefDK on GitHub at `https://github.com/opscode/chef-dk`

# Using the hosted Chef platform

If you want to get started with Chef right away (without the need to install your own Chef server) or want a third party to give you a **Service Level Agreement** (**SLA**) for your Chef server, you can sign up for hosted Chef by Chef Software, Inc. Chef Software, Inc. operates Chef as a cloud service. It's quick to set up and gives you full control, using users and groups to control the access permissions to your Chef setup. We'll configure knife, Chef's command-line tool to interact with hosted Chef, so that you can start managing your nodes.

## Getting ready

Before being able to use hosted Chef, you need to sign up for the service. There is a free account for up to five nodes.

Visit `http://manage.chef.io/signup` and register for a free trial or a free account.

I registered as the user `webops` with an organization short name of `awo`.

After registering your account, it is time now to prepare your organization to be used with your `chef-repo` repository.

## How to do it...

Carry out the following steps in order to interact with the hosted Chef:

1.  Create the configuration directory for your Chef client on your local workstation:

    **mma@laptop:~/chef-repo $ mkdir .chef**

2.  Navigate to `http://manage.chef.io/organizations`. After logging in, you can start downloading your validation keys and configuration file.

3.  Select your organization to be able to see its contents using the web UI.

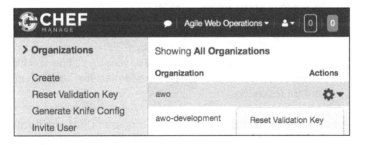

Regenerate the validation key for your organization and save it as `<your-organization-short-name>-validator.pem` in the `chef` directory inside your `chef-repo` repository.

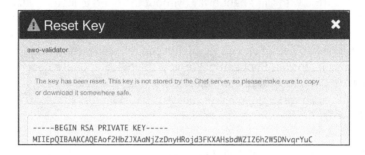

4. Generate the `knife` config and put the downloaded `knife.rb` into the `.chef` directory inside your `chef-repo` directory, as well. Make sure you have downloaded your user's private key from `https://www.chef.io/account/password` and replace `webops` with the username you chose for hosted Chef, and `awo` with the short name you chose for your organization:

```
current_dir = File.dirname(__FILE__)
log_level                  :info
log_location               STDOUT
node_name                  "webops"
client_key                 "#{current_dir}/webops.pem"
validation_client_name     "awo-validator"
validation_key             "#{current_dir}/awo-validator.pem"
chef_server_url            "https://api.chef.io/organizations/awo"
cache_type                 'BasicFile'
cache_options( :path =>    "#{ENV['HOME']}/.chef/checksums" )
cookbook_path              ["#{current_dir}/../cookbooks"]
```

Take a look at the following code:

> `.chef/*.pem`
>
> `.chef/encrypted_data_bag_secret`

You should add the preceding code to your `.gitingore` file inside `chef-repo` to avoid your credentials from ending up in your Git repository.

5. Use knife to verify that you can connect to your hosted Chef organization. It should only have your validator client, so far. Instead of `awo`, you'll see your organization's short name:

```
mma@laptop:~/chef-repo $ knife client list
awo-validator
```

## How it works...

Hosted Chef uses two private keys (called validators):

- ▶ one for the organization
- ▶ one for every user.

You need to tell knife where it can find these two keys in your `knife.rb` file.

The following two lines of code in your `knife.rb` file tell the knife about which organization to use and where to find its private key. The `validation_key` is used to allow new clients to authenticate the Chef server before getting their own Client key:

```
validation_client_name    "awo-validator"
validation_key            "#{current_dir}/awo-validator.pem"
```

The following line of code in your `knife.rb` file tells the knife where to find your users' private key. It is used by your local workstation to authenticate the Chef server:

```
client_key                "#{current_dir}/webops.pem"
```

Also, the following line of code in your `knife.rb` file tells knife that you are using hosted Chef. You will find your organization name as the last part of the URL:

```
chef_server_url           "https://api.chef.io/organizations/awo"
```

Using the `knife.rb` file and your two validators knife, you can now connect to your organization hosted by Chef Software, Inc.

You do not need your own self-hosted Chef server, nor do you need to use Chef client local mode in this setup.

## There's more...

This setup is good for you if you do not want to worry about running, scaling, and updating your own Chef server and if you're happy with saving all your configuration data in the Cloud (under the control of Chef Software, Inc.).

 If you need to have all your configuration data within your own network boundaries, you can install Chef server on premises by choosing "ON PREMISES CHEF" at `https://www.chef.io/chef/choose-your-version/` or install the Open Source version of Chef server directly from GitHub at `https://github.com/chef/chef`.

## See also

> ▸ Learn more about the various Chef products at `https://www.chef.io/chef/`
>
> ▸ You can find the source code of the Chef server on GitHub at `https://github.com/chef/chef`

# Managing virtual machines with Vagrant

Developing Chef cookbooks requires you to run your work in progress cookbooks multiple times on your nodes. To make sure they work, you need a clean, initial state of your nodes every time you run them. You can achieve this by using a **virtual machine** (**VM**). However, manually setting up and destroying VMs is tedious and breaks your development flow.

Vagrant is a command-line tool, which provides you with a configurable, reproducible, and portable development environment by enabling you to manage VMs. It lets you define and use preconfigured disk images to create new VMs from. Also, you can configure Vagrant to use provisioners such as Shell scripts, Puppet, or Chef to bring your VM into the desired state.

In this recipe, we will see how to use Vagrant to manage VMs using VirtualBox and Chef client as the provisioner.

## Getting ready

Download and install VirtualBox at `https://www.virtualbox.org/wiki/Downloads`.

Download and install Vagrant at `https://www.vagrantup.com/downloads.html`.

Install the Omnibus Vagrant plugin to enable Vagrant to install the Chef client on your VM by running the following command:

```
mma@laptop:~/chef-repo $ vagrant plugin install vagrant-omnibus
Installing the 'vagrant-omnibus' plugin. This can take a few minutes...
Installed the plugin 'vagrant-omnibus (1.4.1)'!
```

## How to do it...

Let's create and boot a virtual node by using Vagrant:

1. Visit `https://github.com/opscode/bento` and choose a Vagrant box to base your VMs on. We'll use `opscode-ubuntu-14.10` in this example.

2. The URL of the `opscode-ubuntu-14.10` box is `https://opscode-vm-bento.s3.amazonaws.com/vagrant/virtualbox/opscode_ubuntu-14.10_chef-provisionerless.box`.

3. Edit your new `Vagrantfile`. Make sure that you replace `<YOUR-ORG>` with the name of your organization on the Chef server. Use the name and URL of the box file you noted down in the first step as `config.vm.box` and `config.vm.box_url`:

**mma@laptop:~/chef-repo $ subl Vagrantfile**

```
Vagrant.configure("2") do |config|
  config.vm.box = "opscode-ubuntu-14.10"
  config.vm.box_url = "https://opscode-vm-bento.s3.amazonaws.com/
vagrant/virtualbox/opscode_ubuntu-14.10_chef-provisionerless.box"
  config.omnibus.chef_version = :latest

  config.vm.provision :chef_client do |chef|
    chef.provisioning_path = "/etc/chef"
    chef.chef_server_url = "https://api.chef.io/
organizations/<YOUR_ORG>"
    chef.validation_key_path = ".chef/<YOUR_ORG>-validator.pem"
    chef.validation_client_name = "<YOUR_ORG>-validator"
    chef.node_name = "server"
  end
end
```

4. Create your virtual node using Vagrant:

**mma@laptop:~/chef-repo $ vagrant up**

```
Bringing machine 'server' up with 'virtualbox' provider...
...TRUNCATED OUTPUT...
==> default: Importing base box 'opscode-ubuntu-14.10'...
...TRUNCATED OUTPUT...
==> default: Installing Chef 11.16.4 Omnibus package...
...TRUNCATED OUTPUT...
==> default: Running provisioner: chef_client...
==> default: Creating folder to hold client key...
==> default: Uploading chef client validation key...
Generating chef JSON and uploading...
==> default: Running chef-client...
==> default: [2014-12-01T22:00:54+00:00] INFO: *** Chef 11.16.4
***
...TRUNCATED OUTPUT...
```

5. Log in to your virtual node using SSH:

**mma@laptop:~/chef-repo $ vagrant ssh**

```
Welcome to Ubuntu 14.10 (GNU/Linux 3.16.0-23-generic x86_64)

 * Documentation:  https://help.ubuntu.com/
```

```
Last login: Mon Oct 27 02:22:37 2014 from 10.0.2.2

vagrant@server:~$
```

6. Log out of your virtual node:

   **vagrant@server:~$ exit**

   **mma@laptop:~/chef-repo $**

7. Validate that the Chef server knows your new virtual machine as a client called server:

   **mma@laptop:~/chef-repo $ knife client list**

   ```
   awo-validator
   server
   ```

8. Go to https://manage.chef.io/organizations/<YOUR ORGANIZATION>/ nodes and validate that your new virtual machine shows up as a registered node:

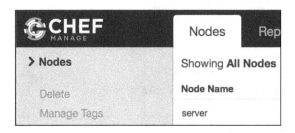

## How it works...

The `Vagrantfile` is written in a Ruby **Domain Specific Language** (**DSL**) to configure the Vagrant virtual machines. We want to boot a simple Ubuntu VM. Let's go through the `Vagrantfile` step by step.

First, we create a `config` object. Vagrant will use this `config` object to configure the VM:

```
Vagrant.configure("2") do |config|
end
```

Inside the `config` block, we tell Vagrant which VM image to use, in order to boot the node:

```
config.vm.box = "opscode-ubuntu-14.10"
config.vm.box_url = "https://opscode-vm-bento.s3.amazonaws.com/
vagrant/virtualbox/opscode_ubuntu-14.10_chef-provisionerless.box"
```

We want to boot our VM using a so-called Bento Box, provided by Chef. We use Ubuntu Version 14.10 here.

If you have never used the box before, Vagrant will download the image file (a few hundred megabytes) when you run `vagrant up` for the first time.

As we want our VM to have the Chef client installed, we tell the omnibus vagrant plugin to use the latest version of Chef client:

```
config.omnibus.chef_version = :latest
```

After selecting the VM image to boot, we configure how to provision the box by using Chef. The Chef configuration happens in a nested Ruby block:

```
config.vm.provision :chef_client do |chef|
...
end
```

Inside this Chef block, we need to instruct Vagrant on how to hook up our virtual node to the Chef server. First, we need to tell Vagrant where to store all the Chef stuff on your node:

```
chef.provisioning_path = "/etc/chef"
```

Vagrant needs to know the API endpoint of your Chef server. If you use hosted Chef, it is `https://api.chef.io/organizations/<YOUR_ORG>`. You need to replace `<YOUR_ORG>` with the name of the organization that you created in your account on hosted Chef. If you are using your own Chef server, change the URL accordingly:

```
chef.chef_server_url = "https://api.chef.io/organizations/<YOUR_ORG>"
```

While creating your organization on hosted Chef, you must download your private key. Tell Vagrant where to find this file:

```
chef.validation_key_path = ".chef/<YOUR_ORG>—validator.pem"
```

Also, you need to tell Vagrant as to which client it should validate itself against the Chef server:

```
chef.validation_client_name = "<YOUR_ORG>-validator"
```

Finally, you should tell Vagrant how to name your node:

```
chef.node_name = "server"
```

After configuring your `Vagrantfile`, all you need to do is run the basic Vagrant commands such as `vagrant up`, `vagrant provision`, and `vagrant ssh`. To stop your VM, just run the `vagrant halt` command.

## There's more...

If you want to start from scratch again, you will have to destroy your VM and delete both the client and the node from your Chef server by running the following command:

```
mma@laptop:~/chef-repo $ vagrant destroy
```

```
mma@laptop:~/chef-repo $ knife node delete server -y && knife client
delete server -y
```

Alternatively, you may use the Vagrant Butcher plugin found at `https://github.com/cassianoleal/vagrant-butcher`.

 Don't blindly trust Vagrant boxes downloaded from the Web; you never know what they contain.

## See also

▶ Find the Vagrant documentation at `http://docs.vagrantup.com/v2/getting-started/index.html`

▶ You can use a Vagrant plugin for VMware instead of VirtualBox and find it at `http://www.vagrantup.com/vmware`

▶ You can use a Vagrant plugin for Amazon AWS instead of VirtualBox and find the same at `https://github.com/mitchellh/vagrant-aws`

# Creating and using cookbooks

Cookbooks are an essential part of Chef. You can easily create them using the Chef executable installed by the Chef DK. In this recipe (and many of the following recipes), I will assume that you're using a Chef server to manage your infrastructure. You can either set up your own cookbook or use the hosted Chef as described previously. You'll use the command-line tool knife to interact with the Chef server.

In this recipe, we'll create and apply a simple cookbook using the Chef and knife command-line tools.

## Getting ready

Make sure you have Chef DK installed and a node available for testing. Check out the installation instructions at `http://learn.chef.io` if you need help here.

Edit your `knife.rb` file (usually found in the hidden `.chef` directory) and add the following three lines to it, filling in your own values:

```
cookbook_copyright "your company"
cookbook_license "apachev2"
cookbook_email "your email address"
```

 The Apache 2 license is the most commonly found in cookbooks, but you're free to choose whichever suits your needs. If you put `none` as `cookbook_license`, knife will put `"All rights reserved"` into your recipe's metadata file.

Chef will use the preceding values as default whenever you create a new cookbook.

We assume that you have a node called `server` registered with your Chef server, as described in the *Managing virtual machines with Vagrant* section in this chapter.

## How to do it...

Carry out the following steps to create and use cookbooks:

1. Create a cookbook named `my_cookbook` by running the following command:

   **mma@laptop:~/chef-repo $ chef generate cookbook cookbooks/my_cookbook**

   ```
   Compiling Cookbooks...
   Recipe: code_generator::cookbook
   ```

   ```
   ...TRUNCATED OUTPUT...
   ```

   Before ChefDK was introduced, the only way to generate cookbooks was to use `knife cookbook create my_cookbook`

2. Upload your new cookbook on the Chef server:

   **mma@laptop:~/chef-repo $ knife cookbook upload my_cookbook**

   ```
   Uploading my_cookbook      [0.1.0]
   Uploaded 1 cookbook.
   ```

3. Add the cookbook to your node's run list. In this example, the name of the node is server:

   **mma@laptop:~/chef-repo $ knife node run_list add server 'recipe[my_cookbook]'**

   ```
   server:
     run_list: recipe[my_cookbook]
   ```

4. Run the Chef client on your node:

```
user@server:~$ sudo chef-client
```

 If you're using a Vagrant VM as your server, you need to make sure to run vagrant up and vagrant ssh in order to be able to execute the Chef client on the node.

## How it works...

The chef executable helps you to manage your local Chef development environment. We used it here to generate the cookbook.

Knife is the command-line interface for the Chef server. It uses the RESTful API exposed by the Chef server to do its work and helps you to interact with the Chef server.

The knife command supports a host of commands structured as follows:

```
knife <subject> <command>
```

The <subject> used in this section is either cookbook or node. The commands we use are upload for the cookbook, and run_list add for the node.

## See also

▶ Learn how to set up your Chef server in the *Using the hosted Chef platform* recipe in this chapter

# Inspecting files on your Chef server with knife

Sometimes, you may want to peek into the files stored on your Chef server. You might not be sure about an implementation detail of that specific cookbook version, which is currently installed on your Chef server, and need to look it up. Knife can help you out by letting you show various aspects of the files stored on your Chef server.

## Getting ready

Make sure that you have the iptables cookbook installed locally and uploaded on your Chef server.

1. Install the iptables community cookbook by executing the following command and code lines:

```
mma@laptop:~/chef-repo $ knife cookbook site install iptables
```

```
Installing iptables to /Users/mma/work/chef-repo/cookbooks
...TRUNCATED OUTPUT...
```

Take a look at the following error:

```
ERROR: IOError: Cannot open or read ../chef-repo/
cookbooks/iptables/metadata.rb!
```

If you get the preceding error, your cookbook only has a `metadata.json` file. Make sure that you delete it and create a valid `metadata.rb`, file instead.

2. Upload the `iptables` cookbook on your Chef server by executing the following given command and code lines:

**mma@laptop:~/chef-repo $ knife cookbook upload iptables**

```
Uploading iptables        [0.14.0]
Uploaded 1 cookbook.
```

## How to do it...

Let's find out how knife can help you to look into a cookbook stored in your Chef server:

1. First, you want to find out the current version of the cookbook you're interested in. In our case, we're interested in the `iptables` cookbook:

   **mma@laptop:~/work/chef_helpster $ knife cookbook show iptables**

   **iptables    0.14.0**

2. Then, you can look up the definitions of the `iptables` cookbook, using the version number that you found out in the previous step:

   **mma@laptop:~/chef-repo $ knife cookbook show iptables 0.14.0**
   **definitions**

   ```
   checksum:      45c0b77ff10d7177627694827ce47340
   name:          iptables_rule.rb
   path:          definitions/iptables_rule.rb
   specificity:   default
   url:           https://s3.amazonaws.com/opscode-platform...
   ```

3. Now, you can even show the contents of the `iptables_rule.rb` definition file, as stored on the server:

   **mma@laptop:~/chef-repo $ knife cookbook show iptables 0.14.0**
   **definitions iptables_rule.rb**

   ```
   #
   # Cookbook Name:: iptables
   ```

```
# Definition:: iptables_rule
#
#
define :iptables_rule, :enable => true, :source => nil, :variables
=> {} do
...TRUNCATED OUTPUT...
end
```

## How it works...

The `knife cookbook show` subcommand helps you understand what exactly is stored on the Chef server. It lets you drill down into specific sections of your cookbooks and see the exact content of the files stored in your Chef server.

## There's more...

Since Chef 11, you can pass patterns to the `knife show` command to tell it what exactly you want to see. Showing the contents of the `iptables_rule` definition can be done as follows, in addition to the way we described previously:

**mma@laptop:~/work/chef_helpster $ knife show cookbooks/iptables/ definitions/\***

```
cookbooks/iptables/definitions/iptables_rule.rb:
#
# Cookbook Name:: iptables
# Definition:: iptables_rule
#
#
define :iptables_rule, :enable => true, :source => nil, :variables =>
{} do
...TRUNCATED OUTPUT...
end
```

## See also

▶   To find some more examples on knife show, visit `http://docs.chef.io/knife_ show.html`

# Defining cookbook dependencies

Quite often, you might want to use features of other cookbooks in your own cookbooks. For example, if you want to make sure that all packages required for compiling software written in C are installed, you might want to include the `build-essential` cookbook, which does just that. Chef server needs to know about such dependencies in your cookbooks. You declare them in a cookbook's metadata.

## Getting ready

Make sure you have a cookbook named `my_cookbook`, and the `run_list` command of your node includes `my_cookbook`, as described in the *Creating and using cookbooks* recipe in this chapter.

## How to do it...

Edit the metadata of your cookbook in the file `cookbooks/my_cookbook/metadata.rb` to add a dependency to the `build-essential` cookbook:

```
mma@laptop:~/chef-repo $ subl cookbooks/my_cookbook/metadata.rb

    ...
    depends 'build-essential'
    depends 'apache2', '>= 1.0.4'
```

## How it works...

If you want to use a feature of another cookbook inside your cookbook, you will need to include the other cookbook in your recipe using the `include_recipe` directive:

```
    include_recipe 'build-essential'
```

To tell the Chef server that your cookbook requires the `build-essential` cookbook, you need to declare that dependency in the `metadata.rb` file. If you uploaded all the dependencies to your Chef server either using `berks install` and `berks upload` or `knife cookbook upload ...`, the Chef server will then send all the required cookbooks to the node.

The first `depends` call tells the Chef server that your cookbook depends on the latest version of the `build-essential` cookbook.

The second `depends` call tells the Chef server that your cookbook depends on a version of the `apache2` cookbook, which is greater or equal to the version `1.0.4`. You may use any of these version constraints with your depends calls:

- ► < (less than)
- ► <= (less than or equal to)
- ► = (equal to)
- ► >= (greater than or equal to)
- ► ~> (approximately greater than)
- ► > (greater than)

## There's more...

If you include another recipe inside your recipe, without declaring the cookbook dependency in your `metadata.rb` file, `Foodcritic` will warn you:

**mma@laptop:~/chef-repo $ foodcritic cookbooks/my_cookbook**

```
FC007: Ensure recipe dependencies are reflected in cookbook metadata:
cookbooks/my_cookbook/recipes/default.rb:9
```

 `Foodcritic` will just return an empty line, if it doesn't find any issues.

Additionally, you can declare conflicting cookbooks through the `conflicts` call:

```
conflicts "nginx"
```

Of course, you can use version constraints exactly the way you did with `depends`.

## See also

- ► Read more on how you can find out what is uploaded on your Chef server in the *Inspecting files on your Chef server with knife* recipe in this chapter
- ► Find out how to use `foodcritic` in the *Flagging problems in your Chef cookbooks* recipe in *Chapter 2, Evaluating and Troubleshooting Cookbooks and Chef Runs*

# Managing cookbook dependencies with Berkshelf

It's a pain to manually ensure that you have installed all the cookbooks that another cookbook depends on. You have to download each and every one of them manually only to find out that with each downloaded cookbook, you inherit another set of dependent cookbooks.

And even if you use `knife cookbook site install`, which installs all the dependencies locally for you, your cookbook directory and your repository get cluttered with all those cookbooks. Usually, you don't really care about all those cookbooks and don't want to see or manage them.

This is where Berkshelf comes into play. It works like Bundler for Ruby gems, managing cookbook dependencies for you. Berkshelf downloads all the dependencies you defined recursively and helps you to upload all cookbooks to your Chef server.

Instead of polluting your Chef repository, it stores all the cookbooks in a central location. You just commit your Berkshelf dependency file (called `Berksfile`) to your repository, and every colleague or build server can download and install all those dependent cookbooks based on it.

Let's see how to use Berkshelf to manage the dependencies of your cookbook.

## Getting ready

Make sure you have a cookbook named `my_cookbook` and the `run_list` of your node includes `my_cookbook`, as described in the *Creating and using cookbooks* recipe.

## How to do it...

Berkshelf helps you to keep those utility cookbooks out of your Chef repository. This makes it much easier to maintain the cookbooks, which really matter.

Let's see how to write a cookbook by running a bunch of utility recipes and manage the required cookbooks with Berkshelf:

1. Edit your cookbook's metadata:

   ```
   mma@laptop:~/chef-repo $ subl cookbooks/my_cookbook/metadata.rb


   . . .
   depends "chef-client"
   depends "apt"
   depends "ntp"
   ```

2. Edit your cookbook's default recipe:

   **mma@laptop:~/chef-repo $ subl cookbooks/my_cookbook/recipes/ default.rb**

   ```
   ...
   include_recipe "chef-client"
   include_recipe "apt"
   include_recipe "ntp"
   ```

3. Run Berkshelf to install all the required cookbooks:

   **mma@laptop:~/chef-repo $ cd cookbooks/my_cookbook**

   **mma@laptop:~/chef-repo/cookbooks/my_cookbook $ berks install**

   ```
   Resolving cookbook dependencies...
   Fetching 'my_cookbook' from source at .
   Fetching cookbook index from https://supermarket.chef.io...
   Installing apt (2.6.0) from https://supermarket.chef.io ([opscode]
   https://supermarket.chef.io/api/v1)
   ...TRUNCATED OUTPUT...
   ```

4. Upload all the cookbooks on the Chef server:

   **mma@laptop:~/chef-repo/cookbooks/my_cookbook $ berks upload**

   ```
   Using my_cookbook (0.1.0)
   ...TRUNCATED OUTPUT...
   Uploading windows (1.34.8) to: 'https://api.chef.io:443/
   organizations/awo
   ```

## How it works...

Berkshelf comes with the Chef DK.

We create our cookbook and tell it to use a few basic cookbooks.

Instead of making us manually install all the cookbooks using `knife cookbook site install`, `chef generate` creates a Berksfile, besides the `metadata.rb` file.

The Berksfile is pretty simple. It tells Berkshelf to use the Chef supermarket as the default source for all cookbooks:

```
source "https://supermarket.chef.io"
```

It tells Berkshelf to read the `metadata.rb` file to find all the required cookbooks. This is the simplest way when working inside a single cookbook. Please see the following *There's more...* section to find an example of a more advanced usage of the Berksfile.

After telling Berkshelf where to find all the required cookbook names, we use it to install all those cookbooks:

**berks install**

Berkshelf stores cookbooks in ~/.berkshelf/cookbooks, by default. This keeps your Chef repository clutter-free. Instead of having to manage all the required cookbooks inside your own Chef repository, Berkshelf takes care of them. You simply need to check in Berksfile with your recipe, and everyone using your recipe can download all the required cookbooks by using Berkshelf.

To make sure that there's no mix-up with different cookbook versions when sharing your cookbook, Berkshelf creates a file called Berksfile.lock alongside Berksfile. Here, you'll find the exact versions of all the cookbooks that Berkshelf installed:

```
DEPENDENCIES
  my_cookbook
    path: .
    metadata: true

GRAPH
  apt (2.6.0)
  chef-client (3.9.0)
    cron (>= 1.2.0)
    logrotate (>= 1.2.0)
    windows (~> 1.11)
  chef_handler (1.1.6)
  cron (1.6.1)
  logrotate (1.7.0)
  my_cookbook (0.1.0)
    apt (>= 0.0.0)
    chef-client (>= 0.0.0)
    ntp (>= 0.0.0)
  ntp (1.6.8)
  windows (1.34.8)
    chef_handler (>= 0.0.0)
```

Berkshelf will only use the exact versions specified in the Berksfile.lock file, if it finds this file.

Finally, we use Berkshelf to upload all the required cookbooks on the Chef server:

**berks upload**

## There's more...

Berkshelf integrates tightly with Vagrant via the `vagrant-berkshelf` plugin. You can set up Berkshelf and Vagrant in such a way that Berkshelf installs and uploads all the required cookbooks on your Chef server whenever you execute `vagrant up` or `vagrant provision`. You'll save all the work of running `berks install` and `berks upload` manually before creating your node with Vagrant.

Let's see how you can integrate Berkshelf and Vagrant.

First, you need to install the Berkshelf plugin for Vagrant:

**mma@mma-mbp:~/work/chef-repo (master)$ vagrant plugin install vagrant-berkshelf**

```
    Installing the 'vagrant-berkshelf' plugin. This can take a few
    minutes...
    Installed the plugin 'vagrant-berkshelf (4.0.1)'!
```

Then, you need to tell Vagrant that you want to use the plugin. You do this by enabling the plugin in `Vagrantfile`:

**mma@mma-mbp:~/work/chef-repo (master)$ subl Vagrantfile**

```
    config.berkshelf.enabled = true
```

Then, you need a Berksfile in the root directory of your Chef repository to tell Berkshelf which cookbooks to install on each Vagrant run:

```
    source 'https://supermarket.chef.io'

    cookbook 'my_cookbook', path: 'cookbooks/my_cookbook'
```

Eventually, you can start your VM using Vagrant. Berkshelf will first download and then install all the required cookbooks in the Berkshelf, and upload them on the Chef server. Only after all the cookbooks are made available on the Chef server by Berkshelf, will Vagrant go on:

**mma@mma-mbp:~/work/chef-repo $ vagrant up**

```
    Bringing machine 'server' up with 'virtualbox' provider...

    ==> default: Loading Berkshelf datafile...
    ==> default: Updating Vagrant's Berkshelf...
```

```
==> default: Resolving cookbook dependencies...
==> default: Fetching 'my_cookbook' from source at cookbooks/my_
cookbook
==> default: Fetching cookbook index from https://supermarket.getchef.
com...
...TRUNCATED OUTPUT...
```

This way, using Berkshelf together with Vagrant, saves a lot of manual steps and gets faster cycle times for your cookbook development.

## See also

▸ For the full documentation of Berkshelf, please visit `http://berkshelf.com/`

▸ Please find the Berkshelf source code at `https://github.com/RiotGames/berkshelf`

▸ Please find the Vagrant Berkshelf plugin source code at `https://github.com/riotgames/vagrant-berkshelf`

▸ The *Managing virtual machines with Vagrant* recipe in this chapter

# Downloading and integrating cookbooks as vendor branches into your Git repository

The Chef community offers a wide variety of ready-made cookbooks for many major software packages. They're a great starting point for your own infrastructure. However, usually you need to modify these cookbooks to suit your needs. Modifying your local copy of a community cookbook leaves you with the dilemma of not being able to update to the latest version of the community cookbook without losing your local changes.

## Getting ready

You'll need to make sure that your local Git repository is clean and does not have any uncommitted changes:

**mma@laptop:~/chef-repo $ git status**

```
# On branch master
nothing to commit (working directory clean)
```

## How to do it...

Carry out the following given steps:

1.  Go to `https://supermarket.chef.io/cookbooks` and search for the cookbook you need. In our example, we will use the `mysql` cookbook, which you can find by typing `mysql` in the search box and hitting enter. All we need is to note down the exact name of the cookbook; in this case, it's simply `mysql`.

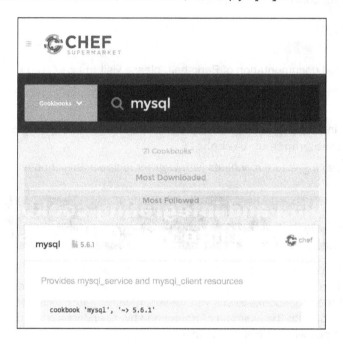

2.  Use knife to pull down the cookbook and integrate it with your local repository:

    ```
    mma@laptop:~/chef-repo $ knife cookbook site install mysql
    ```

    ```
    Installing mysql to /Users/mma/work/chef-repo/cookbooks
    ...TRUNCATED OUTPUT...
    ```

    Verify the downloaded cookbooks:

    ```
    mma@laptop:~/chef-repo $ cd cookbooks
    mma@laptop:~/chef-repo/cookbooks $ ls -l
    ```

    ```
    total 8
    ```

```
-rw-r--r--    1 mma   staff   3064 27 Sep  2013 README.md
```

```
drwxr-xr-x+ 10 mma   staff    340  7 Dez 20:43 mysql
drwxr-xr-x+ 12 mma   staff    408  7 Dez 20:43 yum
drwxr-xr-x+  9 mma   staff    306  7 Dez 20:43 yum-mysql-community
```

Validate the Git status:

**mma@laptop:~/chef-repo/cookbooks $ git status**

```
# On branch master
# Your branch is ahead of 'origin/master' by 3 commits.
#
nothing to commit (working directory clean)
```

3. You might have noticed that your local branch received three commits. Let's take a look at those:

**mma@laptop:~/chef-repo/cookbooks $ git log**

```
commit 271d3de3b95bdc32d68133cdc91cb04e09625f59
Author: Matthias Marschall <mm@agileweboperations.com>
Date:   Sun Dec 7 20:43:50 2014 +0100

    Import yum version 3.5.1

commit cc72319ca7989df26e0ba7c3a76f78f6a7a7a4e2
Author: Matthias Marschall <mm@agileweboperations.com>
Date:   Sun Dec 7 20:43:44 2014 +0100

    Import yum-mysql-community version 0.1.10

commit 30984edb00c12177e25558bdfcd519da508b3ac5
Author: Matthias Marschall <mm@agileweboperations.com>
Date:   Sun Dec 7 20:43:38 2014 +0100

    Import mysql version 5.6.1
```

The `knife` command successfully downloaded and imported the `mysql` cookbook as well as its dependencies.

## How it works...

Knife executes a set of commands to download the desired cookbook and to integrate it with your local repository.

Let's take a look at the output of the `knife cookbook site install` command again and go through it step-by-step:

1. First, the command makes sure that you're on the master branch of your repository:

   **Checking out the master branch.**

2. The next step is to create a new vendor branch for the `mysql` cookbook, if none exists so far:

   **Creating pristine copy branch chef-vendor-mysql.**

3. Then, knife downloads the tarball, removes any older version, uncompresses the new tarball, and removes it after successfully extracting its contents into a new cookbook directory:

   ```
   Downloading mysql from the cookbooks site at version 5.6.1 to /
   Users/mma/work/chef-repo/cookbooks/mysql.tar.gz
   Cookbook saved: /Users/mma/work/chef-repo/cookbooks/mysql.tar.gz
   Removing pre-existing version.
   Uncompressing mysql version 5.6.1.
   Removing downloaded tarball
   ```

4. Now, it's time to commit the newly extracted files to the vendor branch:

   ```
   1 files updated, committing changes
   ```

5. Finally, Git tags the branch with the current version of the cookbook:

   ```
   Creating tag cookbook-site-imported-mysql-5.6.1
   ```

The `knife cookbook site install` command executes all the previously mentioned steps for all the cookbooks the desired cookbook depends on, by default.

Eventually, you end up with a separate branch, the so-called vendor branch, for every downloaded cookbook integrated into your master branch and nicely tagged as shown:

**mma@laptop:~/chef-repo$ git branch -a**

```
    chef-vendor-iptables
    chef-vendor-mysql
  * master
    remotes/origin/master
```

This approach enables you to change whatever you like in your master branch and still pull down newer versions of the community cookbook. Git will automatically merge both versions or ask you to remove conflicts manually; these are standard Git procedures.

## There's more...

If you want to integrate the desired cookbook into another branch, use the `--branch BRANCH_NAME` parameter.

**mma@laptop:~/chef-repo [experimental] $ knife cookbook site install mysql --branch experimental**

```
Installing mysql to /Users/mma/work/chef-repo/cookbooks
Checking out the experimental branch.
Pristine copy branch (chef-vendor-mysql) exists, switching to it.
Downloading mysql from the cookbooks site at version 5.6.1 to /Users/
mma/work/chef-repo/cookbooks/mysql.tar.gz
Cookbook saved: /Users/mma/work/chef-repo/cookbooks/mysql.tar.gz
Removing pre-existing version.
Uncompressing mysql version 5.6.1.
removing downloaded tarball
No changes made to mysql
Checking out the experimental branch.
...TRUNCATED OUTPUT...
```

As you can see, instead of checking out the master branch, the `knife cookbook site install` command uses the experimental branch now.

You can use the `-D` switch when running the command in order to avoid downloading all the cookbooks that your desired cookbook depends on.

**mma@laptop:~/chef-repo $ knife cookbook site install mysql -D**

```
Installing mysql to /Users/mma/work/chef-repo/cookbooks
Checking out the master branch.
Pristine copy branch (chef-vendor-mysql) exists, switching to it.
Downloading mysql from the cookbooks site at version 5.6.1 to /Users/
mma/work/chef-repo/cookbooks/mysql.tar.gz
Cookbook saved: /Users/mma/work/chef-repo/cookbooks/mysql.tar.gz
Removing pre-existing version.
Uncompressing mysql version 5.6.1.
removing downloaded tarball
No changes made to mysql
Checking out the master branch.
```

You can see that the command stopped after dealing with the `mysql` cookbook. It has not yet gotten the other cookbooks.

## See also

▸   You can use Berkshelf to manage cookbooks and their dependencies for you, which makes the preceding approach obsolete. See the *Managing cookbook dependencies with Berkshelf* recipe in this chapter.

# Using custom knife plugins

Knife comes with a set of commands out of the box. The built-in commands deal with the basic elements of Chef-like cookbooks, roles, data bags, and so on. However, it would be nice to use knife for more than just the basic stuff. Fortunately, knife comes with a plugin API and there are already a host of useful knife plugins built by the makers of Chef and the Chef community.

## Getting ready

Make sure you have an account at Amazon Web Services (AWS) if you want to follow along and try out the `knife-ec2` plugin. There are knife plugins available for most Cloud providers. Go through the *There's more...* section of this recipe for the list.

## How to do it...

Let's see which knife plugins are available, and try to use one to manage Amazon EC2 instances:

1.  List the knife plugins that are shipped as Ruby gems using the `chef` command-line tool:

    **mma@laptop:~/chef-repo $ chef gem search -r knife-**

    ```
    *** REMOTE GEMS ***
    ...TRUNCATED OUTPUT...

    knife-azure (1.3.0)
    ...TRUNCATED OUTPUT...
    knife-ec2 (0.10.0)
    ...TRUNCATED OUTPUT...
    ```

2.  Install the EC2 plugin to manage servers in the Amazon AWS Cloud:

    **mma@laptop:~/chef-repo $ chef gem install knife-ec2**

    ```
    Building native extensions.  This could take a while...
    ...TRUNCATED OUTPUT...
    Fetching: knife-ec2-0.10.0.gem (100%)
    ```

```
Successfully installed knife-ec2-0.10.0
...TRUNCATED OUTPUT...


6 gems installed
```

3. List all the available instance types in AWS using the `knife ec2` plugin. Please use your own AWS credentials instead of XXX and YYYYY:

**mma@laptop:~/chef-repo $ knife ec2 flavor list --aws-access-key-id XXX --aws-secret-access-key YYYYY**

```
ID              Name                            Arch    RAM
Disk    Cores
c1.medium     High-CPU Medium                   32-bit
1740.8  350 GB    5
...TRUNCATED OUTPUT...
m2.xlarge     High-Memory Extra Large           64-bit
17510.  420 GB    6.5
t1.micro      Micro Instance                    0-bit   613
0 GB      2
```

## How it works...

Knife looks for plugins at various places.

First, it looks into the `.chef` directory, which is located inside your current Chef repository, to find the plugins specific to this repository:

```
./.chef/plugins/knife/
```

Then, it looks into the `.chef` directory, which is located in your home directory, to find the plugins that you want to use in all your Chef repositories:

```
~/.chef/plugins/knife/
```

Finally, it looks for installed gems. Knife will load all the code from any `chef/knife/` directory found in your installed Ruby gems. This is the most common way of using plugins developed by Chef or the Chef community.

## There's more...

There are hundreds of knife plugins, including plugins for most of the major Cloud providers, as well as the major virtualization technologies, such as VMware, vSphere, and Openstack, amongst others.

## See also

▶ To learn how to write your own knife plugins, see the *Creating custom knife plugins* recipe in *Chapter 2, Evaluating and Troubleshooting Cookbooks and Chef Runs*

▶ Find a list of supported Cloud providers at `http://docs.chef.io/plugin_knife.html`

# Deleting a node from the Chef server

Bootstrapping a node not only installs Chef on that node, but creates a client object on the Chef server as well. Running the Chef client on your node uses the client object to authenticate itself against the Chef server on each run.

Additionally, to registering a client, a node object is created on the Chef server. The node object is the main data structure, which you can use to query node data inside your recipes.

## Getting ready

Make sure you have at least one node registered on your Chef server that is safe to remove.

## How to do it...

Let's delete the node and client object to completely remove a node from the Chef server.

1. Delete the node object:

   ```
   mma@laptop:~/chef-repo $ knife node delete my_node

   Do you really want to delete my_node? (Y/N) y
   Deleted node[my_node]
   ```

2. Delete the client object:

   ```
   mma@laptop:~/chef-repo $ knife client delete my_node

   Do you really want to delete my_node? (Y/N) y
   Deleted client[my_node]
   ```

## How it works...

To keep your Chef server clean, it's important to not only manage your node objects but to also take care of your client objects, as well.

Knife connects to the Chef server and deletes the node object with a given name, using the Chef server RESTful API.

The same happens while deleting the client object on the Chef server.

After deleting both objects, your node is totally removed from the Chef server. Now, you can reuse the same node name with a new box or virtual machine.

## There's more...

It is a bit tedious and error prone when you have to issue two commands. To simplify things, you can use a knife plugin called `playground`.

1. Run the `chef` command-line tool to install the knife plugin:

   ```
   mma@laptop:~/chef-repo $ chef gem install knife-playground

   ...TRUNCATED OUTPUT...
   Installing knife-playground (0.2.2)
   ```

2. Run the `knife pg clientnode delete` subcommand:

   ```
   mma@laptop:~/chef-repo $ knife pg clientnode delete my_node

   Deleting CLIENT my_node...
   Do you really want to delete my_node? (Y/N) y
   Deleted client[my_node]
   Deleting NODE my_node...
   Do you really want to delete my_node? (Y/N) y
   Deleted node[my_node]
   ```

## See also

- ▶ Read about how to do this when using Vagrant in the *Managing virtual machines with Vagrant* recipe in this recipe
- ▶ Read about how to set up your Chef server and register your nodes in the *Using the hosted Chef platform* recipe in this chapter

# Developing recipes with local mode

If running your own Chef server seems like an overkill and you're not comfortable with using the hosted Chef, you can use local mode to execute cookbooks.

## Getting ready

1.  Create a cookbook named `my_cookbook` by running the following command:

    **mma@laptop:~/chef-repo $ chef generate cookbook cookbooks/my_ cookbook**

    ```
    Compiling Cookbooks...
    Recipe: code_generator::cookbook
    ...TRUNCATED OUTPUT...
    ```

2.  Edit the default recipe of `my_cookbook` so that it creates a temporary file:

    **mma@laptop:~/chef-repo $ subl cookbooks/my_cookbook/recipes/ default.rb**

    ```
    file "/tmp/local_mode.txt" do
        content "created by chef client local mode"
    end
    ```

## How to do it...

Let's run `my_cookbook` on your local workstation using Chef client's local mode:

1.  Run the Chef client locally with `my_cookbook` in the run list:

    **mma@laptop:~/chef-repo $ chef-client -z -o my_cookbook**

    ```
    [2014-12-11T22:54:44+01:00] INFO: Starting chef-zero on host
    localhost, port 8889 with repository at repository at /Users/mma/
    work/chef-repo
    [2014-12-11T22:54:44+01:00] INFO: Forking chef instance to
    converge...
    Starting Chef Client, version 11.18.0.rc.1
    [2014-12-11T22:54:44+01:00] INFO: *** Chef 11.18.0.rc.1 ***
    [2014-12-11T22:54:44+01:00] INFO: Chef-client pid: 20179
    [2014-12-11T22:54:47+01:00] WARN: Run List override has been
    provided.
    [2014-12-11T22:54:47+01:00] WARN: Original Run List: []
    [2014-12-11T22:54:47+01:00] WARN: Overridden Run List: [recipe[my_
    cookbook]]
    [2014-12-11T22:54:47+01:00] INFO: Run List is [recipe[my_
    cookbook]]
    [2014-12-11T22:54:47+01:00] INFO: Run List expands to [my_
    cookbook]
    [2014-12-11T22:54:47+01:00] INFO: Starting Chef Run for webops
    ```

2. Validate that the Chef client run creates the desired temporary file:

```
mma@laptop:~/chef-repo $ cat /tmp/local_mode.txt
```

```
created by chef client local mode%
```

## How it works...

The `-z` parameter switches the Chef client into local mode. Local mode uses chef-zero—a simple, in-memory version of the Chef server provided by Chef DK—when converging the local workstation.

By providing the `-o` parameter, you override the run list of your local node so that the Chef client executes the default recipe from `my_cookbook`.

## There's more...

Chef-zero saves all modifications made by your recipes to the local file system. It creates a JSON file containing all node attributes for your local workstation in the `nodes` directory. This way, the next time you run the Chef client in local mode, it will be aware of any changes your recipes made to the node.

### Running knife in local mode

You can use knife in local mode, too. To set the run list of your node named `laptop` (instead of having to override it with `-o`), you can run the following command:

```
mma@laptop:~/chef-repo $ knife node run_list add -z laptop 'recipe[my_
cookbook]'
```

### Moving to hosted Chef or your own Chef server

When you're done editing and testing your cookbooks on your local workstation with chef-zero, you can seamlessly upload them to hosted Chef or your own Chef server:

```
mma@laptop:~/chef-repo $ knife upload /
```

```
laptop:
  run_list: recipe[my_cookbook]
```

## See also

▶ You can find the source code of chef-zero at `https://github.com/opscode/chef-zero`

▶ Read more about the Chef client's local mode and how it relates to Chef solo at `https://www.chef.io/blog/2013/10/31/chef-client-z-from-zero-to-chef-in-8-5-seconds/`

# Using roles

Roles are there in Chef to group nodes with similar configuration. Typical cases are to have roles for web servers, database servers, and so on.

You can set custom run lists for all the nodes in your roles and override attribute values from within your roles.

Let's see how to create a simple role.

## Getting ready

For the following examples, I assume that you have a node named `server` and that you have at least one cookbook (I'll use the `ntp` cookbook) registered with your Chef server.

## How to do it...

Let's create a role and see what we can do with it.

1. Create a role:

   **mma@laptop:~/chef-repo $ subl roles/web_servers.rb**

   ```
   name "web_servers"
   description "This role contains nodes, which act as web servers"
   run_list "recipe[ntp]"
   default_attributes 'ntp' => {
     'ntpdate' => {
       'disable' => true
     }
   }
   ```

2. Upload the role on the Chef `server`:

   **mma@laptop:~/chef-repo $ knife role from file web_servers.rb**

   ```
   Updated Role web_servers!
   ```

3. Assign the role to a node called `server`:

   **mma@laptop:~/chef-repo $ knife node run_list add server 'role[web_servers]'**

   ```
   server:
     run_list: role[web_servers]
   ```

4. Run the Chef client:

   **user@server:~$ sudo chef-client**

```
...TRUNCATED OUTPUT...
[2014-12-25T13:28:24+00:00] INFO: Run List is [role[web_servers]]

[2014-12-25T13:28:24+00:00] INFO: Run List expands to [ntp]

...TRUNCATED OUTPUT...
```

## How it works...

You define a role in a Ruby file inside the `roles` folder of your Chef repository. A role consists of a `name` attribute and a `description` attribute. Additionally, a role usually contains a role-specific run list and role-specific attribute settings.

Every node, which has a role in its run list, will have the role's run list expanded into its own. This means that all the recipes (and roles), which are in the role's run list, will be executed on your nodes.

You need to upload your role on your Chef server by using the `knife role from file` command.

Only then should you add the role to your node's run list.

Running the Chef client on a node having your role in its run list will execute all the recipes listed in the role.

The attributes you define in your role will be merged with attributes from environments and cookbooks, according to the precedence rules described at `https://docs.chef.io/roles.html#attribute-precedence`.

## See also

- ▸ Find out how roles can help you in finding nodes in the *Using search to find nodes* recipe in *Chapter 4, Writing Better Cookbooks*
- ▸ Learn more about in the *Overriding attributes* recipe in *Chapter 4, Writing Better Cookbooks*
- ▸ Read everything about roles at `https://docs.chef.io/roles.html`

# Using environments

Having separate environments for development, testing, and production are good ways to be able to develop and test cookbook updates and other configuration changes in isolation. Chef enables you to group your nodes into separate environments so as to support an ordered development flow.

## Getting ready

For the following examples, I assume that you have a node named `server` in the `_default` environment and that you have at least one cookbook (I'll use the `ntp` cookbook) registered with your Chef server.

## How to do it...

Let's see how to manipulate environments using knife.

 This is only a good idea if you want to play around. For serious work, please create files describing your environments and put them under version control as described in the *There's more...* section of this recipe.

1. Create your environment on the fly using knife. The following command will open your shell's default editor so that you can modify the environment definition:

    Make sure you've set your `EDITOR` environment variable to your preferred one.

   ```
   mma@laptop:~/chef-repo $ knife environment create book
   {
     "name": "book",
     "description": "",
     "cookbook_versions": {
     },
     "json_class": "Chef::Environment",
     "chef_type": "environment",
     "default_attributes": {
     },
     "override_attributes": {
     }
   }
   Created book
   ```

2. List the available environments:

   ```
   mma@laptop:~/chef-repo $ knife environment list
   _default
   book
   ```

3. List the nodes for all the environments:

   **mma@laptop:~/chef-repo $ knife node list**

   ```
   server
   ```

4. Verify that the node `server` is not in the `book` environment yet by listing nodes in the `book` environment only:

   **mma@laptop:~/chef-repo $ knife node list -E book**

   **mma@laptop:~/chef-repo $**

5. Change the environment of `server` to `book` using knife:

   **mma@laptop:~/chef-repo $ knife node environment set server book**

   ```
   server:
     chef_environment: book
   ```

6. List the nodes of the `book` environment again:

   **mma@laptop:~/chef-repo $ knife node list -E book**

   ```
   server
   ```

7. Use specific cookbook versions and override certain attributes for the environment:

   **mma@laptop:~/chef-repo $ knife environment edit book**

   ```
   {
     "name": "book",
     "description": "",
     "cookbook_versions": {
       "ntp": "1.6.8"
     },
     "json_class": "Chef::Environment",
     "chef_type": "environment",
     "default_attributes": {
     },
     "override_attributes": {
       "ntp": {
         "servers": ["0.europe.pool.ntp.org", "1.europe.pool.ntp.
   org", "2.europe.pool.ntp.org", "3.europe.pool.ntp.org"]
       }
     }
   }
   Saved book
   ```

## How it works...

A common use of environments is to promote cookbook updates from development to staging and then into production. Additionally, they enable you to use different cookbook versions on separate sets of nodes and environment-specific attributes. You might have nodes with lesser memory in your staging environment as in your production environment. By using environment-specific default attributes, you can, for example, configure your MySQL service to consume lesser memory on staging than on production.

 The Chef server always has an environment called `_default`, which cannot be edited or deleted. All the nodes go in there if you don't specify any other environment.

Be aware that roles are not environment-specific. You may use environment-specific run lists, though.

The node's environment can be queried using the `node.chef_environment` method inside your cookbooks.

## There's more...

If you want your environments to be under version control (and you should), a better way to create a new environment is to create a new Ruby file in the `environments` directory inside your Chef repository:

```
mma@laptop:~/chef-repo $ cd environments
mma@laptop:~/chef-repo $ subl book.rb
name "book"
```

You should add, commit, and push your new environment file to GitHub:

```
mma@laptop:~/chef-repo $ git add environments/book.rb
mma@laptop:~/chef-repo $ git commit -a -m "the book env"
mma@laptop:~/chef-repo $ git push
```

Now, can create the environment on the Chef server from the newly created file using knife:

```
mma@laptop:~/chef-repo $ knife environment from file book.rb
Created Environment book
```

 You have to deal with two artifact storages here. You have to use your version control system and knife / Berkshelf to sync your local changes to your Chef server. The Chef server is not aware of any changes that you do when using your version control system and vice versa.

There is a way to migrate all the nodes from one environment to another by using `knife exec`:

```
mma@laptop:~/chef-repo $ knife exec -E 'nodes.transform("chef_
environment:_default") { |n| n.chef_environment("book")
```

You can limit your search for nodes in a specific environment:

```
mma@laptop:~/chef-repo $ knife search node "chef_environment:book"

    1 item found
```

## See also

> ▸ If you want to set up a virtual machine as a node, see the *Managing virtual machines with Vagrant* recipe in this chapter

> ▸ Read more about environments at `https://docs.chef.io/environments.html`

# Freezing cookbooks

Uploading broken cookbooks that override your working ones is a major pain and can result in widespread outage throughout your infrastructure. If you have a cookbook version that is known to work, it's a good idea to freeze this version so that no one can overwrite the same version with broken code. When used together with version constraints that are specified in your environment manifests, freezing cookbooks can keep your production servers safe from accidental changes.

## Getting ready

Make sure you have at least one cookbook (I'll use the `ntp` cookbook) registered with your Chef server.

## How to do it...

Let's see what happens if we freeze a cookbook.

1. Upload a cookbook and freeze it:

   ```
   mma@laptop:~/chef-repo $ knife cookbook upload ntp --freeze

   Uploading ntp            [1.6.8]
   Uploaded 1 cookbook.
   ```

2. Try to upload the same cookbook version again:

   ```
   mma@laptop:~/chef-repo $ knife cookbook upload ntp
   ```

```
Uploading ntp                [1.6.8]
ERROR: Version 1.6.8 of cookbook ntp is frozen. Use --force to
override.
WARNING: Not updating version constraints for ntp in the
environment as the cookbook is frozen.
ERROR: Failed to upload 1 cookbook.
```

3. Change the cookbook version:

```
mma@laptop:~/chef-repo $ subl cookbooks/ntp/metadata.rb
```

```
...
version          "1.6.9"
```

4. Upload the cookbook again:

```
mma@laptop:~/chef-repo $ knife cookbook upload ntp
```

```
Uploading ntp                [1.6.9]
Uploaded 1 cookbook.
```

## How it works...

By using the `--freeze` option when uploading a cookbook, you tell the Chef server that it should not accept any changes to the same version of the cookbook anymore. This is important if you're using environments and want to make sure that your production environment cannot be broken by uploading a corrupted cookbook.

By changing the version number of your cookbook, you can upload the new version. Then you can make, for example, your staging environment use that new cookbook version.

## There's more...

To support a more elaborate workflow, you can use the `knife-spork knife` plugin. It helps multiple developers work on the same Chef server and repository without treading on each other's toes. You can find more information about it at `https://github.com/jonlives/knife-spork`.

## See also

▶ Check out Seth Vargo's talk about Chef + Environments = Safer Infrastructure at `https://speakerdeck.com/sethvargo/chef-plus-environments-equals-safer-infrastructure`

# Running Chef client as a daemon

While you can run the Chef client on your nodes manually whenever you change something in your Chef repository, it's sometimes preferable to have the Chef client run automatically every so often. Letting the Chef client run automatically makes sure that no box misses out any updates.

## Getting ready

You need to have a node registered with your Chef server. It needs to be able to run `chef-client` without any errors.

## How to do it...

Let's see how to start the Chef client in the daemon mode so that it runs automatically.

1. Start the Chef client in the daemon mode, running every 30 minutes:

   **`user@server:~$ sudo chef-client -i 1800`**

2. Validate that the Chef client runs as daemon:

   **`user@server:~$ ps auxw | grep chef-client`**

## How it works...

The `-i` parameter will start the Chef client as a daemon. The given number is the seconds between each Chef client run. In the previous example, we specified 1,800 seconds, which results in the Chef client running every 30 minutes.

You can use the same command in a service startup script.

## There's more...

Instead of running the Chef client as a daemon, you can use a Cronjob to run it every so often:

**`user@server:~$ subl /etc/cron.d/chef_client`**

```
PATH=/usr/local/bin:/usr/bin:/bin
# m h dom mon dow user command
*/15 * * * * root chef-client -l warn | grep -v 'retrying [1234]/5 in'
```

This cronjob will run the Chef client every 15 minutes and swallow the first four retrying warning messages. This is important to avoid Cron sending out e-mails if the Chef server is a little slow and the Chef client needs a few retries.

 It is possible to initiate a Chef client run at any time by sending the `SIGUSR1` signal to the Chef client daemon:

```
user@server:~$ sudo killall -USR1 chef-client
```

# Using chef-shell

Writing cookbooks is hard. Being able to try out parts of a recipe interactively and using breakpoints really helps to understand how your recipes work.

Chef comes with chef-shell, which is essentially an interactive Ruby session with Chef. In chef-shell, you can create attributes, write recipes, and initialize Chef runs, among other things. Chef-shell allows you to evaluate parts of your recipes on the fly before uploading them to your Chef server and executeing complete cookbooks on your nodes.

## How to do it...

Running chef-shell is straightforward.

1. Start chef-shell in standalone mode:

```
mma@laptop:~/chef-repo $ chef-shell

loading configuration: none (standalone chef-shell session)
Session type: standalone
Loading......done.



This is the chef-shell.
 Chef Version: 11.18.0
 http://www.chef.io/chef
 http://docs.chef.io/


run `help' for help, `exit' or ^D to quit.

Ohai2u mma@laptop!
chef >
```

2. Switch to the attributes mode in chef-shell:

```
chef > attributes_mode
```

3. Set an attribute value to be used inside the recipe later:

```
chef:attributes > set[:title] = "Chef Cookbook"

 => "Chef Cookbook"

chef:attributes > quit

 => :attributes

chef >
```

4. Switch to the recipe mode:

```
chef > recipe_mode
```

5. Create a file resource inside a recipe, using the title attribute as content:

```
chef:recipe > file "/tmp/book.txt" do
chef:recipe >       content node.title
chef:recipe ?> end

 => <file[/tmp/book.txt] @name: "/tmp/book.txt" @noop: nil @
before: nil @params: {} @provider: Chef::Provider::File @allowed_
actions: [:nothing, :create, :delete, :touch, :create_if_missing]
@action: "create" @updated: false @updated_by_last_action: false
@supports: {} @ignore_failure: false @retries: 0 @retry_delay:
2 @source_line: "(irb#1):1:in `irb_binding'" @elapsed_time: 0 @
resource_name: :file @path: "/tmp/book.txt" @backup: 5 @diff: nil
@cookbook_name: nil @recipe_name: nil @content: "Chef Cookbook">

chef:recipe >
```

6. Initiate a Chef run to create the file with the given content:

```
chef:recipe > run_chef

[2014-12-12T22:26:42+01:00] INFO: Processing file[/tmp/book.txt]
action create ((irb#1) line 1)
...TRUNCATED OUTPUT...
 => true
```

## How it works...

Chef-shell starts an **interactive Ruby Shell** (**IRB**) session, which is enhanced with some Chef-specific features. It offers certain modes, such as `attributes_mode` or `recipe_mode`, which enable you to write commands like you would put them into attributes file or recipes.

Entering a resource command into the recipe context will create the given resource, but not run it yet. It's like Chef reading your recipe files and creating the resources but not yet running them. You can run all the resources you created within the recipe context using the `run_chef` command. This will execute all the resources on your local box and physically change your system. To play around with temporary files, your local box might do, but if you're going to do more invasive stuff, such as installing or removing packages, installing services, and so on, you might want to use chef-shell from within a Vagrant VM.

## There's more...

Not only can you run chef-shell in standalone mode but you can also in Chef client mode. If you run it in Chef client mode, it will load the complete run list of your node and you'll be able to tweak it inside the chef-shell. You start the Chef client mode by using the run it `--client` parameter:

```
mma@laptop:~/chef-repo $ chef-shell --client
```

You can configure which Chef server to connect it to in a file called `chef-shell.rb`, in the same way as you do in the `client.rb` file on your local workstation.

You can use chef-shell to manage your Chef server, for example, listing all nodes:

```
chef > nodes.list
[node[my_server]]
```

You can put breakpoints into your recipes. If it hits a breakpoint resource, chef-shell will stop the execution of the recipe and you'll be able to inspect the current state of your Chef run:

```
breakpoint "name" do
  action :break
end
```

## See also

▶   Read more about the chef-shell at `https://docs.chef.io/chef_shell.html`

# 2
# Evaluating and Troubleshooting Cookbooks and Chef Runs

*"Most people spend more time and energy going around problems than in trying to solve them."*

*Henry Ford*

In this chapter, we'll cover the following recipes:

- ▶ Testing your Chef cookbooks
- ▶ Flagging problems in your Chef cookbooks
- ▶ Test-driven development for cookbooks using ChefSpec
- ▶ Integration testing your Chef cookbooks with Test Kitchen
- ▶ Showing affected nodes before uploading cookbooks
- ▶ Overriding a node's run list to execute a single recipe
- ▶ Using why-run mode to find out what a recipe might do
- ▶ Debugging Chef client runs
- ▶ Inspecting the results of your last Chef run
- ▶ Raising and logging exceptions in recipes
- ▶ Diff-ing cookbooks with knife
- ▶ Using community exception and report handlers
- ▶ Creating custom handlers

# Introduction

Developing cookbooks and making sure your nodes converge to the desired state is a complex endeavor. You need transparency about what is really happening. This chapter will cover a lot of ways to see what's going on and make sure that everything is working as it should. From running basic checks on your cookbooks to a fully test driven development approach, we'll see what the Chef ecosystem has to offer.

# Testing your Chef cookbooks

You know how annoying this is: you tweak a cookbook, upload it to your Chef server, start a Chef run on your node and, boom! It fails. What's even more annoying is that it fails not because a black hole absorbed your node and the whole data center that node lives in, but because you missed a mundane comma in the default recipe of the cookbook you just tweaked. Fortunately, there's a very quick and easy way to find such simple glitches before you go all in and try to run your cookbooks on real nodes.

## Getting ready

Install the `ntp` cookbook by running the following code:

**mma@laptop:~/chef-repo $ knife cookbook site install ntp**

```
Installing ntp to /Users/mma/work/chef-repo/cookbooks
...TRUNCATED OUTPUT...
Cookbook ntp version 1.7.0 successfully installed
```

## How to do it...

Carry out the following steps to test your cookbooks:

1.  Run `knife cookbook test` on a working cookbook, for example, the `ntp` cookbook:

    **mma@laptop:~/chef-repo $ knife cookbook test ntp**

    ```
    checking ntp
    Running syntax check on ntp
    Validating ruby files
    Validating templates
    ```

2. Now, let's break something in the `ntp` cookbook's default recipe by removing the comma at the end of the `node['ntp']['varlibdir'],` line:

**mma@laptop:~/chef-repo $ subl cookbooks/ntp/recipes/default.rb**

```
...
[ node['ntp']['varlibdir'],
  node['ntp']['statsdir'] ].each do |ntpdir|
  directory ntpdir do
    owner node['ntp']['var_owner']
    group node['ntp']['var_group']
    mode 0755
  end
end
```

3. Run the `test` command again:

**mma@laptop:~/chef-repo $ knife cookbook test ntp**

```
checking ntp
Running syntax check on ntp
Validating ruby files
FATAL: Cookbook file recipes/default.rb has a ruby syntax error:
FATAL: cookbooks/ntp/recipes/default.rb:25: syntax error,
unexpected tIDENTIFIER, expecting ']'
FATAL:    node['ntp']['statsdir'] ].each do |ntpdir|
FATAL:           ^
FATAL: cookbooks/ntp/recipes/default.rb:25: syntax error,
unexpected ']', expecting $end
FATAL:    node['ntp']['statsdir'] ].each do |ntpdir|
FATAL:                            ^
```

## How it works...

`knife cookbook test` executes a Ruby syntax check on all Ruby files within the cookbook as well as on all ERB templates. It loops through all Ruby files and runs `ruby -c` against each of them. The `ruby -c` command causes Ruby to check the syntax of the script and quit without running it.

After going through all Ruby files, `knife cookbook test` goes through all ERB templates and pipes the rendered version created by `erubis -x` through `ruby -c`.

## There's more...

The `knife cookbook test` command does only a very simple syntax check on the Ruby files and ERB templates. There exists a whole ecosystem of additional tools such as Foodcritic (a lint check for Chef cookbooks), ChefSpec (behavior-driven testing for Chef), and Test-kitchen (an integration testing tool to run cookbooks on virtual servers), and then some. You can go fully test driven, if you want!

## See also

- ▶ If you want to write automated tests for your cookbooks, read the *Test-driven development for cookbooks using ChefSpec* recipe in this chapter
- ▶ If you want to run full integration tests for your cookbooks, read the *Integration testing your Chef cookbooks with Test Kitchen* recipe in this chapter

# Flagging problems in your Chef cookbooks

Writing solid Chef recipes can be quite challenging. There are a couple of pitfalls, which you can easily overlook. Also, writing cookbooks in a consistent style is even harder. You might wonder what the proven ways to write cookbooks are. Foodcritic tries to identify possible issues with the logic and style of your cookbooks.

In this section, you'll learn how to use Foodcritic on some existing cookbooks.

## Getting ready

Install the `mysql` cookbook by running the following code:

**mma@laptop:~/chef-repo $ knife cookbook site install mysql 6.0.0**

```
Installing mysql to /Users/mma/work/chef-repo/cookbooks
...TRUNCATED OUTPUT...
Cookbook mysql version 6.0.0 successfully installed
```

## How to do it...

Let's see how Foodcritic reports findings:

1. Run `foodcritic` on your cookbook:

   **mma@laptop:~/chef-repo $ foodcritic ./cookbooks/mysql**

   ```
   ...TRUNCATED OUTPUT...
   ```

```
FC001: Use strings in preference to symbols to access node
attributes: ./cookbooks/mysql/libraries/helpers.rb:273
FC005: Avoid repetition of resource declarations: ./cookbooks/
mysql/libraries/provider_mysql_service.rb:77
...TRUNCATED OUTPUT...
```

2. Get a detailed list of the reported sections inside the `mysql` cookbook by using the `-C` flag:

**mma@laptop:~/chef-repo $ foodcritic -C ./cookbooks/mysql**

```
...TRUNCATED OUTPUT...
FC001: Use strings in preference to symbols to access node
attributes
273|          @pkginfo.set[:suse]['11.3']['5.5'][:server_package] =
'mysql'
 274|
 275|          @pkginfo
 276|        end
cookbooks/mysql/libraries/provider_mysql_service.rb
FC005: Avoid repetition of resource declarations
  74|          end
  75|
  76|          # Support directories
  77|          directory "#{new_resource.name} :create #{etc_dir}"
do
  78|            path etc_dir
  79|            owner new_resource.run_user
  80|            group new_resource.run_group
```

## How it works...

Foodcritic defines a set of rules and checks your recipes against each of them. It comes with rules concerning various areas: style, correctness, attributes, strings, portability, search, services, files, metadata, and so on. Running Foodcritic against a cookbook tells you which of its rules matched a certain part of your cookbook. By default, it gives you a short explanation of what you should do along the concerned file and line number.

If you run `foodcritic -C`, it displays the excerpts of the places where it found the rules to match.

In the preceding example, it didn't like that the `mysql` cookbook uses symbols to access node attributes instead of strings:

```
@pkginfo.set[:suse]['11.3']['5.5'][:server_package] = 'mysql'
```

This could be rewritten as follows:

```
@pkginfo.set['suse']['11.3']['5.5']['server_package'] = 'mysql'
```

## There's more...

Some of the rules, especially the ones from the styles section, are opinionated. You're able to exclude certain rules or complete sets of rules, such as style, when running Foodcritic:

```
mma@laptop:~/chef-repo $ foodcritic -t '~style' ./cookbooks/mysql
mma@laptop:~/chef-repo $
```

In this case, the tilde negates the tag selection to exclude all rules with the `style` tag. Running without the tilde would run the style rules exclusively:

```
mma@laptop:~/chef-repo $ foodcritic -t style ./cookbooks/mysql
```

If you want to run `foodcritic` in a **continuous integration** (**CI**) environment, you can use the `-f` parameter to indicate which rules should fail the build:

```
mma@laptop:~/chef-repo $ foodcritic -f style ./cookbooks/mysql
    ...TRUNCATED OUTPUT...
    FC001: Use strings in preference to symbols to access node attributes:
    ./cookbooks/mysql/libraries/helpers.rb:273
    FC005: Avoid repetition of resource declarations: ./cookbooks/mysql/
    libraries/provider_mysql_service.rb:77
mma@laptop:~/chef-repo $ echo $?
    3
```

In this example, we tell Foodcritic to fail if any rule of the style group fails. In our case, it returns a non-zero exit code instead of zero, as it would if either no rule matches or we omit the `-f` parameter. That non-zero exit code would fail your build on your continuous integration server.

## See also

- ▶ Learn how to make sure that your cookbooks compile in the *Testing your Chef cookbooks* recipe in this chapter
- ▶ Check out strainer, a tool to test multiple things, such as Foodcritic and `knife test` as well as other stuff, at once at `http://github.com/customink/strainer`

# Test-driven development for cookbooks using ChefSpec

**Test-driven development** (**TDD**) is a way to write unit tests before writing any recipe code. By writing the test first, you design what your recipe should do and ensure that your test is for real because it should fail, as long as you haven't written your recipe code.

As soon as you've completed your recipe, your unit tests should pass.

ChefSpec is built on the popular **RSpec** framework and offers a tailored syntax to test Chef recipes.

Let's develop a very simple recipe using the TDD approach with ChefSpec.

## Getting ready

Make sure you have a cookbook called `my_cookbook` and `run_list` of your node includes `my_cookbook`, as described in the *Creating and using cookbooks* recipe in *Chapter 1, Chef Infrastructure*.

## How to do it...

Let's write a failing test first and then a recipe, which will pass the test:

1. Create the `spec` directory for your cookbook:

   ```
   mma@laptop:~/chef-repo $ mkdir cookbooks/my_cookbook/spec
   ```

2. Create your `spec` file:

   ```
   mma@laptop:~/chef-repo $ subl
     cookbooks/my_cookbook/spec/default_spec.rb
   require 'chefspec'
   describe 'my_cookbook::default' do
     let(:chef_run) {
       ChefSpec::ServerRunner.new(
         platform:'ubuntu', version:'12.04'
       ).converge(described_recipe)
     }

     it 'creates a greetings file, containing the platform
       name' do
       expect(chef_run).to
         render_file('/tmp/greeting.txt').with_content('Hello!
   ubuntu!')
     end
   end
   ```

3.  Run `rspec` to make sure that your `spec` fails (you've not written your recipe yet):

    **mma@laptop:~/chef-repo $ rspec**
    **cookbooks/my_cookbook/spec/default_spec.rb**

    ```
    F

    Failures:

      1) my_cookbook::default creates a greetings file, containing the
    platform name
         Failure/Error: expect(chef_run.converge(described_recipe)).to
    create_file_with_content('/tmp/greeting.txt','Hello! ubuntu!')
           File content:
             does not match expected:
           Hello! ubuntu!
         # ./cookbooks/my_cookbook/spec/default_spec.rb:11:in `block
    (2 levels) in <top (required)>'

    Finished in 0.11152 seconds
    1 example, 1 failure

    Failed examples:

    rspec ./cookbooks/my_cookbook/spec/default_spec.rb:10 # my_
    cookbook::default creates a greetings file, containing the
    platform name
    ```

4.  Edit your cookbook's default recipe:

    **mma@laptop:~/chef-repo $ subl**
    **cookbooks/my_cookbook/recipes/default.rb**

    ```
    template '/tmp/greeting.txt' do
      variables greeting: 'Hello!'
    end
    ```

5.  Create a directory for the `template` resource used in your cookbook:

    **mma@laptop:~/chef-repo $ mkdir**
    **cookbooks/my_cookbook/templates**

6.  Create the template file:

    **mma@laptop:~/chef-repo $ subl**
    **cookbooks/my_cookbook/templates/greeting.txt.erb**

    ```
    <%= @greeting %> <%= node['platform'] %>!
    ```

7. Run `rspec` again to check whether your test succeeds now:

```
mma@laptop:~/chef-repo $ rspec
  cookbooks/my_cookbook/spec/default_spec.rb

Finished in 0.7316 seconds (files took 1.89 seconds to load)
1 example, 0 failures
```

## How it works...

First, you need to set up a basic infrastructure in order to use RSpec with Chef. The ChefDK comes with ChefSpec preinstalled but your cookbook needs a directory called `spec`, in which all your tests will live.

When everything is set up, we're ready to start. Following the **Test First** approach of TDD, we create our spec before we write our recipe.

Every spec needs the `chefspec` gem:

```
require 'chefspec'
```

The main part of every spec is a `describe` block, where you tell RSpec which recipe you want to test. Here, you want to test the `default` recipe of your cookbook:

```
describe 'my_cookbook::default' do
  ...
end
```

Now, it's time to create the object that simulates the Chef run. Note that ChefSpec will not really run your recipe, but simulate a Chef run so that you can verify whether certain expectations you have about your recipe hold true.

By using RSpec's `let` call, you create a variable called `chef_run`, which you can use later to define your expectations.

The `chef_run` variable is a `ChefSpec::ServerRunner` object. We want to simulate a Chef run on Ubuntu 12.04. The parameters `platform` and `version`, which we pass to the constructor during the `ChefSpec::ServerRunner.new` call, populate the automatic node attributes so that it looks as though we performed our Chef run on an Ubuntu 12.04 node. ChefSpec uses **Fauxhai** to simulate the automatic node attributes as they would occur on various operating systems:

```
let(:chef_run) {
    ChefSpec::ServerRunner.new(
      platform:'ubuntu', version:'12.04'
    ).converge(described_recipe)
}
```

You can retrieve the recipe under test using the `described_recipe` call instead of typing `my_cookbook::default` again. Using `described_recipe` instead of the recipe name will keep you from repeating the recipe name in every it-block. It will keep your spec **DRY** (**Don't Repeat Yourself**):

```
ChefSpec::ChefRunner.new(...).converge(described_recipe)
```

Finally, we define what we expect our recipe to do.

We describe what we expect our recipe to do with the `it`-statements. Our description of the `it`-call will show up in the error message, if this test fails:

```
it 'creates a greetings file, containing the platform name' do
  ...
end
```

Now it's finally time to formulate our exact expectations. We use the standard RSpec syntax to define our expectations:

```
expect(...).to ...
```

Every expectation works on the simulated Chef run object, which was defined earlier.

We use a ChefSpec-specific matcher called `render_file` with the filename and chain it with a call to `with_content` to tell our spec what our recipe should do.

```
... render_file('/tmp/greeting.txt').with_content('Hello! ubuntu!')
```

On the ChefSpec site, you will find the complete list of custom matchers that you can use to test your recipes in the ChefSpec README at `https://github.com/sethvargo/chefspec#making-assertions`.

After defining our spec, it's time to run it and check whether it fails:

```
$ rspec cookbooks/my_cookbook/spec/default_spec.rb
```

Next, we write our recipe. We use the template resource to create a file with the contents as specified in the spec.

Finally, we run `rspec` again to see our spec pass!

## There's more...

You can modify your node attributes before simulating the Chef run:

```
it 'uses a node attribute as greeting text' do
  chef_run.node.override['my_cookbook']['greeting'] = "Go!"
  expect(chef_run).to
    render_file('/tmp/greeting.txt').with_content('Go! ubuntu!')
end
```

Running `rspec` after adding the preceding test to our spec fails, as expected, because our recipe does not handle the node parameter `['my_cookbook']['greeting']` yet:

```
.F

Failures:

  1) my_cookbook::default uses a node attribute as greeting text
     Failure/Error: expect(chef_run.converge(described_recipe)).to
       create_file_with_content('/tmp/greeting.txt','Go! ubuntu!')
       File content:
       Hello! ubuntu! does not match expected:
       Go! ubuntu!
       # ./cookbooks/my_cookbook/spec/default_spec.rb:16:in `block
         (2 levels) in <top (required)>'

Finished in 0.25295 seconds
2 examples, 1 failure

Failed examples:

rspec ./cookbooks/my_cookbook/spec/default_spec.rb:14 #
  my_cookbook::default uses a node attribute as greeting text
```

Now, we modify our recipe to use the node attribute:

```
node.default['my_cookbook']['greeting'] = "Hello!"

template '/tmp/greeting.txt' do
  variables greeting: node['my_cookbook']['greeting']
end
```

This makes, our tests pass again:

```
..
Finished in 0.25078 seconds
2 examples, 0 failures
```

## See also

- ▸ The ChefSpec repository on GitHub at `https://github.com/sethvargo/chefspec`
- ▸ The source code of Fauxhai at `https://github.com/customink/fauxhai`

- ▶ A talk by Seth Vargo showing an example developing a cookbook test-driven at `http://www.confreaks.com/videos/2364-mwrc2013-tdding-tmux`
- ▶ The RSpec website at `http://rspec.info/`

# Integration testing your Chef cookbooks with Test Kitchen

Verifying that your cookbooks really work when converging a node is essential. Only if you can trust your cookbooks, you are ready to run them anytime on your production servers.

Test Kitchen is Chef's integration testing framework. It enables you to write tests, which run after a VM is instantiated and converged, using your cookbook. Your tests run in that VM and can verify that everything works as expected.

This is in contrast to ChefSpec, which only simulates a Chef run. Test Kitchen boots up a real node and runs Chef on it. Your tests see the real thing.

Let's see how you can write such integration tests for your cookbooks.

## Getting ready

Make sure you have a cookbook named `my_cookbook`, as described in the *Creating and using cookbooks* recipe in *Chapter 1, Chef Infrastructure*.

Make sure you have Vagrant installed, as described in the *Managing virtual machines with Vagrant* recipe in *Chapter 1, Chef Infrastructure*.

## How to do it...

Let's create a very simple recipe and use Test Kitchen and `Serverspec` to run a full integration test with Vagrant:

1. Edit your cookbook's default recipe:

   ```
   mma@laptop:~/chef-repo $ subl
     cookbooks/my_cookbook/recipes/default.rb

   file "/tmp/greeting.txt" do
     content node['my_cookbook']['greeting']
   end
   ```

2. Edit your cookbook's default attributes:

   ```
   mma@laptop:~/chef-repo $ mkdir -p cookbooks/my_cookbook/attributes
   ```

```
mma@laptop:~/chef-repo $ subl
  cookbooks/my_cookbook/attributes/default.rb

default['my_cookbook']['greeting'] = "Ohai, Chefs!"
```

3. Change to your cookbook directory:

```
mma@laptop:~/chef-repo $ cd cookbooks/my_cookbook
```

4. Initialize Test Kitchen for your cookbook:

```
mma@laptop:~/chef-repo/cookbooks/my_cookbook $ kitchen init

      create  .kitchen.yml
      create  test/integration/default
Successfully installed kitchen-vagrant-0.16.0
1 gem installed
```

5. Edit the generated Test Kitchen configuration file to only test against Ubuntu 14.04:

```
mma@laptop:~/chef-repo/cookbooks/my_cookbook $ subl .kitchen.yml

 ...
 platforms:
   - name: ubuntu-14.04
 ...
```

6. Create a directory for your Serverspec files inside your cookbook:

```
mma@laptop:~/chef-repo/cookbooks/my_cookbook $ mkdir -p test/
integration/default/serverspec
```

7. Create your spec, defining what you expect your cookbook to do:

```
mma@laptop:~/chef-repo/cookbooks/my_cookbook $ subl test/
integration/default/serverspec/greeting_spec.rb
require 'serverspec'

# Required by serverspec
set :backend, :exec

describe file('/tmp/greeting.txt') do
its(:content) { should match 'Ohai, Chefs!' }
end
```

8. Run Test Kitchen:

```
mma@laptop:~/chef-repo/cookbooks/my_cookbook $ kitchen test

-----> Starting Kitchen (v1.2.1)
...TRUNCATED OUTPUT...
```

```
Bringing machine 'default' up with 'virtualbox' provider...
...TRUNCATED OUTPUT...
Finished creating <default-ubuntu-1404> (0m50.31s).
-----> Converging <default-ubuntu-1404>...
...TRUNCATED OUTPUT...
-----> Installing Chef Omnibus (true)
...TRUNCATED OUTPUT...
Starting Chef Client, version 12.0.3
...TRUNCATED OUTPUT...
Recipe: my_cookbook::default
...TRUNCATED OUTPUT...
      Chef Client finished, 1/1 resources updated in 6.450780111
seconds
...TRUNCATED OUTPUT...
Uploading /tmp/busser/suites/serverspec/greeting_spec.rb
(mode=0644)
-----> Running serverspec test suite
-----> Installing Serverspec..
...TRUNCATED OUTPUT...
-----> serverspec installed (version 2.7.1)
...TRUNCATED OUTPUT...
File "/tmp/greeting.txt"
  content
    should match "Ohai, Chefs!"

Finished in 0.09647 seconds (files took 0.26995 seconds to load)
1 example, 0 failures
      Finished verifying <default-ubuntu-1404> (0m15.46s).
-----> Destroying <default-ubuntu-1404>...
...TRUNCATED OUTPUT...
-----> Kitchen is finished. (2m13.66s)
```

## How it works...

First, we create a very simple recipe, which writes the value of a node attribute to a file.

Then, it's time to configure Test Kitchen. You do this by running `kitchen init`, which creates a `.kitchen.yml` file in your cookbook directory. It consists of four parts:

1. Part one defines which driver you want Test Kitchen to use to create virtual machines (VMs) for testing. We use Vagrant to spin up VMs:

   ```
   driver:
     name: vagrant
   ```

2. Part two defines how you want to use Chef on your test VMs. We don't want to use a Chef server, so we keep the default Chef solo:

   **provisioner:**
   ```
     - name: chef_solo
   ```

3. Part three defines on which platforms you want to test your cookbook. To keep things simple, we only define Ubuntu 14.04 here. Test Kitchen will always create and destroy new instances. You do not have to fear any side effects with Vagrant VMs you spin up using your `Vagrantfile`:

   ```
   platforms:
   - name: ubuntu-14.04
   ```

4. Part four defines the test suites. We define one called `default`. We include our `my_cookbook::default` recipe here so that we're able to test what it does:

   ```
   suites:
   - name: default
     run_list:
     - recipe[my_cookbook::default]
     attributes:
   ```

Now, it's time to create our specs using Serverspec. Test Kitchen uses a naming convention inside the `test/integration` directory to discover the test framework to use for each test suite. In our case, we run the `default` test suite by using `serverspec` as the testing framework. That's why our directory structure looks like this:

```
test/integration/default/serverspec
```

We call our spec `greeting_spec.rb` and put it inside the aforementioned directory, so that Test Kitchen will automatically pick it up and run it.

After some boilerplate code, we describe what we expect our recipe to do:

```
describe file('/tmp/greeting.txt') do
  its(:content) { should match 'Ohai, Chefs!' }
end
```

`Serverspec` provides you with custom RSpec matchers to verify the status of your systems. You can find a complete list of the supported resource types here: `http://serverspec.org/resource_types.html`.

Finally, we can run Test Kitchen. It will first make sure that no old VMs are around and then create a new one. It installs Chef on that brand new VM and starts a Chef run. Test Kitchen uses **Busser** to install the desired test framework (as defined by the directory structure below `test/integration`) and execute our specs after the node converges.

If everything works, Test Kitchen destroys the VM again.

If something fails, Test Kitchen keeps the VM and you can analyze it by running `kitchen login`.

## There's more...

You don't have to run `kitchen test` every time you change something. If you change your cookbook, you can run `kitchen converge` to re-apply your changes to an existing VM.

To run your test suite after your node converged, you use `kitchen verify`.

Test Kitchen does not only support Vagrant but a host of other cloud providers such as OpenStack, EC2, Rackspace, Joyent, and many more. Just make sure you use the matching driver in your `.kitchen.yml` file.

You can define multiple different platforms, such as other Ubuntu versions or CentOS and so on, by adding them to the platforms definition in `.kitchen.yml`:

```
platforms:
- name: centos-6.4
```

>  You find Test Kitchen's log files inside your cookbook in the `.kitchen/logs` directory.

If you defined multiple platforms but want to run a Test Kitchen command against only one of them, you can add a regular expression matching the desired platform to your command: `kitchen test default-ubuntu-14.04` or `kitchen test 14`.

If you want to know the status of the various VMs managed by Test Kitchen, you can list them as follows:

**mma@laptop:~/chef-repo/cookbooks/my_cookbook $ kitchen list**

```
Instance              Driver    Provisioner   Last Action
default-ubuntu-1404   Vagrant   ChefSolo      Converged
```

## See also

- Find Test Kitchen at `http://kitchen.ci`
- Find the source code for Test Kitchen and the associated tools (including drivers for cloud providers and Busser plugins for other test frameworks) on GitHub at `https://github.com/test-kitchen`
- Find Serverspec at `http://serverspec.org`

# Showing affected nodes before uploading cookbooks

You know how it goes. You tweak a cookbook to support your new server and upload it to your Chef server. Your new node converges just fine and you're happy. Well, until your older production server picks up your modified cookbook during an automated Chef client run and spits its guts at you. Obviously, you forgot that your old production server was still using the cookbook you tweaked. Luckily, there is the `knife preflight` command, which can show you all the nodes using a certain cookbook before you upload it to your Chef server.

## Getting ready

For the following example, we assume that you have at least one role using the `ntp` cookbook in its run list and that you have multiple servers with this role and/or the `ntp` cookbook in their run list directly.

Use Chef to install the `knife-preflight` gem:

```
mma@laptop:~/chef-repo $ chef gem install knife-preflight

    Fetching gem metadata from https://rubygems.org/
    ...TRUNCATED OUTPUT...
    Installing knife-preflight (0.1.7)
```

## How to do it...

Let's see how `preflight` works on the `ntp` cookbook:

Run the `preflight` command to find out which nodes and roles have the `ntp` cookbook in their expanded run lists. You'll obviously see your nodes and roles in the output instead of the exact ones listed here:

```
mma@laptop:~/chef-repo $ knife preflight ntp

    Searching for nodes containing ntp OR ntp::default in their
      expanded run_list...
    2 Nodes found
    www-staging.example.com
    cms-staging.example.com
    Searching for roles containing ntp OR ntp::default in their
      expanded run_list...
    3 Roles found
    your_cms_role
    your_www_role
```

```
your_app_role
Found 6 nodes and 3 roles using the specified search
  criteria
```

## How it works...

There are multiple ways for a cookbook to get executed on a node:

- You can assign the cookbook directly to a node by adding it to the node's run list
- You can add a cookbook to a role and add the role to the node's run list
- You can add a role to the run list of another role and add that other role to the node's run list
- A cookbook can be a dependency of another used cookbook and many more

No matter how a cookbook ended up in a node's run list, the `knife preflight` command will catch it because Chef stores all expanded lists of roles and recipes in node attributes. The `knife preflight` command issues a search for exactly those node attributes.

Eventually, the `knife preflight` command is a nicer way to run `knife search node recipes:ntp -a name` and `knife search node roles:ntp -a name`.

> When using the `knife preflight` command (or trying to search for the `recipes` and `roles` attributes of a node), it is important to be aware of the fact that those attributes are only filled after a Chef client runs. If you change anything in your run lists but do not run the Chef client, neither `knife preflight` nor `knife search` will pick up your changes.

## See also

- Learn how to find and use other knife plugins in the *Using custom knife plugins* recipe in *Chapter 1, Chef Infrastructure*
- The source code of the `knife-preflight` plugin is available from GitHub at `https://github.com/jonlives/knife-preflight`

# Overriding a node's run list to execute a single recipe

We all have those snowflake environments that are built using Chef, but we're not comfortable with running the Chef client anymore. We know that some cookbooks have been enhanced but never tested against this specific environment. The risk of bringing it down by a Chef client run is pretty high.

However, even though we do not dare do a full Chef client run, we might need to run, for example, the users cookbook, in order to add a new colleague to our snowflake environment. This is where Chef client's feature to override a run list to execute a single recipe comes in very handy.

 Don't overuse this feature! Make sure you fix your environment so that you're comfortable to run Chef client whenever you need to!

## Getting ready

To follow along with the following example, you'll need a node hooked up to your Chef server having multiple recipes and/or roles in its run list.

## How to do it...

Let's see how to run a single recipe out of a bigger run list on your node:

1. Show the data for your node. In this example, my node has the role base in its run list. Depending on your setup, you'll find other data here:

```
mma@laptop:~/chef-repo $ knife node show www.example.com

...TRUNCATED OUTPUT…
Run List:     role[base]
Roles:        base
Recipes:      chef-client::delete_validation, runit, chef-client
...TRUNCATED OUTPUT…
```

2. Run chef-client, overriding its run list. In our example, we want to run the default recipe of the users cookbook. Please replace recipe[users] with whatever you want to run on your node:

```
user@server:~$ chef-client -o 'recipe[users]'

Starting Chef Client, version 12.0.3
[2014-12-23T10:58:10+00:00] WARN: Run List override has been provided.
[2014-12-23T10:58:10+00:00] WARN: Original Run List: []
[2014-12-23T10:58:10+00:00] WARN: Overridden Run List: [recipe[users]]
resolving cookbooks for run list: ["users"]
...TRUNCATED OUTPUT...
```

## How it works...

Usually, the node uses the run list stored on the Chef server. The `-o` parameter simply ignores the node's run list and uses whatever the value of the `-o` parameter is as the run list for the current Chef run. It will not persist the passed run list. The next Chef client run (without the `-o` parameter) will use the run list stored on the Chef server again.

## See also

- ► Read more about Chef run lists at `http://docs.chef.io/nodes.html#about-run-lists`
- ► You might want to read more about it in the *Showing affected nodes before uploading cookbooks* recipe in this chapter

# Using why-run mode to find out what a recipe might do

`why-run` mode lets each resource tell you what it would do during a Chef client run, assuming certain prerequisites. This is great because it gives you a glimpse about what might really happen on your node when you run your recipe for real.

However, because Chef converges a lot of resources to a desired state, `why-run` will never be accurate for a complete run. Nevertheless, it might help you during development while you're adding resources step-by-step to build the final recipe.

In this section, we'll try out `why-run` mode to see what it tells us about our Chef client runs.

## Getting ready

To try out `why-run` mode, you need a node where you can execute the Chef client and at least one cookbook that is available on that node.

## How to do it...

Let's try to run the `ntp` cookbook in `why-run` mode:

1. Override the current run list to run the `ntp` recipe in `why-run` mode on a brand new box:

    ```
    user@server:~$ sudo chef-client -o 'recipe[ntp]' --why-run
    ```

```
...TRUNCATED OUTPUT...
Converging 10 resources
Recipe: ntp::default
  * apt_package[ntp] action install
    - Would install version 1:4.2.6.p5+dfsg-3ubuntu2 of package
ntp
  * apt_package[ntpdate] action install (up to date)
  * directory[/var/lib/ntp] action create
    - Would create new directory /var/lib/ntp
    - Would change mode from '' to '0755'
...TRUNCATED OUTPUT...
   * service[ntp] action enable
    * Service status not available. Assuming a prior action would
have installed the service.
    * Assuming status of not running.
    * Could not find /etc/init/ntp.conf. Assuming service is
disabled.
    - Would enable service service[ntp]
...TRUNCATED OUTPUT...
Chef Client finished, 10/11 resources would have benne updated
```

2.  Install the `ntp` package manually to see the difference in `why-run`:

    **user@server:~$ sudo apt-get install ntp**

    ```
    ...TRUNCATED OUTPUT...
    0 upgraded, 2 newly installed, 0 to remove and 1 not
      upgraded.
    ...TRUNCATED OUTPUT...
    ```

3.  Run `why-run` for the `ntp` recipe again (now with the installed `ntp` package):

    **user@server:~$ sudo chef-client -o recipe['ntp'] --why-run**

    ```
    ...TRUNCATED OUTPUT...
    Converging 10 resources
    Recipe: ntp::default
      * apt_package[ntp] action install (up to date)
      * apt_package[ntpdate] action install (up to date)
      * directory[/var/lib/ntp] action create (up to date)
    ...TRUNCATED OUTPUT...
     Chef Client finished, 5/11 resources would have been updated
    ```

## How it works...

The `why-run` mode is the *no-operations* mode for the Chef client. Instead of providers modifying the system, it tries to tell what the Chef run would attempt to do.

It's important to know that `why-run` makes certain assumptions; if it cannot find the command needed to find out about the current status of a certain service, it assumes that an earlier resource would have installed the needed package for that service and that therefore, the service would be started. We see this when the `ntp` cookbook tries to enable the `ntp` service:

```
* Service status not available. Assuming a prior action would
  have installed the service.
* Assuming status of not running.
* Could not find /etc/init/ntp.conf. Assuming service is disabled.
- Would enable service service[ntp]
```

Additionally, `why-run` shows diffs of modified files. In our example, those differences show the whole files, as they do not exist yet. This feature is more helpful if you already have `ntp` installed and your next Chef run would only change a few configuration parameters.

 `why-run` mode will execute the `not_if` and `only_if` blocks. It is assumed that the code within the `not_if` and `only_if` blocks will not modify the system but only do some checks.

## See also

▶ Read more about `why-run` mode at `http://docs.chef.io/nodes.html#about-why-run-mode`

▶ Read more about the issues with dry runs in configuration management at `http://blog.afistfulofservers.net/post/2012/12/21/promises-lies-and-dryrun-mode/`

# Debugging Chef client runs

Sometimes you get obscure error messages when running the Chef client and you have a hard time finding any clue about where to look for the error. Is your cookbook broken? Do you have a networking issue? Is your Chef server down? Only by looking at the most verbose log output do you have a chance to find out.

## Getting ready

You need a Chef client hooked up to the hosted Chef or your own Chef server.

## How to do it...

Let's see how we can ask the Chef client to print debug messages:

1. Run the Chef-client with `debug` output:

   **user@server:~$ sudo chef-client -l debug**

   ...TRUNCATED OUTPUT...
   [2014-12-27T21:38:34+00:00] DEBUG: Chef::HTTP calling Chef::HTTP::
   RemoteRequestID#handle_request
   [2014-12-27T21:38:34+00:00] DEBUG: Chef::HTTP calling Chef::HTTP::
   ValidateContentLength#handle_request
   [2014-12-27T21:38:34+00:00] DEBUG: Initiating GET to https://api.
   opscode.com/organizations/awo/nodes/server
   [2014-12-27T21:38:34+00:00] DEBUG: ---- HTTP Request Header Data:
   ----
   [2014-12-27T21:38:34+00:00] DEBUG: Accept: application/json
   [2014-12-27T21:38:34+00:00] DEBUG: Accept-Encoding: gzip;q=1.0,def
   late;q=0.6,identity;q=0.3
   [2014-12-27T21:38:34+00:00] DEBUG: X-OPS-SIGN:
   ...TRUNCATED OUTPUT...
   [2014-12-27T21:38:34+00:00] DEBUG: HOST: api.opscode.com:443
   [2014-12-27T21:38:34+00:00] DEBUG: X-REMOTE-REQUEST-ID: d4b07248-
   d522-4181-bf02-1405c3ccb110
   [2014-12-27T21:38:34+00:00] DEBUG: ---- End HTTP Request Header
   Data ----
   [2014-12-27T21:38:35+00:00] DEBUG: ---- HTTP Status and Header
   Data: ----
   [2014-12-27T21:38:35+00:00] DEBUG: HTTP 1.1 200 OK
   [2014-12-27T21:38:35+00:00] DEBUG: server: ngx_openresty
   [2014-12-27T21:38:35+00:00] DEBUG: date: Sat, 27 Dec 2014 21:38:35
   GMT
   [2014-12-27T21:38:35+00:00] DEBUG: content-type: application/json
   [2014-12-27T21:38:35+00:00] DEBUG: transfer-encoding: chunked
   [2014-12-27T21:38:35+00:00] DEBUG: connection: close
   [2014-12-27T21:38:35+00:00] DEBUG: x-ops-api-info:
   flavor=hec;version=12.0.0;oc_erchef=0.29.2
   [2014-12-27T21:38:35+00:00] DEBUG: content-encoding: gzip
   [2014-12-27T21:38:35+00:00] DEBUG: ---- End HTTP Status/Header
   Data ----
   [2014-12-27T21:38:35+00:00] DEBUG: Chef::HTTP calling Chef::HTTP::
   ValidateContentLength#handle_response
   [2014-12-27T21:38:35+00:00] DEBUG: HTTP server did not include
   a Content-Length header in response, cannot identify truncated
   downloads.

```
[2014-12-27T21:38:35+00:00] DEBUG: Chef::HTTP calling Chef::HTTP::
RemoteRequestID#handle_response
[2014-12-27T21:38:35+00:00] DEBUG: Chef::HTTP calling Chef::HTTP::
Authenticator#handle_response
[2014-12-27T21:38:35+00:00] DEBUG: Chef::HTTP calling
Chef::HTTP::Decompressor#handle_response
...TRUNCATED OUTPUT...
```

## How it works...

The -l option on the Chef-client run sets the log level to debug. In the debug log level, the Chef client shows more or less everything it does, including every request to the Chef server.

## There's more...

The debug log level is the most verbose one. You're free to use debug, info, warn, error, or fatal with the -l switch.

You can configure the log level in your /etc/chef/client.rb file, using the log_level directive:

```
...
log_level :debug
...
```

## See also

► Read more about log levels in the *Raising and logging exceptions in recipes* section in this chapter.

# Inspecting the results of your last Chef run

More often than we like to admit, Chef client runs fail. Especially when developing new cookbooks, we need to know what exactly went wrong.

Even though Chef prints all the details to stdout, you might want to look at it again, for example, after clearing your shell window.

## Getting ready

You need to have a broken cookbook in your node's run list.

## How to do it...

Carry out the following steps:

1. Run the Chef client with your broken cookbook:

   ```
   user@server:~$ sudo chef-client
   ================================================================
   ==============
   Recipe Compile Error in /var/chef/cache/cookbooks/my_cookbook/
   recipes/default.rb
   ================================================================
   ==============
   NoMethodError
   -------------
   undefined method `each' for nil:NilClass


   Cookbook Trace:
   ---------------
     /var/chef/cache/cookbooks/my_cookbook/recipes/default.rb:7:in
   `from_file'


   Relevant File Content:
   ----------------------
   /var/chef/cache/cookbooks/my_cookbook/recipes/default.rb:

     3:  # Recipe:: default
     4:  #
     5:  # Copyright (c) 2014 The Authors, All Rights Reserved.
     6:
     7>> nil.each {}
     8:
   ```

2. Look into the `stracktrace` file to find out what happened in more detail:

   ```
   user@server:~$ sudo less /var/chef/cache/chef-stacktrace.out
   ```

   ```
   Generated at 2014-12-27 21:52:06 +0000
   NoMethodError: undefined method `each' for nil:NilClass
   ```

```
/var/chef/cache/cookbooks/my_cookbook/recipes/default.rb:10:in
`from_file'
/opt/chef/embedded/apps/chef/lib/chef/mixin/from_file.rb:30:in
`instance_eval'
/opt/chef/embedded/apps/chef/lib/chef/mixin/from_file.rb:30:in
`from_file'
/opt/chef/embedded/apps/chef/lib/chef/cookbook_version.rb:245:in
`load_recipe'
```

## How it works...

The Chef client reports errors to `stdout`, by default. If you missed that output, you need to look into the files Chef generated to find out what went wrong.

## See also

> ▶ Read how to produce the debug output on `stdout` in the *Logging debug messages* section in this chapter.

# Raising and logging exceptions in recipes

Running your own cookbooks on your nodes might lead into situations where it does not make any sense to continue the current Chef run. If a critical resource is offline or a mandatory configuration value cannot be determined, it is time to bail out.

However, even if things are not that bad, you might want to log certain events while executing your recipes. Chef offers the possibility to write your custom log messages and exit the current run, if you choose to do so.

In this section, you'll learn how to add log statements and stop Chef runs using exceptions.

## Getting ready

You need to have at least one cookbook you can modify and run on a node. The following example will use the `ntp` cookbook.

## How to do it...

Let's see how to add our custom log message to a recipe:

1. Add log statements to the `ntp` cookbook's default recipe:

   ```
   mma@laptop:~/chef-repo $ subl cookbooks/ntp/recipes/default.rb
   ```

```
Chef::Log.info('** Going to install the ntp service
  now...')

service node['ntp']['service'] do
  supports :status => true, :restart => true
  action [ :enable, :start ]
end

Chef::Log.info('** ntp service installed and started
  successfully!')
```

2. Upload the modified cookbook to the Chef server:

   **mma@laptop:~/chef-repo $ knife cookbook upload ntp**

   ```
   Uploading ntp              [1.7.0]
   Uploaded 1 cookbook.
   ```

3. Run the Chef client on the node:

   **user@server:~$ sudo chef-client**

   ```
   ...TRUNCATED OUTPUT...
   [2014-12-27T13:53:19+00:00] INFO: Storing updated cookbooks/ntp/
   TESTING.md in the cache.
   [2014-12-27T13:53:19+00:00] INFO: ** Going to install the ntp
   service now...
   [2014-12-27T13:53:19+00:00] INFO: ** ntp service installed and
   started successfully!
   [2014-12-27T13:53:19+00:00] INFO: Processing package[ntp] action
   install (ntp::default line 21)
   ...TRUNCATED OUTPUT...
   ```

4. Raise an exception from within the ntp default recipe:

   **mma@laptop:~/chef-repo $ subl cookbooks/ntp/recipes/default.rb**

   ```
   Chef::Application.fatal!('Ouch!!! Bailing out!!!')
   ```

5. Upload the modified cookbook to the Chef server:

   **mma@laptop:~/chef-repo $ knife cookbook upload ntp**

   ```
   Uploading ntp              [1.7.0]
   Uploaded 1 cookbook.
   ```

6. Run the Chef client on the node again:

   **user@server:~$ sudo chef-client**

   ```
   ...TRUNCATED OUTPUT...
   [2014-12-28T11:09:44+00:00] FATAL: 'Ouch!!! Bailing out!!!
   ...TRUNCATED OUTPUT...
   ```

## How it works...

The `fatal!(msg)` method logs the given error message through `Chef::Log.fatal(msg)` and then exits the Chef client process using `Process.exit` with the exit code `-1`.

## There's more...

You might want to exit the Chef client run without logging a `fatal` message. You can do so by using the `exit!(msg)` method in your recipe. It will log the given message as `debug` and exit the Chef client, the same as it does when calling `fatal!(...)`.

## See also

▸ Read the documentation for the `fatal!` method here: `http://www.rubydoc.info/gems/chef/Chef/Application#fatal%21-class_method`

▸ Find a detailed description about how to abort a Chef run here: `http://stackoverflow.com/questions/14290397/how-do-you-abort-end-a-chef-run`

# Diff-ing cookbooks with knife

When working with a Chef server, you often need to know what exactly is already uploaded to it. You edit files like recipes or roles locally, and commit and push them to GitHub.

However, before you're ready to upload your edits to the Chef server, you want to verify your changes. To do this, you need to run a diff between the local version of your files against the version already uploaded to the Chef server.

## Getting ready

You need to have at least one cookbook you can modify and which is uploaded to your Chef server.

## How to do it...

After changing a recipe, you can diff it against the current version stored on the Chef server.

Let knife show you the differences between your local version of `my_cookbook` and the version stored on the Chef server, by running:

```
mma@laptop:~/chef-repo $ knife diff cookbooks/my_cookbook
```

```
diff --knife cookbooks/my_cookbook/recipes/default.rb cookbooks/my_
cookbook/recipes/default.rb
--- cookbooks/my_cookbook/recipes/default.rb    2014-12-29
21:02:50.000000000 +0100
+++ cookbooks/my_cookbook/recipes/default.rb    2014-12-29
21:02:50.000000000 +0100
@@ -7,5 +7,6 @@
 #file "/tmp/greeting.txt" do
 #   content node['my_cookbook']['greeting']
 #end
-nil.each {}
+Chef::Application.fatal!('Ouch!!! Bailing out!!!')
+
```

## How it works...

The `diff` verb for knife treats the Chef server like a file server mirroring your local file system. This way, you can run diffs by comparing your local files against files stored on the Chef server.

## There's more...

If you want to show diffs of multiple cookbooks at once, you can use wildcards when running `knife diff`:

**mma@laptop:~/chef-repo $ knife diff cookbooks/\***

```
diff --knife remote/cookbooks/backup_gem/recipes/default.rb
  cookbooks/backup_gem/recipes/default.rb
...TRUNCATED OUTPUT...
diff --knife remote/cookbooks/backup_gem/metadata.rb
  cookbooks/backup_gem/metadata.rb
...TRUNCATED OUTPUT...
```

You can limit `knife diff` to only list files, which have been changed instead of the full diff:

**mma@laptop:~/chef-repo $ knife diff --name-status cookbooks/my_cookbook**

```
M    cookbooks/my_cookbook/recipes/default.rb
```

The `M` indicates that the file `cookbooks/my_cookbook/recipes/default.rb` is modified.

## See also

▶ Find some more examples on how to use `knife diff` here: `http://docs.chef.io/knife_diff.html`

# Using community exception and report handlers

When running your Chef client as a daemon on your nodes, you usually have no idea whether everything works as expected. Chef comes with a feature named **Handler**, which helps you to find out what's going on during your Chef client runs.

There are a host of community handlers available, for example, to report Chef client run results to IRC, via email, to Campfire, Nagios, or Graphite. You name it.

In this section, we'll see how to install an IRC handler as an example. The same method is applicable to all other available handlers.

 For a full list of available community handlers, go to `http://docs.chef.io/community_plugin_report_handler.html`

## Getting ready

In order to install community exception and report handlers, you need to add the `chef_handler` cookbook to your `Berksfile` first:

**mma@laptop:~/chef-repo $ subl Berksfile**

```
cookbook 'chef_handler'
```

## How to do it...

Let's see how to install and use one of the community handlers:

1. Create your own cookbook to install community exception and report handlers:

   **mma@laptop:~/chef-repo $ chef generate cookbook cookbooks/my_handlers**

   ```
   Compiling Cookbooks...
   Recipe: code_generator::cookbook
     * directory[/Users/mma/work/chef-repo/cookbooks/my_handlers]
   action create
       - create new directory /Users/mma/work/chef-repo/cookbooks/
   my_handlers
   ...TRUNCATED OUTPUT...
   ```

2. Make your `my_handlers` cookbook aware of the fact that it needs the `chef_handler` cookbook by adding the dependency to its metadata:

**mma@laptop:~/chef-repo $ subl**
  **cookbooks/my_handlers/metadata.rb**

```
depends 'chef_handler'
```

3. Add the IRC handler to your `my_handlers` cookbook (make sure you use your own URI for the `irc_uri` argument):

**mma@laptop:~/chef-repo $ subl**
  **cookbooks/my_handlers/recipes/default.rb**

```
include_recipe 'chef_handler'

chef_gem "chef-irc-snitch"

chef_handler 'IRCSnitch' do
  source File.join(Gem::Specification.find{|s| s.name ==
    'chef-irc-snitch'}.gem_dir,
    'lib', 'chef-irc-snitch.rb')
  arguments :irc_uri => "irc://nick:password@irc.example.
com:6667/#admins"
  action :enable
end
```

4. Upload your `my_handlers` cookbook to your Chef server:

**mma@laptop:~/chef-repo $ knife cookbook upload my_handlers**

```
Uploading my_handlers    [0.1.0]
Uploaded 1 cookbook.
```

5. Run the Chef client on your node to install your handlers:

**user@server:~$ sudo chef-client -o recipe[my_handlers]**

```
...TRUNCATED OUTPUT...
  * chef_handler[IRCSnitch] action enable
    - load /opt/chef/embedded/lib/ruby/gems/2.1.0/gems/chef-irc-
snitch-0.2.1/lib/chef-irc-snitch.rb[2014-12-29T10:19:25+00:00]
INFO: Enabling chef_handler[IRCSnitch] as a report handler

    - enable chef_handler[IRCSnitch] as a report handler
[2014-12-29T10:19:25+00:00] INFO: Enabling chef_handler[IRCSnitch]
as a exception handler

    - enable chef_handler[IRCSnitch] as a exception handler
```

## How it works...

The `chef_handler` **Light Weight Resource Provider** (**LWRP**) provided by the `chef_handler` cookbook helps you enable and configure any custom handler without the need to manually modify `client.rb` on all your nodes.

Typically, you would install the desired community handler as a gem. You do this using the `chef_gem` resource.

You can pass an attributes Hash to the `Handler` class and you need to tell the LWRP where it can find the `Handler` class. The default should be `chef/handlers/...` but more often than not, this is not the case. We will search through all our installed Ruby gems to find the right one and append the path to the `.rb` file, where the `Handler` class is defined.

The LWRP will take care of enabling the handler, if you tell it to do so by using `enable true`.

## There's more...

If you want, you can install your handler manually by editing `client.rb` on your nodes.

If your desired handler is not available as a Ruby gem, you can install it in `/var/chef/handlers` and use this directory as the source when using the `chef_handler` LWRP.

## See also

▸ Read more about Exception and Report handlers at `http://docs.chef.io/handlers.html`

# Creating custom handlers

Chef handlers can be very helpful to integrate Chef with your tool chain. If there is no handler readily available for the tools you are using, it's pretty simple to write your own.

We'll have a look at how to create an exception handler, reporting Chef client run failures to **Flowdock**, a web-based team inbox and chat tool.

## Getting ready...

As we want to publish information to a Flowdock inbox, you need to sign up for an account at `http://www.flowdock.com`. Also, we need to install the API client as a Ruby gem in order to be able to post to our team inbox from Chef.

Install the `flowdock` gem on your local development box:

**mma@laptop:~/chef-repo $ chef gem install flowdock**

```
...TRUNCATED OUTPUT...
Fetching: flowdock-0.5.0.gem (100%)
Successfully installed flowdock-0.5.0
2 gems installed
```

## How to do it...

Carry out the following steps to create a custom handler to post Chef run failures to Flowdock:

1. Create your handler class:

   **mma@laptop:~/work/chef-handler-flowdock $ mkdir -p lib/chef/handler**

   **mma@laptop:~/work/chef-handler-flowdock $ subl lib/chef/handler/flowdock_handler.rb**

```ruby
require 'chef/handler'
require 'flowdock'

class Chef
  class Handler
    class FlowdockHandler < Chef::Handler

      def initialize(options = {})
        @from = options[:from] || nil
        @flow = Flowdock::Flow.new(:api_token =>
          options[:api_token],
          :source => options[:source] || "Chef client")
      end

      def report
        if run_status.failed?
          content = "Chef client raised an exception:<br/>"
          content << run_status.formatted_exception
          content << "<br/>"
          content << run_status.backtrace.join("<br/>")

          @from = {:name => "root", :address =>
            "root@#{run_status.node.fqdn}"} if @from.nil?

          @flow.push_to_team_inbox(:subject => "Chef client
            run on #{run_status.node} failed!",
```

```
                    :content => content,
                    :tags => ["chef",
                      run_status.node.chef_environment,
                      run_status.node.name], :from => @from)
              end
            end
          end
        end
      end
```

2. Copy the handler to your node:

```
user@server:~$ sudo mkdir -p /var/chef/handlers
```

```
mma@laptop:~/work/chef-handler-flowdock $ scp
   lib/chef/handler/flowdock_handler.rb
   user@server:/var/chef/handlers/flowdock_handler.rb
```

3. Enable the handler in `client.rb` on your node. Replace FLOWDOCK_API_TOKEN with your own token:

```
user@server:~$ subl /etc/chef/client.rb
```

```
require '/var/chef/handlers/flowdock_handler'
exception_handlers <<
   Chef::Handler::FlowdockHandler.new(:api_token =>
   "FLOWDOCK_API_TOKEN")
```

If you have a failing Chef client run on your node, your handler will report it to your Flowdock flow.

## How it works...

To create a Chef handler, your class needs to extend `Chef::Handler`. It should have two methods: `initialize` and `report`. Chef will call the `report` method at the end of every Chef client run.

The handler class can access `run_status` of the Chef client run to retrieve information about the run, for example, the current `node` object, `success?` or `failed?`, and the exception (if any). You will find a full list of the supported attributes at `http://docs.chef.io/handlers.html#run-status-object`

As we only want to report exceptions, we will execute our logic inside the `report` method only if the Chef run fails

## There's more...

Instead of manually installing the handler on all your nodes, you can create a cookbook called my_handlers to do it for you (see the *Using community exception and report handlers* recipe in this chapter). The default recipe of your my_handlers cookbook should look like this:

```
include_recipe "chef_handler"
chef_gem "flowdock"
remote_file "#{node["chef_handler"]["handler_path"]}/flowdock_handler.
rb" do
  source "https://raw.githubusercontent.com/mmarschall/chef-handler-
flowdock/master/lib/chef/handler/flowdock_handler.rb"
end
chef_handler "Chef::Handler::FlowdockHandler" do
  source "#{node["chef_handler"]["handler_path"]}/flowdock_handler.rb"
  arguments :api_token =>  "FLOWDOCK_API_TOKEN"
  action :enable
end
```

In our example, we create the Flowdock API client in the initialize method. If you use the LWRP to install the handler, the initialize method will receive an options Hash from the arguments call inside the chef_handler provider.

## See also

- ▸ If you just want to use an existing handler, read the *Using community exception and report handlers* recipe in this chapter

# 3
# Chef Language and Style

*"Style is what separates the good from the great."*

*Bozhidar Batsov*

In this chapter, we will cover the following recipes:

- ▶ Using community Chef style
- ▶ Using attributes to dynamically configure recipes
- ▶ Using templates
- ▶ Mixing plain Ruby with Chef DSL
- ▶ Installing Ruby gems and using them in recipes
- ▶ Using libraries
- ▶ Using definitions
- ▶ Creating your own **Lightweight Resource Providers (LWRP)**
- ▶ Extending community cookbooks by using application wrapper cookbooks
- ▶ Creating custom Ohai plugins
- ▶ Creating custom knife plugins

# Introduction

If you want to automate your infrastructure, you will end up using most of Chef's language features. In this chapter, we will take a look at how to use the Chef **Domain Specific Language** (**DSL**) from basic to advanced level. We will end the chapter with creating custom plugins for Ohai and knife.

# Using community Chef style

It's easier to read code that adheres to a coding style guide. It is really important to deliver consistently styled code, especially when sharing cookbooks with the Chef community. In this chapter, you'll find some of the most important rules (out of many more—enough to fill a short book on its own) to apply to your own cookbooks.

## Getting ready

As you're writing cookbooks in Ruby, it's a good idea to follow general Ruby principles for readable (and therefore maintainable) code.

Chef Software, Inc. is used to propose Ian Macdonald's *Ruby Style Guide* (`http://www.caliban.org/ruby/rubyguide.shtml#style`), but to be honest, I prefer Bozhidar Batsov's *Ruby Style Guide* (`https://github.com/bbatsov/ruby-style-guide`) due to its clarity.

Let's take a look at the most important rules for Ruby in general and for cookbooks specifically.

## How to do it...

Let's walk through a few Chef styling guideline examples:

1. Use two spaces per indentation level:

   ```
   remote_directory node['nagios']['plugin_dir'] do
     source 'plugins'
   end
   ```

2. Use Unix-style line endings. Avoid Windows line endings by configuring Git accordingly:

   **`mma@laptop:~/chef-repo $ git config --global core.autocrlf true`**

 For more options on how to deal with line endings in Git, go to `https://help.github.com/articles/dealing-with-line-endings`.

3. Align parameters spanning more than one line:

```
variables(
  mon_host: 'monitoring.example.com',
  nrpe_directory: "#{node['nagios']['nrpe']['conf_dir']}/nrpe.d"
)
```

4. Describe your cookbook in `metadata.rb` (you should always use the Ruby DSL as the JSON version will be automatically generated from it).

5. Configure your cookbook to the appropriate version by using Semantic Versioning (`http://semver.org`):

```
version           "1.1.0"
```

6. List the supported operating systems looping through an array by using each parameter:

```
%w(redhat centos ubuntu debian).each do |os|
  supports os
end
```

7. Declare dependencies in `metadata.rb`:

```
depends "apache2", ">= 1.0.4"
depends "build-essential"
```

8. Construct strings from variable values and static parts by using string expansion:

```
my_string = "This resource changed #{counter} files"
```

9. Download temporary files to `Chef::Config['file_cache_path']` instead of `/tmp` or some local directory.

10. Use strings to access node attributes instead of Ruby symbols:

```
node['nagios']['users_databag_group']
```

11. Set attributes in `my_cookbook/attributes/default.rb` by using `default`:

```
default['my_cookbook']['version']    = "3.0.11"
```

12. Create an attribute namespace by using your cookbook name as the first level in `my_cookbook/attributes/default.rb`:

```
default['my_cookbook']['version']    = "3.0.11"
default['my_cookbook']['name']       = "Mine"
```

## How it works...

Using community Chef style helps to increase the readability of your cookbooks. Your cookbooks will be read much more often than changed. Because of this, it usually pays off to put a little extra effort into following a strict style guide when writing cookbooks.

## There's more...

Using Semantic Versioning (see: `http://semver.org`) for your cookbooks helps to manage dependencies. If you change anything that might break cookbooks, depending on your cookbook, you need to consider this as a backwards incompatible API change. In such cases, Semantic Versioning demands that you increase the major number of your cookbook, for example from `1.1.3` to `2.0.0`, resetting minor level and patch levels.

Using Semantic Versioning helps to keep your production systems stable if you freeze your cookbooks (see the *Freezing cookbooks* recipe in *Chapter 1, Chef Infrastructure*).

## See also

▶   If you want to know whether you did everything right, follow the *Flagging problems in your Chef cookbooks* recipe in *Chapter 2, Evaluating and Troubleshooting Cookbooks and Chef Runs*.

# Using attributes to dynamically configure recipes

Imagine some cookbook author has hardcoded the path where the cookbook puts a configuration file—but in a place that does not comply with your rules. Now, you're in trouble! You can either patch the cookbook or rewrite it from scratch. Both options leave you with a lot of work and headaches.

Attributes are there to avoid such headaches. Instead of hardcoding values inside cookbooks, attributes enable authors to make their cookbooks configurable. By overriding default values set in cookbooks, users can inject their own values. Suddenly, it's next to trivial to obey your own rules.

In this section, we'll see how to use attributes in your cookbooks.

## Getting ready

Make sure you have a cookbook called `my_cookbook` and the `run_list` of your node includes `my_cookbook`, as described in the *Creating and using cookbooks* recipe in *Chapter 1, Chef Infrastructure*.

## How to do it...

Let's see how to define and use a simple attribute:

1. Create a default file for your cookbook attributes:

   **mma@laptop:~/chef-repo $ subl cookbooks/my_cookbook/attributes/ default.rb**

2. Add a default attribute:

   ```
   default['my_cookbook']['message'] = 'hello world!'
   ```

3. Use the attribute inside a recipe:

   **mma@laptop:~/chef-repo $ subl cookbooks/my_cookbook/recipes/ default.rb**

   ```
   message = node['my_cookbook']['message']
   Chef::Log.info("** Saying what I was told to say: #{message}")
   ```

4. Upload the modified cookbook to the Chef server (use `--force` or bump the version number in your `metadata.rb` file if Berkshelf has frozen your cookbook earlier):

   **mma@laptop:~/chef-repo $ knife cookbook upload my_cookbook --force**

   ```
   Uploading my_cookbook      [0.1.0]
   ```

5. Run `Chef-client` on your node:

   **user@server:~$ sudo chef-client**

   ```
   ...TRUNCATED OUTPUT...
   [2015-01-13T20:48:21+00:00] INFO: ** Saying what I was told to
   say: hello world!
   ...TRUNCATED OUTPUT...
   ```

## How it works...

Chef loads all attributes from the attribute files before it executes the recipes. The attributes are stored with the node object. You can access all attributes stored with the node object from within your recipes and retrieve their current values.

Chef has a strict order of precedence for attributes: default being the lowest, then comes normal (which is aliased with set), and then override. Additionally, attribute levels set in recipes have precedence over the same level set in an attribute file. Also, attributes defined in roles and environments have the highest precedence.

You will find an overview chart at `http://docs.chef.io/attributes. html#attribute-precedence`.

## There's more...

You can set and override attributes within roles and environments, as well. Attributes defined in roles or environments have the highest precedence (on their respective levels: `default` and `override`):

1. Create a role:

   ```
   mma@laptop:~/chef-repo $ subl roles/german_hosts.rb
   ```

   ```
   name "german_hosts"
   description "This Role contains hosts, which should print out
   their messages in German"
   run_list "recipe[my_cookbook]"
   default_attributes "my_cookbook" => { "message" => "Hallo Welt!" }
   ```

2. Upload the role to the Chef server:

   ```
   mma@laptop:~/chef-repo $ knife role from file german_hosts.rb
   Updated Role german_hosts!
   ```

3. Assign the role to a node called `server`:

   ```
   mma@laptop:~/chef-repo $ knife node run_list add server
   'role[german_hosts]'
   server:
      run_list: role[german_hosts]
   ```

4. Run the Chef client on your node:

   ```
   user@server:~$ sudo chef-client
   ...TRUNCATED OUTPUT...
   [2015-01-13T20:49:49+00:00] INFO: ** Saying what I was told to
   say: Hallo Welt!
   ...TRUNCATED OUTPUT...
   ```

## Calculating values in the attribute files

Attributes set in roles and environments (as shown earlier) have the highest precedence and they're already available when the attribute files get loaded. This enables you to calculate attribute values based on role or environment-specific values:

1. Set an attribute within a role:

   ```
   mma@laptop:~/chef-repo $ subl roles/german_hosts.rb
   ```

   ```
   name "german_hosts"
   ```

```
description "This Role contains hosts, which should print out
their messages in German"
run_list "recipe[my_cookbook]"
default_attributes "my_cookbook" => {
  "hi" => "Hallo",
  "world" => "Welt"
}
```

2. Calculate the message attribute, based on the two attributes `hi` and `world`:

   **mma@laptop:~/chef-repo $ subl cookbooks/my_cookbook/attributes/**
   **default.rb**

   ```
   default['my_cookbook']['message'] = "#{node['my_cookbook']['hi']}
   #{node['my_cookbook']['world']}!"
   ```

3. Upload the modified cookbook to your Chef server and run the Chef client on your node to see that it works, as shown in the preceding example.

## See also

▶ Read more about attributes in Chef at `http://docs.chef.io/attributes.html`

▶ Learn all about how attributes evolved since Chef 0.7 here: `http://www.opscode.com/blog/2013/02/05/chef-11-in-depth-attributes-changes/`

# Using templates

**Configuration Management** is all about configuring your hosts well. Usually, configuration is carried out by using configuration files. Chef's template resource allows you to recreate these configuration files with dynamic values that are driven by the attributes we discussed so far in this chapter.

You can retrieve dynamic values from **data bags**, attributes, or even calculate them on the fly before passing them into a template.

## Getting ready

Make sure you have a cookbook called `my_cookbook` and that the `run_list` of your node includes `my_cookbook`, as described in *Creating and using cookbooks* recipe in *Chapter 1, Chef Infrastructure.*

## How to do it...

Let's see how to create and use a template to dynamically generate a file on your node:

1. Add a template to your recipe:

   **mma@laptop:~/chef-repo $ subl cookbooks/my_cookbook/recipes/default.rb**

   ```
   template '/tmp/message' do
     source 'message.erb'
     variables(
       hi: 'Hallo',
       world: 'Welt',
       from: node['fqdn']
     )
   end
   ```

2. Add the ERB template file:

   **mma@laptop:~/chef-repo $ mkdir -p cookbooks/my_cookbook/templates**

   **mma@laptop:~/chef-repo $ subl cookbooks/my_cookbook/templates/default/message.erb**

   ```
   <%- 4.times do %>
   <%= @hi %>, <%= @world %> from <%= @from %>!
   <%- end %>
   ```

3. Upload the modified cookbook to the Chef server:

   **mma@laptop:~/chef-repo $ knife cookbook upload my_cookbook**

   **Uploading my_cookbook       [0.1.0]**

4. Run the Chef client on your node:

   **user@server:~$ sudo chef-client**

   ```
   ...TRUNCATED OUTPUT...
   [2015-01-14T20:41:21+00:00] INFO: Processing template[/tmp/
   message] action create (my_cookbook::default line 9)
   [2015-01-14T20:41:22+00:00] INFO: template[/tmp/message] updated
   content
   ...TRUNCATED OUTPUT...
   ```

5. Validate the content of the generated file:

   **user@server:~$ sudo cat /tmp/message**

   ```
   Hallo, Welt from vagrant.vm!
   Hallo, Welt from vagrant.vm!
   ```

```
Hallo, Welt from vagrant.vm!
Hallo, Welt from vagrant.vm!
```

## How it works...

Chef uses **Erubis** as its template language. It allows you to use pure Ruby code by using special symbols inside your templates.

You use `<%= %>` if you want to print the value of a variable or Ruby expression into the generated file.

You use `<%- %>` if you want to embed Ruby logic into your template file. We used it to loop our expression four times.

When you use the `template` resource, Chef makes all the variables you pass available as instance variables when rendering the template. We used `@hi`, `@world`, and `@from` in our earlier example.

## There's more...

The node object is available in a template as well. Technically, you could access node attributes directly from within your template:

```
<%= node['fqdn'] %>
```

However, this is not a good idea because it will introduce hidden dependencies to your template. It is better to make dependencies explicit, for example, by declaring the **fully qualified domain name (FQDN)** of your node as a variable for the `template` resource inside your cookbook:

```
template '/tmp/fqdn' do
  source 'fqdn.erb'
  variables(
    fqdn:node['fqdn']
  )
end
```

 Avoid using the node object directly inside your templates because this introduces hidden dependencies to node variables in your templates.

If you need a different template for a specific host or platform, you can put those specific templates into various subdirectories of the templates directory. Chef will try to locate the correct template by searching these directories from the most specific (host) to least specific(default).

You can place `message.erb` in the `cookbooks/my_cookbook/templates/host-server.vm` (`"host-#{node[:fqdn]}"`) directory it should be specific to that host. It should be specific to a certain platform version. You can place it in `cookbooks/my_cookbook/templates/ubuntu-14.04` (`"#{node[:platform]}-#{node[:platorm_version]}"`), and if it is only be platform-specific, you can place it in `cookbooks/my_cookbook/templates/ubuntu` (`"#{node[:platform]}"`). Only if your template is the same for any host or platform, you will place it in the `default` directory.

 Be aware of the fact that the `templates/default` directory means that a template file is the same for all hosts and platforms—it does not correspond to a recipe name.

## See also

▸ Read more about templates at `http://docs.chef.io/templates.html`

# Mixing plain Ruby with Chef DSL

To create simple recipes, you only need to use resources provided by Chef such as `template`, `remote_file`, or `service`. However, as your recipes become more elaborate, you'll discover the need to do more advanced things such as conditionally execute parts of your recipe, looping, or even complex calculations.

Instead of declaring the `gem_package` resource ten times, simply use different name attributes; it is so much easier to loop through an array of gem names creating the `gem_package` resources on the fly.

This is the power of mixing plain Ruby with **Chef Domain Specific Language** (**DSL**). We'll see a few tricks in the following sections.

## Getting ready

Start a Chef-shell on any of your nodes in Client mode to be able to access your Chef server, as shown in the following code:

```
user@server:~$ sudo chef-shell --client

    loading configuration: /etc/chef/client.rb
    Session type: client
    ...TRUNCATED OUTPUT...
    run `help' for help, `exit' or ^D to quit.
    Ohai2u user@server!
    chef >
```

## How to do it...

Let's play around with some Ruby constructs in chef-shell to get a feel for what's possible:

1. Get all nodes from the Chef server by using `search` from the Chef DSL:

```
chef > nodes = search(:node, "hostname:[* TO *]")
=> [#<Chef::Node:0x00000005010d38 @chef_server_rest=nil, @
name="server",
...TRUNCATED OUTPUT...
```

2. Sort your nodes by name by using plain Ruby:

```
chef > nodes.sort! { |a, b| a.hostname <=> b.hostname }.collect {
|n| n.hostname }
 => ["alice", "server"]
```

3. Loop through the nodes, printing their operating systems:

```
chef > nodes.each do |n|
chef > puts n['os']
chef ?> end
linux
windows
 => [node[server], node[alice]]
```

4. Log only if there are no nodes:

```
chef > Chef::Log.warn("No nodes found") if nodes.empty?
=> nil
```

5. Install multiple Ruby gems by using an array, a loop, and string expansion to construct the gem names:

```
chef > recipe_mode
chef:recipe > %w{ec2 essentials}.each do |gem|
chef:recipe > gem_package "knife-#{gem}"
chef:recipe ?> end
=> ["ec2", "essentials"]
```

## How it works...

Chef recipes are Ruby files, which get evaluated in the context of a Chef run. They can contain plain Ruby code, such as `if` statements and loops, as well as Chef DSL elements such as resources (`remote_file`, `service`, `template`, and so on).

Inside your recipes, you can declare Ruby variables and assign them any values. We used the Chef DSL method `search` to retrieve an array of `Chef::Node` instances and stored that array in the variable `nodes`.

Because `nodes` is a plain Ruby array, we can use all methods the array class provides such as `sort!` or `empty?`

Also, we can iterate through the array by using the plain Ruby `each` iterator, as we did in the third example earlier.

Another common thing is to use `if`, `else`, or `case` for conditional execution. In the fourth example earlier, we used `if` to only write a warning to the log file, if the `nodes` array would be empty.

In the last example, we entered recipe mode and combined an array of strings (holding parts of gem names) and the `each` iterator with the Chef DSL `gem_package` resource to install two Ruby gems. To take things one step further, we used plain Ruby string expansion to construct the full gem names (`knife-ec2` and `knife-essentials`) on the fly.

## There's more...

You can use the full power of Ruby in combination with the Chef DSL in your recipes. Here is an excerpt from the default recipe from the `nagios` cookbook, which shows what's possible:

```
# Sort by name to provide stable ordering
nodes.sort! { |a, b| a.name <=> b.name }
# maps nodes into nagios hostgroups
service_hosts = {}
search(:role, ,*:*') do |r|
  hostgroups << r.name
  nodes.select { |n| n[,roles'].include?(r.name) if n[,roles'] }.each
do |n|
    service_hosts[r.name] = n[node[,nagios'][,host_name_attribute']]
  end
end
```

First, they use Ruby to sort an array of nodes by their name attributes.

Then, they define a Ruby variable called `service_hosts` as an empty Hash. After this, you will see some more array methods in action such as `select`, `include?`, and `each`.

## See also

▸ Find out more about how to use Ruby in recipes here: `http://docs.chef.io/chef/dsl_recipe.html`

▸ The *Using community Chef style* recipe in this chapter

▸ The *Using attributes to dynamically configure recipes* recipe in this chapter

# Installing Ruby gems and using them in recipes

Recipes are plain Ruby files. It is possible to use all of Ruby's language features inside your recipes. Most of the time, the built-in Ruby functionality is enough but sometimes you might want to use additional Ruby gems. Connecting to an external application via an API or accessing a MySQL database from within your recipe is an example of where you will need Ruby gems inside your recipes.

Chef lets you install Ruby gems from within a recipe, so that you can use them later.

## Getting ready

Make sure you have a cookbook called `my_cookbook` and that the `run_list` of your node includes `my_cookbook`, as described in *Creating and using cookbooks* recipe in *Chapter 1, Chef Infrastructure*.

## How to do it...

Let's see how we can use the `ipaddress` gem in our recipe:

1. Edit the default recipe of your cookbook, installing a gem to be used inside the recipe:

   **mma@laptop:~/chef-repo $ subl**

   ```
   cookbooks/my_cookbook/recipes/default.rb
   chef_gem 'ipaddress'
   require 'ipaddress'
   ip = IPAddress("192.168.0.1/24")
   Chef::Log.info("Netmask of #{ip}: #{ip.netmask}")
   ```

2. Upload the modified cookbook to the Chef server:

   **mma@laptop:~/chef-repo $ knife cookbook upload my_cookbook**

   ```
   Uploading my_cookbook     [0.1.0]
   ```

3. Run Chef client on your node to see whether it works:

   **user@server $ sudo chef-client**

   ```
   ...TRUNCATED OUTPUT...
   [2014-12-29T22:29:15+01:00] INFO: Netmask of 192.168.0.1:
   255.255.255.0
   ...TRUNCATED OUTPUT...
   ```

## How it works...

A Chef run consists of a *compile* phase, where it instantiates all resources, and an *execute* phase, where Chef runs the resource providers to converge the node.

If you want to use the functionality of a Ruby gem inside your cookbook, you need to install that gem during the *compile* phase. Otherwise, it will not be available during the *execute* phase (only after the Chef run).

The `chef_gem` resource will do exactly that.

The `gem_package` resource, in contrast, installs the gem into the system Ruby. It does that during the *execute* phase of the Chef run. This means that gems installed by `gem_package` cannot be used inside your recipes.

## See also

▶  The *Mixing plain Ruby with Chef DSL* recipe in this chapter

# Using libraries

You can use arbitrary Ruby code within your recipes. As long as your logic isn't too complicated, it's totally fine to keep it inside your recipe. However, as soon as you start using plain Ruby more than Chef DSL, it's time to the move logic into external libraries.

Libraries provide a place to encapsulate Ruby code so that your recipes stay clean and neat.

In this section, we'll create a simple library to see how this works.

## Getting ready

Make sure you have a cookbook called `my_cookbook` and that the `run_list` of your node includes `my_cookbook`, as described in *Creating and using cookbooks* recipe of *Chapter 1, Chef Infrastructure*.

## How to do it...

Let's create a library and use it in a cookbook:

1.  Create a helper method in your own cookbook's library:

    ```
    mma@laptop:~/chef-repo $ mkdir -p cookbooks/my_cookbook/libraries
    mma@laptop:~/chef-repo $ subl cookbooks/my_cookbook/libraries/
    ipaddress.rb
    ```

```
class Chef::Recipe
  def netmask(ipaddress)
    IPAddress(ipaddress).netmask
  end
end
```

2. Use your helper method in a recipe:

    **mma@laptop:~/chef-repo $ subl cookbooks/my_cookbook/recipes/
    default.rb**

    ```
    ip = '10.10.0.0/24'
    mask = netmask(ip) # here we use the library method
    Chef::Log.info("Netmask of #{ip}: #{mask}")
    ```

3. Run the Chef client on your development box to see whether it works:

    **mma@laptop:~/chef-repo $ chef-client -z -o 'recipe[my_cookbook]'**

    ```
    ...TRUNCATED OUTPUT...
    [2014-12-30T21:17:44+01:00] INFO: Netmask of 10.10.0.0/24:
    255.255.255.0
    ...TRUNCATED OUTPUT...
    ```

## How it works...

In your Library code, you can open the Chef::Recipe class and add your new methods.

 This isn't the cleanest, but it is the simplest way of doing it. The following paragraphs will help you find a cleaner way.

```
class Chef::Recipe
  def netmask(ipaddress)
    ...
  end
end
```

Chef automatically loads your library code in the compile phase that enables you to use the methods that you declare inside your recipes of the cookbook:

```
mask = netmask(ip)
```

## There's more...

Opening a class and adding methods pollutes the class's namespace. This might lead to name clashes, for example, if you define a method inside a library of your own cookbook and someone else defines a method with the same name in the library of another cookbook. Another clash would happen if you accidentally use a method name, which Chef defines in its `Chef::Recipe` class.

It's cleaner to introduce your subclasses inside your libraries and define your methods as class methods. This avoids polluting the `Chef::Recipe` namespace are given:

**mma@laptop:~/chef-repo $ subl cookbooks/my_cookbook/libraries/ipaddress.rb**

```
class Chef::Recipe::IPAddress
  def self.netmask(ipaddress)
    IPAddress(ipaddress).netmask
  end
end
```

You can use the method inside your recipes like this:

```
IPAddress.netmask(ip)
```

You can define library methods in chef-shell directly in the root context:

**user@server $ chef-shell --client**

```
chef > class Chef::Recipe::IPAddress
chef ?> def self.netmask(ipaddress)
chef ?>     IPAddress(ipaddress).netmask
chef ?>   end
chef ?> end
```

Now, you can use the library method inside the recipe context:

```
chef > recipe
chef:recipe > IPAddress.netmask('10.10.0.0/24')
 => "255.255.255.0"
```

## See also

▶ Learn more about chef-shell by reading the *Using the Chef console (chef-shell)* recipe in *Creating and using cookbooks* recipe of *Chapter 1, Chef Infrastructure*

▶ The *Mixing plain Ruby with Chef DSL* recipe in this chapter

# Using definitions

Your cookbooks will grow and get pretty long. Silently, some duplication will sneak in, as well. It's time to group resources and give them names in order to regain readability for your cookbook. Also, if you use the same set of resources again and again, it is a good idea to refactor such groups of resources into **definitions**.

In this section, we'll group a set of resources into a definition to make it reusable.

## Getting ready

Make sure you have a cookbook called `my_cookbook` and that the `run_list` file of your node includes `my_cookbook`, as described in *Creating and using cookbooks* recipe of *Chapter 1, Chef Infrastructure*.

## How to do it...

Let's see how to create and use a definition:

1. Create a definition in a new file in your cookbook's `definitions` folder:

   ```
   mma@laptop:~/chef-repo $ mkdir -p cookbooks/my_cookbook/
   definitions
   mma@laptop:~/chef-repo $ subl cookbooks/my_cookbook/definitions/
   capistrano_deploy_dirs.rb

   define :capistrano_deploy_dirs, :deploy_to => '' do
     directory "#{params[:deploy_to]}/releases"
     directory "#{params[:deploy_to]}/shared"
     directory "#{params[:deploy_to]}/shared/system"
   end
   ```

2. Use the definition inside your cookbook's default recipe:

   ```
   mma@laptop:~/chef-repo $ subl cookbooks/my_cookbook/recipes/
   default.rb

   capistrano_deploy_dirs do
     deploy_to "/srv"
   end
   ```

3. Upload the modified cookbook to the Chef server:

   ```
   mma@laptop:~/chef-repo $ knife cookbook upload my_cookbook

   Uploading my_cookbook      [0.1.0]
   ```

4.  Run the Chef client on your node to see whether it works:

```
user@server $ sudo chef-client

...TRUNCATED OUTPUT...
  * directory[/srv/releases] action create[2014-12-
30T16:23:57+00:00] INFO: directory[/srv/releases] created
directory /srv/releases

    - create new directory /srv/releases
  * directory[/srv/shared] action create[2014-12-
30T16:23:57+00:00] INFO: directory[/srv/shared] created directory
/srv/shared

    - create new directory /srv/shared
  * directory[/srv/shared/system] action create[2014-12-
30T16:23:57+00:00] INFO: directory[/srv/shared/system] created
directory /srv/shared/system

    - create new directory /srv/shared/system
...TRUNCATED OUTPUT...
```

## How it works...

Definitions in Chef are like macros: you group a collection of resources and give this group a name. Chef reads the definition and expands its contents into the recipe during the compile phase.

A definition has a name (here, `capistrano_deploy_dirs`) by which you can call it from your recipe. Also, a definition has a list of parameters (here `deploy_to`):

```
define :capistrano_deploy_dirs, :deploy_to => '' do
  ...
end
```

The code inside the definition has access to a Hash called `params`. It contains all the keys you defined after the definition name. Here, Chef will add the three `directory` resources to the execution list:

```
define ...
  directory "#{params[:deploy_to]}/releases"
  directory "#{params[:deploy_to]}/shared"
  directory "#{params[:deploy_to]}/shared/system"
end
```

In your recipes, you can use the definition name instead of putting all the three directory resources. Inside the block, you use dynamically generated methods to fill each parameter with its value:

```
capistrano_deploy_dirs do
  deploy_to "/srv"
end
```

## There's more...

Be aware that definitions are expanded into their containing resources during the compile phase of the Chef run. Definitions are not available during the execution phase. You cannot notify a definition, but only the resources it contains.

You cannot address the definition:

```
notifies :delete, 'capsitrano_deploy_dirs', :immediately
```

However, you *can* address the individual resources inside the definition:

```
notifies :delete, 'directory[/srv/releases], :immediately
```

## See also

▶   Read more about definitions at `http://docs.chef.io/definitions.html`

# Creating your own Lightweight Resource Providers (LWRP)

Chef offers the opportunity to extend the list of available resources by creating a custom **Lightweight Resource Provider** (**LWRP**). By creating your own custom resources, you can simplify writing cookbooks because your own custom resources enrich the Chef DSL and make your recipe code more expressive.

Many of the custom resources in Chef's community cookbooks (and elsewhere) are implemented as LWRPs. So, there are many working examples in the real world, such as `iptables_rule`, `apt_repository`, and many more.

In this section, we will create a very simple LWRP to demonstrate the basic mechanics.

## Getting ready

Create a new cookbook named `greeting` and ensure that the `run_list` of your node includes `greeting`, as described in *Creating and using cookbooks* recipe of *Chapter 1, Chef Infrastructure*.

## How to do it...

Let's see how to build a very simple LWRP to create a text file on your node:

1. Create your custom resource in your `greeting` cookbook:

   **mma@laptop:~/chef-repo $ subl cookbooks/greeting/resources/
   default.rb**

   ```
   actions :create, :remove
   attribute :title, kind_of: String, default: "World"
   attribute :path, kind_of: String, default: "/tmp/greeting.txt"
   ```

2. Create the provider for your resource in your `greeting` cookbook:

   **mma@laptop:~/chef-repo $ subl cookbooks/greeting/providers/
   default.rb**

   ```
   action :create do
     Chef::Log.info "Adding '#{new_resource.name}' greeting as #{new_
   resource.path}"
     file new_resource.path do
       content "#{new_resource.name}, #{new_resource.title}!"
       action :create
     end
   end
   action :remove do
     Chef::Log.info "Removing '#{new_resource.name}' greeting #{new_
   resource.path}"
     file new_resource.path do
       action :delete
     end
   end
   ```

3. Use your new resource by editing your greeting cookbook's default recipe:

   **mma@laptop:~/chef-repo $ subl
   cookbooks/greeting/recipes/default.rb**

   ```
   greeting "Ohai" do
     title "Chef"
     action :create
   end
   ```

4. Run the Chef client on your workstation:

   **mma@laptop:~/chef-repo $ chef-client -z -o 'recipe[greeting]'**

   ```
   ...TRUNCATED OUTPUT...
   ```

```
    * greeting[Ohai] action create[2014-12-30T18:08:21+01:00] INFO:
Processing greeting[Ohai] action create (greeting::default line 6)
[2014-12-30T18:08:21+01:00] INFO: Adding 'Ohai' greeting as /tmp/
greeting.txt
  (up to date)
    * file[/tmp/greeting.txt] action create[2014-12-
30T18:08:21+01:00] INFO: Processing file[/tmp/greeting.txt]
action create (/Users/mma/.chef/local-mode-cache/cache/cookbooks/
greeting/providers/default.rb line 3)
[2014-12-30T18:08:21+01:00] INFO: file[/tmp/greeting.txt] created
file /tmp/greeting.txt

    - create new file /tmp/greeting.txt[2014-12-30T18:08:21+01:00]
WARN: Could not set gid = 0 on /var/folders/fz/dcb5y3qs4m5g1hk8zrx
d948m0000gn/T/.greeting.txt20141230-49531-1rn88me, file modes not
preserved
[2014-12-30T18:08:21+01:00] INFO: file[/tmp/greeting.txt] updated
file contents /tmp/greeting.txt

    - update content in file /tmp/greeting.txt from none to 47c39a
    --- /tmp/greeting.txt    2014-12-30 18:08:21.000000000 +0100
    +++ /var/folders/fz/dcb5y3qs4m5g1hk8zrxd948m0000g
n/T/.greeting.txt20141230-49531-1rn88me    2014-12-30
18:08:21.000000000 +0100
    @@ -1 +1,2 @@
    +Ohai, Chef!
  ...TRUNCATED OUTPUT...
```

5. Validate the content of the generated file:

   **mma@laptop:~/chef-repo $ cat /tmp/greeting.txt**

   Ohai, Chef!

## How it works...

LWRPs live in cookbooks. A custom resource, which you will define in a file called `default.rb` in the `resources` directory of your cookbook, will be available under the cookbook name.

We create `greeting/resources/default.rb` and use it in our default recipe, as follows:

```
greeting "..." do
end
```

Let's see what the resource definition in `greeting/resources/default.rb` looks like.

First, we define the actions, which our resource should support:

```
actions :create, :remove
```

Then, we define attributes you can pass to the resource when using it in your cookbook. In our case, we define two string attributes with their default values:

```
attribute :title, kind_of: String, default: "World"
attribute :path, kind_of: String, default: "/tmp/greeting.txt"
```

Now, we can use those actions and attributes in our recipe:

```
greeting "Ohai" do
  title "Chef"
  action :create
end
```

We defined the resource, now it's time to make it do something. The implementation of a resource lives in one or many providers. You might find multiple providers for the same resource for different operating systems. However, we keep it simple here and create only one provider in `greeting/providers/default.rb`.

The provider has to implement each action defined in the resource. In our case, we need to implement two actions: `create` and `remove`, as shown in the following code:

```
action :create do
  ...
end
action :remove do
  ...
end
```

Now, you can use pure Ruby and the existing Chef resources to make your provider do something. First, we create a log statement and then we use the existing `file` resource to create a text file containing the greeting:

```
Chef::Log.info "Adding '#{new_resource.name}' greeting as #{new_resource.path}"
file new_resource.path do
  ...
end
```

The `new_resource` attribute is a Ruby variable containing the resource definition from the recipe that uses the resource. In our case, `new_resource.name` evaluates to Ohai and `new_resource.path` evaluates to the attributes default value (because we did not use that attribute when using the greeting resource in our cookbook).

Inside the `file` resource, we use our resource's title (`new_resource.title`) attribute to fill the text file:

```
file new_resource.path do
  content "#{new_resource.name}, #{new_resource.title}!"
  action :create
end
```

The `remove` action works in a similar way to the `create` action, but calls the `file` resource's `delete` action, instead.

## There's more...

To simplify the usage of your custom resource, you can define a default action. You declare it using the `default_action` call:

```
default_action :create
```

Now you can use your new resource like this:

```
greeting "Ohai" do
  title "Chef"
end
```

 If you're using plain Ruby code in your providers, you need to make sure that your code is idempotent. This means that it only runs if it has to modify something. You should be able to run your code multiple times on the same machine, without executing unnecessary actions on each run.

If you want your resource to support `why-run` mode, you need to add the following to it:

```
def whyrun_supported?
  true
end
```

Then, you can wrap your code with a `converge_by` block. This will produce the message you pass to it during `why-run` mode, instead of executing the code inside, as shown in the following code:

```
converge_by("Doing something with #{ @new_resource }") do
  ...
end
```

## See also

▶ Read more about what LWRPs are at `http://docs.chef.io/lwrp.html`

▶ You find a more detailed explanation about how to create LWRPs at `http://docs.chef.io/lwrp_custom.html`

▶ Read more about the `why-run` mode in the *Using why-run mode to find out what a recipe might do* in *Chapter 2, Evaluating and Troubleshooting Cookbooks and Chef Runs*

# Extending community cookbooks by using application wrapper cookbooks

Using community cookbooks is great. However, sometimes they do not exactly match your use case. You may need to modify them. If you don't want to use Git vendor branches that are generated by `knife cookbook site install`, you need to use the *library* versus *application* cookbook approach.

In this approach, you don't touch the community (*library*) cookbook. Instead, you include it in your own application cookbook and modify resources from the library cookbook.

Let's see how to extend a community cookbook within your own application cookbook.

## Getting ready

We'll use the `ntp` cookbook as the *library* cookbook and will change a command it executes.

Add the `ntp` cookbook to your Berksfile:

```
mma@laptop:~/chef-repo $ subl Berksfile
source 'https://supermarket.getchef.com'
cookbook 'ntp'
```

## How to do it...

Let's see how we can override the `ntp` cookbook's behavior from within our own cookbook:

1. Create your own *application* cookbook:

   ```
   mma@laptop:~/chef-repo $ chef generate cookbook my-ntp

   Compiling Cookbooks...
   Recipe: code_generator::cookbook
   ```

```
    * directory [/Users/mma/work/chef-repo/cookbooks/my-ntp] action
create
    - create new directory /Users/mma/work/chef-repo/cookbooks/my-
ntp
```

2. Add your new `my-ntp` cookbook to the run list of your node:

   **mma@laptop:~/chef-repo $ knife node run_list add server 'recipe[my-ntp]'**

   **server:**
     **run_list:**
     **recipe[my-ntp]**

3. Add the dependency on the `ntp` cookbook to the `my-ntp` metadata:

   **mma@laptop:~/chef-repo $ subl cookbooks/my-ntp/metadata.rb**

   ```
   version          '0.1.0'
   ...
   depends 'ntp'
   ```

4. Make the `default` recipe from the `ntp` cookbook execute another command, which you defined in your own cookbook:

   **mma@laptop:~/chef-repo $ subl cookbooks/my-ntp/recipes/default.rb**

   ```
   ...
   include_recipe 'ntp::default'
   node.override['ntp']['sync_hw_clock'] = true
   resources("execute[Force sync hardware clock with system clock]").
   command "hwclock --systohc -D"
   ```

5. Upload your cookbook to the Chef server:

   **mma@laptop:~/chef-repo $ knife cookbook upload my-ntp**

   ```
   Uploading my-ntp     [0.1.0]
   ```

6. Run the Chef client on your node:

   **user@server $ sudo chef-client**

   **...TRUNCATED OUTPUT...**

   **[2015-01-02T21:24:54+00:00] INFO: execute[Force sync hardware clock with system clock] ran successfully**

   **- execute hwclock --systohc -D**

   **...TRUNCATED OUTPUT...**

## How it works...

We retrieve and modify the `execute` resource for the `hwclock --systohc` command from the `ntp` cookbook. First, we need to include the recipe, which defines the resource we want to modify the code:

```
include_recipe 'ntp::default'
```

The `resources` method retrieves the given resource. We can then call all the methods on it, which we could also call while defining it in a recipe. In our example, we want to tell the `execute` resource that we want to use a different `command` lines:

```
resources("execute[Force sync hardware clock with system clock]").
command "hwclock --systohc -D"
```

This modification of the resource happens during the compile phase. Only after Chef has evaluated the whole recipe, it will execute all the resources it built during the compile phase.

## There's more...

If you don't want to modify the existing cookbooks, this is currently the only way to modify parts of recipes, which are not meant to be configured via attributes.

I don't like this approach too much. It is the exact same thing as monkey-patching any Ruby class by reopening it in your own source files. This usually leads to brittle code, as your code now depends on implementation details of another piece of code instead of depending on its public interface (in Chef recipes, the public interface is its attributes).

You should be aware of the fact that what you're doing is dangerous. Keep such cookbook modifications in a separate place so that you can easily find out what you did later. If you bury your modifications deep inside your complicated cookbooks, you might experience issues later that are very hard to debug.

## See also

▶ The *Downloading and integrating cookbooks as vendor branches into your Git repository* recipe in *Creating and using cookbooks* recipe of *Chapter 1, Chef Infrastructure*

# Creating custom Ohai plugins

Ohai is the tool used by a Chef client to find out everything about the node's environment. During a Chef client run, Ohai plugin populates the node object with all the information it found about the node such as its operating system, hardware, and so on.

It is possible to write custom Ohai plugins to query additional properties about a node's environment.

 Please note that Ohai data isn't populated until after a successful chef-client run!

In this example, we will see how to query the currently active firewall rules using **iptables** and make them available as node attributes.

## Getting ready

Make sure you have `iptables` installed on your node. See the *Managing firewalls with iptables* recipe in *Chapter 7, Servers and Cloud Infrastructure*.

Make sure you have the `chef-client` cookbook available:

1. Add the `chef-client` cookbook to your `Berksfile`:

   **mma@laptop:~/chef-repo $ subl Berksfile**

   ```
   cookbook 'chef-client'
   ```

2. Add the `chef-client` cookbook to your node's run list:

   **mma@laptop:~/chef-repo $ knife node run_list add server 'chef-client::config'**

   ```
   server:
     run_list:
       recipe[chef-client::config]
   ```

## How to do it...

Let's write a simple Ohai plugin, which lists all the currently active `iptables` rules:

1. Install the `ohai` cookbook:

   **mma@laptop:~/chef-repo $ knife cookbook site install ohai**
   **Installing ohai to /Users/mma/work/chef-repo/cookbooks**
   **...TRUNCATED OUTPUT...**
   **Cookbook ohai version 2.0.1 successfully installed**

2. Add your plugin to the ohai cookbook:

   **mma@laptop:~/chef-repo $ subl cookbooks/ohai/files/default/plugins/iptables.rb**

   ```
   Ohai.plugin(:Iptables) do
   ```

```
    provides "iptables"

    collect_data(:default) do
      iptables Mash.new
      `iptables -S`.each_line.with_index {|line, i| iptables[i] =
line }
    end
end
```

3. Upload the modified `ohai` cookbook to the Chef server:

   **`mma@laptop:~/chef-repo $ knife cookbook upload ohai`**

   **`Uploading ohai    [2.0.1]`**

4. Add the `ohai` cookbook to the run list of your node:

   **`mma@laptop:~/chef-repo $ knife node run_list add server ohai`**

   ```
   server:
     run_list:
       recipe[chef-client::config]
       recipe[ohai]
   ```

5. Run the Chef client on your node:

   **`user@server:~$ sudo chef-client`**

   ```
   ...TRUNCATED OUTPUT...
   [2015-01-02T21:21:55+00:00] INFO: ohai[custom_plugins] reloaded

       - re-run ohai and merge results into node attributes
   ...TRUNCATED OUTPUT...
   ```

6. Validate that the `iptables` rules show up as node attributes, for example, by navigating to your Chef server's management console. The `iptables` rules should show up amongst the other node attributes:

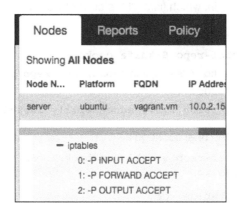

## How it works...

The `chef-client` cookbook configures the Chef client to look for additional Ohai plugins in the `/etc/chef/ohai_plugins` directory by adding this line to `/etc/chef/client.rb`:

```
Ohai::Config[:plugin_path] << "/etc/chef/ohai_plugins"
```

You can simply install the `ohai` cookbook and add your Ohai plugins to the `cookbooks/ohai/files/default/plugins` directory. The `ohai` cookbook will then upload your plugins to your node.

A custom Ohai plugin has only a few basic parts. First, you need to give it a Ruby class name:

```
Ohai.plugin(:Iptables) do
end
```

Then, you need to define which attribute the plugin will populate:

```
provides "iptables"
```

The preceding code tells Ohai that the node attributes you fill will be available under the `iptables` key.

Inside a method called `collect_data`, you define what the plugin should do when it runs. The parameter `:default` says that this `collect_data` method runs on any platform.

You collect the node attributes in a Mash—an extended version of a Hash the code, as follows:

```
iptables Mash.new
```

The preceding line of code creates an empty node attribute.

Then, we run `iptables -S` to list all the currently loaded firewall rules and loop through the lines. Each line gets added to the Mash with its line number as the key:

```
`sudo iptables -S`.each_line.with_index {|line,i|
  iptables[i] = line }
```

Ohai will add the contents of that Mash as node attributes during a Chef client run. We can now use the new `iptables` node attribute in our recipes:

```
node['iptables']
```

## There's more...

You can use your Ohai plugin as a library. This enables you to use the functionality of your Ohai plugins in arbitrary Ruby scripts. Fire up IRB in the `/etc/chef/ohai_plugins` directory and run the following command lines to make the `iptables` attributes accessible in the IRB session:

```
user@server:/etc/chef/ohai_plugins$ sudo /opt/chef/embedded/bin/irb

  >> require 'ohai'
  >> Ohai::Config[:plugin_path] << '.'
  >> o = Ohai::System.new
  >> o.all_plugins
  >> o['iptables']
=> {0=>"-P INPUT ACCEPT\n", 1=>"-P FORWARD ACCEPT\n", 2=>"-P OUTPUT
ACCEPT\n"}
```

## See also

  ▸ Read more about Ohai at `https://docs.chef.io/ohai.html`

  ▸ Learn more about how to create your own custom Ohai plugins at `https://docs.chef.io/ohai_custom.html`

  ▸ Read more about how to distribute Ohai plugins here: `https://docs.chef.io/ohai.html#ohai-cookbook`

  ▸ Find the source code of Ohai here: `https://github.com/opscode/ohai`

  ▸ Find the source code of the Ohai cookbook here: `https://github.com/opscode-cookbooks/ohai`

# Creating custom knife plugins

Knife, the command-line client for the Chef server, has a plugin system. This plugin system enables us to extend the functionality of knife in any way we need it. The `knife-ec2` plugin is a common example; it adds commands such as `ec2 server create` to knife.

In this section, we will create a very basic `custom knife plugin` to learn about all the required building blocks of knife plugins. As knife plugins are pure Ruby programs, which can use any external libraries, there are no limits for what you can make knife do. This freedom enables you to build your whole `DevOps` workflow on knife, if you want to.

Now, let's teach knife how to tweet your name!

## Getting ready

Make sure you have a Twitter user account and created an application with Twitter (`https://apps.twitter.com/app/new`).

While creating your Twitter application, you should set the **OAuth** access level to *Read and write*, so as to enable your application to post your name.

Create an access token by connecting the application to your Twitter account. This will enable your Twitter application (and therefore your knife plugin) to tweet as your Twitter user.

Make sure you have the `twitter` gem installed. It will enable you to interact with Twitter from within your `knife` plugin:

```
mma@laptop:~/chef-repo $ chef gem install twitter
...TRUNCATED OUTPUT...
Successfully installed twitter-5.13.0
5 gems installed
```

## How to do it...

Let's create a knife plugin so that we can tweet by using the following knife command:

```
$ knife tweet "having fun building knife plugins"
```

1. Create a directory for your knife plugin inside your Chef repository:

   ```
   mma@laptop:~/chef-repo $ mkdir -p .chef/plugins/knife
   ```

2. Create your knife plugin:

   ```
   mma@laptop:~/chef-repo $ subl .chef/plugins/knife/knife_twitter.rb
   ```

   ```ruby
   require 'chef/knife'
   module KnifePlugins
     class Tweet < Chef::Knife
       deps do
         require 'twitter'
       end
       banner "knife tweet MESSAGE"
       def run
         client = Twitter::REST::Client.new do |config|
           config.consumer_key = "<YOUR_CONSUMER_KEY>"
           config.consumer_secret = "<YOUR_CONSUMER_SECRET>"
           config.access_token = "<YOUR_ACCESS-TOKEN>"
   ```

```
          config.access_token_secret = "<YOUR_ACCESS_TOKEN_SECRECT>"
        end
        client.update("#{name_args.first} #getchef")
      end
    end
  end
```

3. Send your first tweet:

   **mma@laptop:~/chef-repo $ knife tweet "having fun with building knife plugins"**

4. Validate whether the tweet went live:

## How it works...

There are three ways to make your knife plugins available: in your home directory under `~/.chef/plugins/knife` (so that you can use them for all your Chef repositories), in your Chef repository under `.chef/plugins/knife` (so that every co-worker using that repository can use them), or as a Ruby gem (so that everyone in the Chef community can use them).

We chose the second way, so that everyone working on our Chef repository can check out and use our Twitter knife plugin.

First, we need to include Chef's knife library into our Ruby file in order to be able to create a knife plugin:

```
require 'chef/knife'
```

Then, we define our plugin as follows:

```
module KnifePlugins
  class Tweet < Chef::Knife
    ...
  end
end
```

The preceding code creates the new knife command `tweet`. The command is derived from the class name that we gave our plugin. Each knife plugin needs to extend `Chef::Knife`.

The next step is to load all the dependencies required. Instead of simply putting multiple `require` calls at the beginning of our Ruby file, knife provides the `deps` method (which we can override) to load dependencies lazily on demand:

```
deps do
   require 'twitter'
end
```

Placing `require 'twitter'` inside the `deps` method makes sure that the `twitter` gem will only get loaded if our plugin runs. Not doing so would mean that the `twitter` gem would get loaded on each knife run, no matter whether it would be used or not.

After defining the dependencies, we need to tell the users of our plugin what it does and how to use it. The knife plugin provides the `banner` method to define the message that users see when they call our plugin with the `--help` parameter:

```
banner "knife tweet MESSAGE"
```

Let's see how this works:

**mma@laptop:~/chef-repo $ knife tweet --help**

**knife tweet MESSAGE**

Finally, we need to actually do something. The `run` method is where to place the code we want to execute. In our case, we create a Twitter client passing our authentication credentials:

```
client = Twitter::REST::Client.new do |config|
...
end
```

Then, we send our tweet:

```
client.update("#{name_args.first} #getchef")
```

The `name_args` attribute contains command-line arguments. We take the first one as the message that we send to Twitter and add the `#getchef` hashtag to every message we send.

## There's more...

You can add simple error handling to make sure that the user doesn't send empty tweets by adding this block at the beginning of the run method:

```
run
  unless name_args.size == 1
```

```
        ui.fatal "You need to say something!"
        show_usage
        exit 1
    end
  ...
  end
```

This piece of code gets executed if there isn't exactly one command-line argument available to the `knife tweet` call. In that case, it will print the error message and a user will get the same message when using the `--help` parameter. Then, this block will exit with the error code `1`, without doing anything else.

## See also

- ▶ Read more about how to write custom knife plugins at `https://docs.chef.io/plugin_knife_custom.html`

- ▶ Find the `twitter` gem at `https://github.com/sferik/twitter`

# 4
# Writing Better Cookbooks

*"When you know better, you do better"*

*Maya Angelou*

In this chapter, we will cover the following recipes:

- ▸ Setting the environment variables
- ▸ Passing arguments to shell commands
- ▸ Overriding attributes
- ▸ Using search to find nodes
- ▸ Using data bags
- ▸ Using search to find data bag items
- ▸ Using encrypted data bag items
- ▸ Accessing data bag values from external scripts
- ▸ Getting information about the environment
- ▸ Writing cross-platform cookbooks
- ▸ Finding the complete list of operating systems you can use in cookbooks
- ▸ Making recipes idempotent by using conditional execution

# Introduction

In this chapter, we'll see some of the more advanced topics in action. You'll see how to make your recipes more flexible by using search and data bags, and how to make sure your cookbooks run on different operating systems. You'll gain critical knowledge to create extensible and maintainable cookbooks for your infrastructure.

# Setting the environment variables

You might have experienced this: you try out a command on your node's shell and it works perfectly. Now, you try to execute the very same command from within your Chef recipe but it fails. One reason may be that there are certain environment variables set in your shell, which are not set during the Chef run. You might have set them manually or in your shell start up scripts—it does not really matter. You'll need to set them again in your recipe.

In this section, you will see how to set environment variables needed during a Chef run.

## Getting ready

Make sure you have a cookbook called `my_cookbook`, and that the `run_list` of your node includes `my_cookbook`, as described in the *Creating and using cookbooks* recipe in *Chapter 1, Chef Infrastructure*.

## How to do it...

Let's see how we can set environment variables from within Chef recipes:

1. Set an environment variable to be used during the Chef client run:

```
mma@laptop:~/chef-repo $ subl
  cookbooks/my_cookbook/recipes/default.rb

ENV['MESSAGE'] = 'Hello from Chef'

execute 'print value of environment variable $MESSAGE' do
  command 'echo $MESSAGE > /tmp/message'
end
```

2. Upload the modified cookbook to the Chef server:

```
mma@laptop:~/chef-repo $ knife cookbook upload my_cookbook --force

Uploading my_cookbook    [0.1.0]
```

3. Run the Chef client to create the `tmp` file:

**user@server:~$ sudo chef-client**

```
...TRUNCATED OUTPUT...
[2015-01-02T22:46:30+01:00] INFO: execute[print value of
environment variable $MESSAGE] ran successfully

    - execute echo $MESSAGE > /tmp/message
...TRUNCATED OUTPUT...
```

4. Ensure that it worked:

**user@server:~$ cat /tmp/message**

```
Hello from Chef
```

## How it works...

Ruby exposes the current environment via ENV—a hash to read or modify environment variables. We use ENV to set our environment variable. It is valid for the Ruby process in which the Chef client runs, as well as all child processes run.

The execute resource spawns a child process of the Ruby process by running the Chef client. Because it is a child process, the environment variable we set in the recipe is available to the script code the execute resource runs.

We simply access the environment variable by $MESSAGE, as we would do through the command line.

## There's more...

The execute resource offers a way to pass environment variables to the command it executes.

1. Change the my_cookbook default recipe:

**mma@laptop:~/chef-repo $ subl cookbooks/my_cookbook/recipes/default.rb**

```
execute 'print value of environment variable $MESSAGE' do
  command 'echo $MESSAGE > /tmp/message'
  environment 'MESSAGE' => 'Hello from the execute resource'
end
```

2. Upload the modified cookbook to your Chef server and run the Chef client, as shown in the *How to do it...* section.

3. Validate the contents of the `tmp` file:

**`user@server:~$ cat /tmp/message`**

`Hello from the execute resource`

 Setting an environment variable using `ENV` will make that variable available during the whole Chef run. In contrast, passing it to the execute resource will only make it available for that one command executed by the resource.

## See also

▶ Read more about handling Unix environment variables in Chef at `https://docs.chef.io/environment_variables.html`

# Passing arguments to shell commands

The Chef client enables you to run shell commands by using the `execute` resource. However, how can you pass arguments to such shell commands? Let's assume you want to calculate a value you need to pass to the shell command in your recipe. How can you do that? Let's find out...

## Getting ready

Make sure you have a cookbook called `my_cookbook`, and the `run_list` of your node includes `my_cookbook`, as described in the *Creating and using cookbooks* recipe in *Chapter 1, Chef Infrastructure*.

## How to do it...

Let's see how we can pass Ruby variables into shell commands:

1. Edit your default recipe. You'll pass an argument to a shell command by using an `execute` resource:

```
mma@laptop:~/chef-repo $ subl
  cookbooks/my_cookbook/recipes/default.rb

max_mem = node['memory']['total'].to_i * 0.8

execute 'echo max memory value into tmp file' do
```

```
    command "echo #{max_mem} > /tmp/max_mem"
end
```

2. Upload the modified cookbook to the Chef server:

   **mma@laptop:~/chef-repo $ knife cookbook upload my_cookbook**

   Uploading my_cookbook      [0.1.0]

3. Run the Chef client on your node to create the `tmp` file:

   **user@server:~$ sudo chef-client**

   ```
   ...TRUNCATED OUTPUT...
   [2015-01-02T22:55:20+01:00] INFO: execute[echo max memory value
   into tmp file] ran successfully

       - execute echo 6553.6 > /tmp/max_mem
   ...TRUNCATED OUTPUT...
   ```

4. Validate that it worked:

   **user@server:~$ cat /tmp/max_mem**

   299523.2

## How it works...

We calculate a value, which we want to pass to the command we want to execute. The `node['memory']['total']` call returns a string. We need to convert it to an integer by calling `to_i` on the returned string to be able to multiply it with `0.8`.

As these recipes are Ruby files, you can use string expansion if you need it. One way to pass arguments to shell commands defined by `execute` resources is to use string expansion in the `command` parameter:

```
command "echo #{max_mem} > /tmp/max_mem"
```

In the preceding line, Ruby will replace `#{max_mem}` with the value of the `max_mem` variable that was defined previously. The string, which we pass as a command to the `execute` resource, could look like this (assuming that `node['memory']['total']` returns `1000`):

```
command "echo 800 > /tmp/max_mem"
```

 Be careful! You need to use double quotes if you want Ruby to expand your string.

## There's more...

String expansion works in multi-line strings, as well. You can define them like this:

```
command <<EOC
echo #{message} > /tmp/message
EOC
```

 EOC is the string delimiter. You're free to use whatever you want here. It can be EOF, EOH, STRING, FOO, or whatever you want it to be. Just make sure to use the same delimiter at the beginning and the end of your multi-line string.

We saw another way to pass arguments to shell commands by using environment variables in the previous section.

## See also

▶ The *Mixing plain Ruby with Chef DSL* section in *Chapter 3, Chef Language and Style*
▶ The *Setting the environment variables* section in this chapter

# Overriding attributes

You can set attribute values in attribute files. Usually, cookbooks come with reasonable default values for attributes. However, the default values might not suit your needs. If they don't fit, you can override attribute values.

In this section, we'll look at how to override attributes from within recipes and roles.

## Getting ready

Make sure you have a cookbook called my_cookbook, and that the run_list of your node includes my_cookbook, as described in the *Creating and using cookbooks* recipe in *Chapter 1, Chef Infrastructure*.

## How to do it...

Let's see how we can override attribute values:

1. Edit the default attributes file to add an attribute:

```
mma@laptop:~/chef-repo $ subl
  cookbooks/my_cookbook/attributes/default.rb

default['my_cookbook']['version'] = '1.2.3'
```

2. Edit your `default recipe`. You'll override the value of the `version` attribute and print it to the console:

   **mma@laptop:~/chef-repo $ subl**
     **cookbooks/my_cookbook/recipes/default.rb**

   ```
   node.override['my_cookbook']['version'] = '1.5'
   execute 'echo the cookbook version' do
     command "echo #{node['my_cookbook']['version']}"
   end
   ```

3. Upload the modified cookbook to the Chef server:

   **mma@laptop:~/chef-repo $ knife cookbook upload my_cookbook**

   ```
   Uploading my_cookbook      [0.1.0]
   ```

4. Run the Chef client on your node in order to create the `tmp` file:

   **user@server:~$ sudo chef-client**

   ```
   ...TRUNCATED OUTPUT...
   [2015-01-02T22:59:10+01:00] INFO: execute[echo the path attribute]
   ran successfully

       - execute echo 1.5
   ```

## How it works...

You set a default value for the `version` attribute in your cookbook's default attributes file. Chef evaluates the attributes file early in the Chef run and makes all the attributes defined available via the `node` object. Your recipes can use the `node` object to access the values of the attributes.

The Chef DSL provides various ways to modify attributes, once they are set. In our example, we used the `override` method to change the value of the attribute inside our recipe. After this call, the node will carry the newly set value for the attribute, instead the old value set via the attributes file.

## There's more...

You can override attributes from within roles and environments as well. In the following example, we set the `version` attribute to `2.0.0` (instead of keeping the default value of `1.2.3`):

1. Edit the default attributes file to add an attribute:

   **mma@laptop:~/chef-repo $ subl**
     **cookbooks/my_cookbook/attributes/default.rb**

   ```
   default['my_cookbook']['version'] = '1.2.3'
   ```

2. Use the attribute in your default recipe:

   **mma@laptop:~/chef-repo $ subl**
   **cookbooks/my_cookbook/recipes/default.rb**

   ```
   execute 'echo the path attribute' do
     command "echo #{node['my_cookbook']['version']}"
   end
   ```

3. Upload the modified cookbook to the Chef server:

   **mma@laptop:~/chef-repo $ knife cookbook upload my_cookbook --force**

   ```
   Uploading my_cookbook      [0.1.0]
   ```

4. Create a role named `upgraded_hosts` by creating a file called `roles/upgraded_hosts.rb`:

   **mma@laptop:~/chef-repo $ subl roles/upgraded_hosts.rb**

   ```
   name "upgraded_hosts"

   run_list "recipe[my_cookbook]"
   default_attributes 'my_cookbook' => { 'version' => '2.0.0' }
   ```

5. Upload the role to the Chef server:

   **mma@laptop:~/chef-repo $ knife role from file**
   **upgraded_hosts.rb**

   ```
   Updated Role upgraded_hosts!
   ```

6. Change the `run_list` of your node:

   **mma@laptop:~/chef-repo $ knife node run_list set server**
   **'role[upgraded_hosts]'**

   ```
   server:
       run_list: role[upgraded_hosts]
   ```

7. Run the Chef client on your system:

   **user@server:~$ sudo chef-client**

   ```
   ...TRUNCATED OUTPUT...
   [2015-01-02T23:04:29+00:00] INFO: execute[echo the path attribute]
   ran successfully

       - execute echo 2.0.0
   ```

▶ Learn more about roles at `https://docs.chef.io/roles.html`

▶ Read more about attributes at `https://docs.chef.io/attributes.html`

# Using search to find nodes

If you are running your infrastructure in any type of a virtualized environment, such as a public or private cloud, the server instances that you use will change frequently. Instead of having a well-known set of servers, you destroy and create virtual servers regularly.

Your cookbooks cannot rely on hardcoded server names when you need in this situation, a list of available servers.

Chef provides a way to find nodes by their attributes, for example, their roles. In this section, we'll see how you can retrieve a set of nodes to use them in your recipes.

## Getting ready

Make sure that you have a cookbook called `my_cookbook`, as described in the *Creating and using cookbooks* section in *Chapter 1, Chef Infrastructure*.

## How to do it...

Let's see how we can find all nodes having a certain role:

1. Create a role called `web` that has `my_cookbook` in its run list. This command will open a JSON definition of your role in your default editor. You need to add `"recipe[my_cookbook]"` to `"run_list"`:

   ```
   mma@laptop:~/chef-repo $ knife role create web
   ```

   ```
   ...
     "run_list": [
       "recipe[my_cookbook]"
     ],
   ...
   Created role[web]
   ```

2. Create at least one node that has the new role in its run list. This command will open a JSON definition of your node in your default editor:

   ```
   mma@laptop:~/chef-repo $ knife node create webserver
   ```

   ```
   ...
     "run_list": [
   ```

```
        "role[web]"
    ],
    ...
Created node[webserver]
```

3.  Edit your default recipe to search for all nodes that have the web role:

    **mma@laptop:~/chef-repo $ subl
    cookbooks/my_cookbook/recipes/default.rb**

    ```
    servers = search(:node, "role:web")

    servers.each do |srv|
      log srv.name
    end
    ```

4.  Upload your modified cookbook:

    **mma@laptop:~/chef-repo $ knife cookbook upload my_cookbook**

    ```
    Uploading my_cookbook     [0.1.0]
    ```

5.  Run the Chef client on one of your nodes:

    **user@server:~$ sudo chef-client**

    ```
    ...TRUNCATED OUTPUT...
    [2015-02-19T21:32:00+00:00] INFO: webserver
    ...TRUNCATED OUTPUT...
    ```

## How it works...

The Chef server stores all nodes with their attributes. The attributes are partly auto-detected by using `ohai` (such as name, IP address, CPUs, and so on) and partly configured by you (such as `run_list`). The Chef DSL offers the `search` method to look up nodes based on your search criteria. In the preceding example, we simply used a role as the search criteria. However, you can use any combination of node attributes available to construct your search.

The search method returns a list of node objects, which you can use in your recipe. In the preceding example, we looped through the list of nodes by using the standard Ruby `each` iterator. The current element is available as the variable you declare between the | after the do. In our case, it's a full-blown node object and you can use it to retrieve its attributes, or even to modify it.

## There's more...

Search is a very powerful tool to dynamically identify nodes. You can use Boolean operators to craft more complex queries and you can use search in your cookbooks, as well as with knife. Let's see how you can take search a bit further.

## Using knife to search for nodes

Knife offers the very same search syntax as the `search` method within your recipes. It lets you search for nodes via the command line:

```
mma@laptop:~/chef-repo $ knife search node "role:web"

    3 items found
    Node Name:    web
    ...TRUNCATED OUTPUT...
    Node Name:    web1
    ...TRUNCATED OUTPUT...
    Node Name:    web2
    ...TRUNCATED OUTPUT...
```

## Searching for arbitrary node attributes

In addition to searching for roles, you can search for any attribute of a node. Let's see how you can search for a node that has `ubuntu` as its platform using `knife`:

```
mma@laptop:~/chef-repo $ knife search node "platform:ubuntu"

    3 items found
    Node Name:    web
    ...TRUNCATED OUTPUT...
    Node Name:    vagrant
    ...TRUNCATED OUTPUT...
    Node Name:    db
    ...TRUNCATED OUTPUT...
```

## Using Boolean operators in search

If you want to combine multiple attributes in your search query, you can use Boolean operators such as NOT, AND, and OR:

```
mma@laptop:~/chef-repo $ knife search node 'platform:ubuntu AND
    name:v*'

    1 items found
    Node Name:    vagrant
    ...TRUNCATED OUTPUT...
```

## See also

▸ Read more about search at `https://docs.chef.io/chef_search.html`

▸ Read more about how to use search from within a recipe here: `https://docs.chef.io/dsl_recipe.html#search`

# Using data bags

There are situations where you have data, which you neither want to hard code in your recipes nor store as attributes in your cookbooks. Users, external servers, or database connections are examples of such data. Chef offers so-called **data bags** to manage arbitrary collections of data, which you can use with your cookbooks.

Let's see how we can create and use a data bag and its items.

## Getting ready

In the following example, we want to illustrate the usage of data bags by sending HTTP requests to a configurable HTTP endpoint. We don't want to hardcode the HTTP endpoint in our recipe. That's why we store it as a data bag item in a data bag.

To be able to follow along with the example, you'll need an HTTP endpoint.

One way to establish an HTTP endpoint is to just run `sudo nc -l 80` on any server accessible by your node and use its IP address below.

Another way to establish an HTTP endpoint, which shows us the requests we make, is a free service called `RequestBin`. To use it, follow these steps:

1. Open `http://requestb.in` in your browser and click on **Create a RequestBin**:

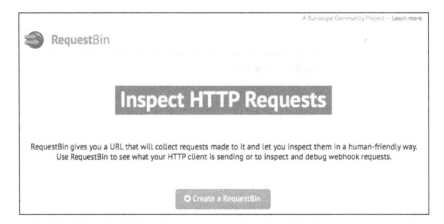

2. Note the URL for your new RequestBin. We'll call it from within our recipe, as shown in screenshot:

```
Bin URL
http://requestb.in/1ka7usr1
```

## How to do it...

Let's create a data bag to hold our HTTP endpoint URL and use it from within our recipe:

1. Create a directory for your data bag:

   ```
   mma@laptop:~/chef-repo $ mkdir data_bags/hooks
   ```

2. Create a data bag item for RequestBin. Make sure to use your own RequestBin URL you noted in the *Getting ready* section:

   ```
   mma@laptop:~/chef-repo $ subl data_bags/hooks/request_bin.json

   {
     "id": "request_bin",
     "url": "http://requestb.in/<YOUR_REQUEST_BIN_ID>"
   }
   ```

3. Create the data bag on the Chef server:

   ```
   mma@laptop:~/chef-repo $ knife data bag create hooks

   Created data_bag[hooks]
   ```

4. Upload your data bag item to the Chef server:

   ```
   mma@laptop:~/chef-repo $ knife data bag from file hooks
       request_bin.json

   Updated data_bag_item[hooks::request_bin]
   ```

5. Edit the default recipe of `my_cookbook` in order to retrieve the RequestBin URL from your data bag:

   ```
   mma@laptop:~/chef-repo $ subl
       cookbooks/my_cookbook/recipes/default.rb

   hook = data_bag_item('hooks', 'request_bin')
   http_request 'callback' do
     url hook['url']
   end
   ```

6. Upload your modified cookbook to the Chef server:

```
mma@laptop:~/chef-repo $ knife cookbook upload my_cookbook

Uploading my_cookbook    [0.1.0]
```

7. Run the Chef client on your node to test whether the HTTP request to your RequestBin was executed:

```
user@server:~$ sudo chef-client

...TRUNCATED OUTPUT...
[2015-01-02T20:08:20+01:00] INFO: http_request[callback] GET to
http://requestb.in/1ka7usr1 successful

    - http_request[callback] GET to http://requestb.in/1ka7usr1
...TRUNCATED OUTPUT...
```

8. Check your RequestBin. The request should show up there:

## How it works...

A data bag is a named collection of structured data entries. You define each data entry called a data bag item in a JSON file. You can search for data bag items from within your recipes to use the data stored in the data bag.

In our example, we created a data bag called hooks. A data bag is a directory within your Chef repository and you can use knife to create it on the Chef server.

Then, we created a data bag item with the name request_bin in a file called request_bin.json inside the data bag's directory and uploaded it to the Chef server as well.

Our recipe retrieves the data bag item using the data_bag_item method, taking the data bag name as the first parameter and the item name as the second parameter.

Then, we create an `http_request` resource by passing it the `url` attribute of the data bag item. You can retrieve any attribute from a data bag item using the Hash notation `hook['url']`.

## See also

▸ Read more about data bags at `https://docs.chef.io/data_bags.html`

# Using search to find data bag items

You might want to execute code in your recipe multiple times—once for each data bag item, such as for each user or each HTTP end point.

You can use search to find certain data bag items and loop through search results to execute code multiple times.

Let's see how we can make our recipes more dynamic by searching for data bag items.

## Getting ready

Follow the *Getting ready* and *How to do it...* (steps 1 to 4) sections in the *Using data bags* recipe in this chapter. You might want to add a few more HTTP end points to your data bag.

## How to do it...

Let's create a recipe to search for data bag items and call the `http_request` resource for everyone:

1.  Edit the default recipe of `my_cookbook` to retrieve all HTTP hooks, which should be called by your recipe from your data bag:

    ```
    mma@laptop:~/chef-repo $ subl
      cookbooks/my_cookbook/recipes/default.rb
    ```

    ```
    search(:hooks, '*:*').each do |hook|
      http_request 'callback' do
        url hook['url']
      end
    end
    ```

2.  Upload your modified recipe to the Chef server, run the Chef client on your node, and verify that your HTTP endpoint received the HTTP request as described in *How to do it...* (steps 6 to 8) sections in the *Using data bags* recipe in this chapter.

## How it works...

Our recipe uses the `search` method to retrieve all items from the data bag called `hooks`. The first parameter of the `search` method is the name of the data bag (as Ruby symbol). The second parameter is the search query—in our case, we're looking for all data bag items by using `*:*`. Using the `each` iterator, we loop through every data bag item found. Inside the Ruby block, which gets executed for each item, we can access the item by using the variable `hook`.

We create an `http_request` resource for each data bag item, passing the URL stored in the item as the `url` parameter to the resource. You can access arbitrary attributes of your data bag item using a Hash-like notation.

## There's more...

You can use various search patterns to find certain data bag items, some examples are shown here:

▶ `search(:hooks, "id:request_bin")`

▶ `search(:hooks, "url:*request*")`

## See also

▶ The *Using data bags* recipe in this chapter

▶ The *Using search to find nodes* recipe in this chapter

▶ Find out what else is possible with data bag search at `http://docs.chef.io/data_bags.html#with-search`

# Using encrypted data bag items

Data bags are a great way to store user- and application-specific data. Before long, you'll want to store passwords and private keys in data bags as well. However, you might (and should) be worried about uploading confidential data to a Chef server.

Chef offers encrypted data bag items to enable you to put confidential data into data bags, thus reducing the implied security risk.

## Getting ready

Make sure you have a Chef repository and can access your Chef server.

## How to do it...

Let's create and encrypt a data bag item and see how we can use it:

1. Create a directory for your encrypted data bag:

   **mma@laptop:~/chef-repo $ mkdir data_bags/accounts**

2. Create a data bag item for a Google account:

   **mma@laptop:~/chef-repo $ subl data_bags/accounts/google.json**

   ```
   {
     "id": "google",
     "email": "some.one@gmail.com",
     "password": "Oh! So secret?"
   }
   ```

3. Create the data bag on the Chef server:

   **mma@laptop:~/chef-repo $ knife data bag create accounts**

   ```
   Created data_bag[accounts]
   ```

4. Upload your data bag item to the Chef server, encrypting it on the fly:

   **mma@laptop:~/chef-repo $ knife data bag from file accounts google.json --secret 'Open sesame!'**

   ```
   Updated data_bag_item[accounts::google]
   ```

 Be careful! Using the `--secret` command-line switch is dangerous because it will show up in your shell history and log files. Take a look at the *There's more...* section of this recipe to find out how to use a private key instead of a plaintext `secret`.

5. Verify that your data bag item is encrypted:

   **mma@laptop:~/chef-repo $ knife data bag show accounts google**

   ```
   email:
     cipher:           aes-256-cbc
     encrypted_data:
       DqYu8DnI8E1XQ5I/
       jNyaFZ7LVXIzRUzuFjDHJGHymgxd9cbUJQ48nYJ3QHxi
       3xyE

     iv:               B+eQ1hD35PfadjUwe+e18g==

     version:          1
   ```

```
id:          google
password:
  cipher:          aes-256-cbc
  encrypted_data:
    m3bGPmp6cObnmHQpGipZYHNAcxJYkIfx4udsM8GPt7cT1ecOw+
    IuLZk0Q9F8
  2pX0

  iv:              Bp5jEZG/cPYMRWiUX1UPQA==

  version:         1
```

6.  Now let's take a look at the decrypted data bag by providing the `secret` keys:

    **mma@laptop:~/chef-repo $ knife data bag show accounts google -
    -secret 'Open sesame!'**

    ```
    email:   some.one@gmail.com
    id:      google
    password: Oh! So secret?
    ```

## How it works...

Passing `--secret` to the `knife` command that is creating the data bag item encrypts the contents of the data bag.

> The primary purpose of encrypting is to protect data on the Chef server. You still need to securely distribute the `secret` keys manually.
>
> The ID of the data bag item will not be encrypted because the Chef server needs it to work with the data bag item.

Chef uses a shared secret to encrypt and decrypt data bag items. Everyone having access to the shared secret will be able to decrypt the contents of the encrypted data bag item.

## There's more...

Accessing encrypted data bag items from the command line with `knife` is usually not what you want. Let's take a look at how to use encrypted data bag items in real life.

### Using a private key file

Instead of passing the shared secret via the command line, you can create an **openssl** format private key and pass its file location to the `knife` command:

```
mma@laptop:~/chef-repo $ knife data bag from file accounts
  google.json --secret-file .chef/data_bag_secret_key.pem
```

You can create an `openssl` format private key like this:

`mma@laptop:~/chef-repo $ openssl genrsa -out .chef/ data_bag_secret_key.pem 1024`

The preceding command assumes that you have a file called `data_bag_secret_key.pem` in the `.chef` directory.

To enable your node to decrypt the data bag item, you need to `scp` your secret key file to your node and place it in the `/etc/chef/` directory. If you're using Vagrant, you can run `vagrant ssh-config; scp -P 2222 .chef/data_bag_secret_key.pem 127.0.0.1`:

 The initial bootstrap procedure for a node will put the key in the right place on the node, if one already exists in your Chef repository.

Make sure that `/etc/chef/client.rb` points to your `data_bag_secret_key.pem` file:

`encrypted_data_bag_secret "/etc/chef/data_bag_secret_key.pem"`

Now, you can access the decrypted contents of your data bag items in your recipe:

```
google_account = Chef::EncryptedDataBagItem.load("accounts",
  "google")
log google_account["password"]
```

Chef will look for the file configured in `client.rb` and use the secret given there to decrypt the data bag item.

## See also

▸ The *Using data bags* recipe in this chapter
▸ Learn more about encrypted data bag items at `http://docs.chef.io/data_bags.html#encrypt-a-data-bag-item`

# Accessing data bag values from external scripts

Sometimes, you cannot put a server under full Chef control (yet). In such cases, you might want to be able to access the values managed in Chef data bags from scripts, which are not maintained by Chef. The easiest way to do this is to dump the data bag values (or any node values for that matter) into a JSON file and let your external script read them from there.

## Getting ready

Make sure you have a cookbook called `my_cookbook`, and that the `run_list` of your node includes `my_cookbook`, as described in the *Creating and using cookbooks* recipe in *Chapter 1, Chef Infrastructure*.

Create a data, as shown in the following steps, so that we can use its values later:

1. Create the data bag:

```
mma@laptop:~/chef-repo $ mkdir data_bags/servers
mma@laptop:~/chef-repo $ knife data bag create servers

Created data_bag[servers]
```

2. Create the first data bag item:

```
mma@laptop:~/chef-repo $ subl data_bags/servers/backup.json

{
  "id": "backup",
  "host": "10.0.0.12"
}

mma@laptop:~/chef-repo $ knife data bag from file servers
  backup.json

Updated data_bag_item[servers::backup]
```

## How to do it...

Let's create a JSON file that contains data bag values by using our cookbook, so that external scripts can access those values:

1. Edit your cookbook's default recipe:

```
mma@laptop:~/chef-repo $ subl
  cookbooks/my_cookbook/recipes/default.rb

file "/etc/backup_config.json" do
  owner "root"
  group "root"
  mode 0644
  content data_bag_item('servers', 'backup')['host'].to_json
end
```

2. Upload the modified cookbook to the Chef server:

```
mma@laptop:~/chef-repo $ knife cookbook upload my_cookbook

Uploading my_cookbook    [0.1.0]
```

3. Run the Chef client on your node:

```
user@server:~$ sudo chef-client

...TRUNCATED OUTPUT...
[2015-01-08T21:02:24+01:00] INFO: file[/etc/backup_config.json]
created file /etc/backup_config.json

    - create new file /etc/backup_config.json
  [2015-01-08T21:02:24+01:00] INFO: file[/etc/backup_config.json]
updated file contents / etc/backup_config.json

    - update content in file / etc/backup_config.json from none to
adc6de
...TRUNCATED OUTPUT...
```

4. Validate the content of the generated file:

```
user@server:~$ cat /etc/backup_config.json

"10.0.0.12"
```

5. Now, you can access the `backup_config.json` file from within your external scripts, which are not managed by Chef.

## How it works...

The file resource creates a `JSON` file in the `/etc` directory. It gets the file's content directly from the data bag by using the `data_bag_item` method. This method expects the name of the data bag as the first argument and the name of the data bag item as the second argument. We then can access the host value from the data bag item and convert it to JSON.

The file resource uses this JSON converted value as its content and writes it to disk.

Now, any external script can read the value from that file.

## There's more...

If you are sure that your data bag values don't get modified by the Chef client run on the node, you could use the Chef API directly from your script.

## See also

▸ Read more about how to do this at `https://stackoverflow.com/questions/10318919/how-to-access-current-values-from-a-chef-data-bag`

▸ The *Using data bags* recipe in this chapter to learn how to handle data bags

# Getting information about the environment

Sometimes, your recipes need to know details about the environment they are modifying. I'm not talking about Chef environments but about things such as Linux kernel versions, existing users, and network interfaces.

Chef provides all this information via the `node` object. Let's take a look at how to retrieve it.

## Getting ready

Log in to any of your Chef managed nodes and start the chef-shell:

```
user@server:~$ sudo chef-shell --client
chef >
```

## How to do it...

Let's play around with the node object and take a look at what information it stores:

1. List which information is available. The example shows the keys available on a Vagrant VM. Depending on what kind of server you work on, you'll find different data, as shown in the following:

   ```
   chef > node.keys.sort
   ```

   ```
   => ["block_device", "chef_packages", "command", "counters",
   "cpu", "current_user", "dmi", "domain", "etc", "filesystem",
   "fqdn", "hostname", "idletime", "idletime_seconds", "ip6address",
   "ipaddress", "kernel", "keys", "languages", "lsb", "macaddress",
   "memory", "network", "ntp", "ohai_time", "os", "os_version",
   "platform", "platform_family", "platform_version", "recipes",
   "roles", "root_group", "tags", "uptime", "uptime_seconds",
   "virtualization"]
   ```

2. Get a list of network interfaces available:

   ```
   chef > node['network']['interfaces'].keys.sort
   ```

   ```
   => ["eth0", "lo"]
   ```

3. List all the existing user accounts:

   ```
   chef > node['etc']['passwd'].keys.sort
   ```

   ```
   => ["backup", "bin", "daemon", "games", "gnats", "irc", "libuuid",
   "list", "lp", "mail", "man", "messagebus", "news", "nobody",
   "ntp", "proxy", "root", "sshd", "sync", "sys", "syslog", "uucp",
   "vagrant", "vboxadd", "www-data"]
   ```

4. Get the details of the root user:

```
chef > node['etc']['passwd']['root']
```

```
=> {"dir"=>"/root", "gid"=>0, "uid"=>0, "shell"=>"/bin/bash",
"gecos"=>"root"}
```

5. Get the code name of the installed Ubuntu distribution:

```
chef > node['lsb']['codename']
```

```
=> "utopic"
```

6. Find out which kernel modules are available:

```
chef > node['kernel']['modules'].keys.sort
```

```
=> ["auth_rpcgss", "dm_crypt", "drm", "e1000", "fscache", "i2c_
piix4", "ip_tables", "iptable_filter", "lockd", "mac_hid",
"nfs", "nfs_acl", "nfsd", "parport", "parport_pc", "pata_acpi",
"ppdev", "psmouse", "serio_raw", "sunrpc", "vboxguest", "vboxsf",
"vboxvideo", "x_tables"]
```

## How it works...

Chef uses Ohai to retrieve a node's environment. It stores the data found by Ohai with the node object in a Hash-like structure called a **Mash**. In addition to providing key-value pairs, it adds methods to the node object to query the keys directly.

Instead of using node['lsb']['codename'], you could use node.lsb.codename as well.

## There's more...

You can use the exact same calls that we used in chef-shell inside your recipes.

## See also

▶ Ohai is responsible for filling the node with all that information. Read more about Ohai at https://docs.chef.io/ohai.html

# Writing cross-platform cookbooks

Imagine you have written a great cookbook for your Ubuntu node and now you need to run it on that CentOS server. Ouch! It will most probably fail miserably. Package names might be different and configuration files are in different places.

Luckily, Chef provides you with a host of features to write cross-platform cookbooks. With just a few simple commands, you can make sure that your cookbook adapts to the platform that your node is running on. Let's take a look at how to do this...

## Getting ready

Make sure you have a cookbook called `my_cookbook`, and that the `run_list` of your node includes `my_cookbook`, as described in the *Creating and using cookbooks* recipe in *Chapter 1, Chef Infrastructure*.

## How to do it...

Retrieve the node's platform and execute the conditional logic in your cookbook depending on the platform:

1. Log a message only if your node is on Ubuntu:

    ```
    mma@laptop:~/chef-repo $ subl
      cookbooks/my_cookbook/recipes/default.rb
    ```

    ```
    Log.info("Running on ubuntu") if node.platform == 'ubuntu'
    ```

2. Upload the modified cookbook to your Chef server:

    ```
    mma@laptop:~/chef-repo $ knife cookbook upload my_cookbook --force
    ```

    ```
    Uploading my_cookbook      [0.1.0]
    Uploaded 1 cookbook.
    ```

3. Log in to your node and run the Chef client to see whether it works:

    ```
    user@server:~$ sudo chef-client
    ```

    ```
    ...TRUNCATED OUTPUT...
    [2015-01-08T21:24:39+01:00] INFO: Running on Ubuntu
    ...TRUNCATED OUTPUT...
    ```

4. If you are not interested in a specific platform but you only need to know whether you run on a Debian derivative, you can place the following line in your default recipe:

    ```
    Log.info("Running on a debian derivative") if
      platform_family?('debian')
    ```

5. Upload the modified cookbook and run the Chef client on an Ubuntu node will show:

    ```
    [2015-01-08T21:25:20+01:00] INFO: Running on a debian
      derivative
    ```

## How it works...

Ohai discovers the current node's operating system and stores it as a platform attribute with the node object. You can access it like any other attribute by using the Hash syntax, as follows:

```
node['platform']
```

Alternatively, you can use the method style syntax, as follows:

```
node.platform
```

Chef knows which operating systems belong together. You can use this knowledge by using the `platform_family` method from the Chef DSL.

You can then use basic Ruby conditionals, such as `if`, `unless`, or even `case` to make your cookbook do platform-specific things.

## There's more...

Let's take a closer look at what else is possible.

### Avoiding case statements to set values based on the platform

The Chef DSL offers the convenience methods `value_for_platform` and `value_for_platform_family`. You can use them to avoid complex case statements and use a simple Hash instead. The `runit` cookbook, for example, uses `value_for_platform` to pass the start command for the `runit` service to the `execute` resource:

```
execute "start-runsvdir" do
  command value_for_platform(
    "debian" => { "default" => "runsvdir-start" },
    "ubuntu" => { "default" => "start runsvdir" },
    "gentoo" => { "default" => "/etc/init.d/runit-start start" }
  )
  action :nothing
end
```

The command will be `runsvdir-start` on Debian, `start runsvdir` on Ubuntu, and will use an `init.d` script on Gentoo.

Some of the built-in resources have platform-specific providers. These platform-specific providers will automatically be used by Chef. For example, the `group` resource uses one of the following providers depending on the platform:

`Chef::Provider::Group::Dscl` on Mac OS X

`Chef::Provider::Group::Pw` on FreeBSD

`Chef::Provider::Group::Usermod` on Solaris

### Declaring support for specific operating systems in your cookbook's metadata

If your cookbook is written for a well-defined set of operating systems, you should list the supported platforms in your cookbook's metadata:

```
mma@laptop:~/chef-repo $ subl
  cookbooks/my_cookbook/recipes/metadata.rb

    supports 'ubuntu'
```

If your cookbook supports multiple platforms, you can use a nice Ruby shortcut to list all the platforms as a Ruby array of strings (using the `%w` shortcut) and loop through that array to call `supports` for each platform:

```
%w(debian ubuntu redhat centos fedora scientific amazon oracle).each
do |os|
    supports os
end
```

## See also

▸ The *Mixing plain Ruby with Chef DSL* recipe in *Chapter 3, Chef Language and Style*

▸ The `runit` cookbook at `https://github.com/hw-cookbooks/runit`

# Finding the complete list of operating systems you can use in cookbooks

You want to write cookbooks that work on different operating systems, such as Ubuntu, RedHat, Debian, or Windows.

Inside your cookbooks, you need to distinguish between these different platforms. And you need to tell your cookbook which platforms it supports. However, you don't know which platform values you can use inside `metadata.rb` or your recipes.

In this section, we'll look at a very simple way to ask Chef which values it defines for a platform.

## How to do it...

Let's use plain Ruby to find out all the possible values for `platform` and use a subset of those in `metadata.rb`:

1. Print a list of supported platforms by querying the `Chef::Platform` class:

   **`mma@laptop:~/chef-repo/cookbooks $ ruby -rchef -e`**
   **`'puts Chef::Platform.platforms.keys.sort.join(", ")'`**

   ```
   aix, amazon, arch, centos, cloudlinux, debian, default, exherbo,
   fedora,
   ...TRUNCATED OUTPUT...
   ubuntu, windows, xcp, xenserver
   ```

2. Tell the users of your cookbook which platforms it supports:

   **`mma@laptop:~/chef-repo/cookbooks $ subl`**
   **`my_cookbook/metadata.rb`**

   ```
   . . .

   %w(debian ubuntu mac_os_x).each do |os|
     supports os
   end
   ```

## How it works...

Chef maintains a set of supported operating system platforms it runs on in the `Chef::Platform` class. To query this class for the list of platforms, we use the Ruby command line.

We need to require the `chef` gem by adding an `-r` parameter to the `ruby` call.

The `-e` parameter contains the Ruby code that we want to execute. In our case, we use `puts` to print the result of our query to the console.

The `Chef::Platform` class holds a collection called **platforms**. We get its keys, sort them, and join the contents of the resulting Ruby array to a comma-separated string:

```
Chef::Platform.platforms.keys.sort.join(", ")
```

## There's more...

Each platform in the `Chef::Platforms` collection not only has the platform name as the key, but a set of default providers as well.

Providers contain the platform-specific implementation details for resources. For example, the package resource has providers to use Apt on Ubuntu, but Yum on RedHat:

**mma@laptop:~/chef_helpster $ irb**

```
2.1.0 :001 > require 'chef'
 => true
2.1.0 :002 > Chef::Platform.platforms[:ubuntu]
 => {:default=>{:package=>Chef::Provider::Package::Apt,
    :service=>Chef::Provider::Service::Debian,
    :cron=>Chef::Provider::Cron, :mdadm=>Chef::Provider::Mdadm}}
```

Instead of using the Ruby command line, we can use the Chef classes in the **Interactive Ruby shell** (**IRB**).

You can change how your recipe works, depending on the platform it runs on (example taken from Opscode's apache cookbook):

```
service "apache2" do
  case node[:platform]
  when "centos","redhat","fedora","suse"
    service_name "httpd"
  ...TRUNCATED OUTPUT…
when "arch"
    service_name "httpd"
  end
  supports value_for_platform(
    "debian" => { ... },
    "ubuntu" => { ... },
  ...TRUNCATED OUTPUT...
"default" => { ... }
  )
  action :enable
end
```

This version of the apache cookbook sets up the apache service with different names and commands depending on the platform, and tells Chef which actions may be called to manage the apache service.

Chef sets the node attribute :platform according to the underlying operating system. You can use this node attribute to tailor your recipe code for each platform you need.

## See also

- ▶ To see some examples on how to use the platform values, go to https://docs.chef.io/dsl_recipe.html

# Making recipes idempotent by using conditional execution

Chef manages the configuration of your nodes. It is not simply an installer for new software but you will run the Chef client on the existing nodes, as well as new ones.

To speed up your Chef client runs on the existing nodes, you should make sure that your recipes do not try to re-execute resources, which have already reached the desired state.

Running resources repeatedly will be a performance issue at best and will break your servers at worst. Chef offers a way to tell resources not to run or only to run if a certain condition is met. Let's take a look at how conditional execution of resources works.

## Getting ready

Make sure you have a cookbook called `my_cookbook` and that the `run_list` of your node includes `my_cookbook`, as described in the *Creating and using cookbooks* recipe in *Chapter 1, Chef Infrastructure*.

## How to do it...

Let's see how to use conditional execution in our cookbooks:

1. Edit your default recipe to trigger a callback only if you have set a node attribute called `enabled`:

   **mma@laptop:~/chef-repo $ subl cookbooks/my_cookbook/recipes/default.rb**

   ```
   http_request 'callback' do
     url node['my_cookbook']['callback']['url']
     only_if { node['my_cookbook']['callback']['enabled'] }
   end
   ```

2. Add the attributes to your cookbook:

   **mma@laptop:~/chef-repo $ subl cookbooks/my_cookbook/attributes/default.rb**

   ```
   default['my_cookbook']['callback']['url'] =
     'http://www.chef.io'
   default['my_cookbook']['callback']['enabled'] = true
   ```

3. Upload your modified cookbook to the Chef server:

   **mma@laptop:~/chef-repo $ knife cookbook upload my_cookbook --force**

   ```
   Uploading my_cookbook    [0.1.0]
   ```

4.  Run the Chef client on your node to test whether the HTTP request was executed:

```
user@server:~$ sudo chef-client

...TRUNCATED OUTPUT...
[2015-01-08T21:43:39+01:00] INFO: http_request[callback] GET to
http://www.chef.io successful

   - http_request[callback] GET to http://www.chef.io
...TRUNCATED OUTPUT...
```

## How it works...

You can use `only_if` and `not_if` with every resource. In our example, we passed it a Ruby block. The Ruby block simply queried a node attribute. Because we set the `enabled` attribute to `true`, the Ruby block evaluates it to be `true`. And because we used `only_if`, the resource is executed.

You can use the full power of Ruby to find out whether or not the resource should run. Instead of using the curly braces, you can use `do ... end` to surround a multiline Ruby block.

## There's more...

Instead of passing a Ruby block, you can pass a shell command as well, as shown in the following code:

```
http_request 'callback' do
  url node['my_cookbook']['callback']['url']
  only_if "test -f /etc/passwd"
end
```

In this example, Chef will execute the `test` command in a shell. If the shell command returns the exit code `0`, the resource will run.

## See also

▸   The *Using attributes* recipe in *Chapter 3, Chef Language and Style*

▸   Learn more about conditional execution at: `https://docs.chef.io/resource_common.html#guards`

# 5
# Working with Files and Packages

*"The file is a gzipped tar file. Your browser is playing tricks with you and trying to be smart."*

*Rasmus Lerdorf*

In this chapter, we will cover the following recipes:

- ▶  Creating configuration files using templates
- ▶  Using pure Ruby in templates for conditionals and iterations
- ▶  Installing packages from a third-party repository
- ▶  Installing software from source
- ▶  Running a command when a file is updated
- ▶  Distributing directory trees
- ▶  Cleaning up old files
- ▶  Distributing different files based on the target platform

## Introduction

Moving files around and installing software are the most common tasks undertaken when setting up your nodes. In this chapter, we'll take a look at the various ways in which Chef supports you in dealing with files and software packages.

# Creating configuration files using templates

The term **Configuration Management** already says it loud and clear: your recipes manage the configuration of your nodes. In most cases, the system configuration is held in local files, on disk. Chef uses templates to dynamically create configuration files from given values. It takes such values from data bags or attributes, or even calculates them on the fly before passing them into a template.

Let's see how we can create configuration files by using templates.

## Getting ready

Make sure that you have a cookbook named `my_cookbook` and that the `run_list` of your node includes `my_cookbook`, as described in the *Creating and using cookbooks* recipe in *Chapter 1, Chef Infrastructure*.

## How to do it...

Let's use a template resource to create a configuration file:

1. Edit your cookbook's default recipe:

   **mma@laptop:~/chef-repo $ subl cookbooks/my_cookbook/recipes/default.rb**

   ```
   template "/etc/logrotate.conf" do
     source "logrotate.conf.erb"
     variables(
       how_often: "daily",
       keep: "31"
     )
   end
   ```

2. Add an ERB template file to your recipe in its `default` folder:

   **mma@laptop:~/chef-repo $ mkdir -p cookbooks/my_cookbook/templates/default**

   **mma@laptop:~/chef-repo $ subl cookbooks/my_cookbook/templates/default/logrotate.conf.erb**

   ```
   <%= @how_often %>
   rotate <%= @keep %>
   create
   ```

3.  Upload the modified cookbook to the Chef server:

    **mma@laptop:~/chef-repo $ knife cookbook upload my_cookbook**

    Uploading my_cookbook     [0.1.0]

4.  Run the Chef client on your node:

    **user@server:~$ sudo chef-client**

    ```
    ...TRUNCATED OUTPUT...
    [2015-01-09T10:33:23+01:00] INFO: template[/etc/logrotate.conf]
    updated file contents /etc/logrotate.conf
        - update content in file /etc/logrotate.conf from b44f70 to
    c5c92d
        --- /etc/logrotate.conf     2015-01-08 22:20:17.000000000
    +0100
        +++ /var/folders/fz/dcb5y3qs4m5g1hk8zrxd948m0000g
    n/T/chef-rendered-template20150109-63309-1y6vmk     2015-01-09
    10:33:23.000000000 +0100
        @@ -1,2 +1,4 @@
        -dailyrotate 31create
        +daily
        +rotate 31
        +create
    ...TRUNCATED OUTPUT...
    ```

5.  Validate the content of the generated file:

    **user@server:~$ cat /etc/logrotate.conf**

    ```
    daily
    rotate 31
    create
    ```

## How it works...

If you want to manage any configuration file by using Chef, you have to follow the given steps:

1.  Copy the desired configuration file from your node to your cookbook's `default` directory under the `templates` folder.

2.  Add the extension `.erb` to this copy.

3.  Replace any configuration value that you want to manage with your cookbook with an ERB statement printing out a variable. Chef will create variables for every parameter that you define in the `variables` call in your template resource. You can use it in your template, like this:

    ```
    <%= @variable_name -%>
    ```

4. Create a template resource in your recipe by using the newly created template as the `source`, and pass all the variables you introduced in your ERB file to it.

5. Running your recipe on the node will back up the original configuration file to the `backup_path` that you configured in your `client.rb` file (default is `/var/chef/backup`) and replace it with the dynamically generated version.

 Whenever possible, try using attributes instead of hardcoding values in your recipes.

## There's more...

Be careful when a package update makes changes to the default configuration files. You need to be aware of those changes and merge them manually into your handcrafted configuration file template; otherwise, you'll lose all the configuration settings you changed using Chef.

 To avoid accidental changes, it's usually a good idea to add a comment at the top of your configuration file to say that it is managed by Chef.

## See also

▸ Read everything about templates at `https://docs.chef.io/templates.html`

▸ Learn more about templates in the *Using templates* recipe in *Chapter 3, Chef Language and Style*

# Using pure Ruby in templates for conditionals and iterations

Switching options on and off in a configuration file is a pretty common thing. Since Chef uses ERB as its template language, you can use pure Ruby to control the flow in your templates. You can use conditionals or even loops in your templates.

## Getting ready

Make sure that you have a cookbook called `my_cookbook` and that the `run_list` of your node includes `my_cookbook`, as described in the *Creating and using cookbooks* recipe in *Chapter 1, Chef Infrastructure*.

## How to do it...

Let's create a hypothetical configuration file listing the IP addresses of a given set of backend servers. We only want to print that list and set a flag called `enabled` to `true`:

1. Edit your cookbook's default recipe:

   **mma@laptop:~/chef-repo $ subl cookbooks/my_cookbook/recipes/
   default.rb**

   ```
   template "/tmp/backends.conf" do
     mode "0444"
     owner "root"
     group "root"
     variables({
       :enabled => true,
       :backends => ["10.0.0.10", "10.0.0.11", "10.0.0.12"]
     })
   end
   ```

2. Create your template:

   **mma@laptop:~/chef-repo $ subl cookbooks/my_cookbook/templates/
   default/backends.conf.erb**

   ```
   <%- if @enabled %>
     <%- @backends.each do |backend| %>
       <%= backend %>
     <%- end %>
   <%- else %>
     No backends defined!
   <%- end %>
   ```

3. Upload the modified cookbook to the Chef server:

   **mma@laptop:~/chef-repo $ knife cookbook upload my_cookbook**

   ```
   Uploading my_cookbook    [0.1.0]
   ```

4. Run the Chef client on your node:

   **user@server:~$ sudo chef-client**

   ```
   ...TRUNCATED OUTPUT...
   [2015-01-09T10:37:45+01:00] INFO: template[/tmp/backends.conf]
   created file /tmp/backends.conf
       - create new file /tmp/backends.conf[2015-01-
   09T10:37:45+01:00] WARN: Could not set gid = 0 on /var/folders/fz/
   dcb5y3qs4m5g1hk8zrxd948m0000gn/T/chef-rendered-template20150109-
   63512-1y8uas4, file modes not preserved
   ```

```
[2015-01-09T10:37:45+01:00] INFO: template[/tmp/backends.conf]
updated file contents /tmp/backends.conf
    - update content in file /tmp/backends.conf from none to
68b086
    --- /tmp/backends.conf 2015-01-09 10:37:45.000000000 +0100
    +++ /var/folders/fz/dcb5y3qs4m5g1hk8zrxd948m0000gn
/T/chef-rendered-template20150109-63512-1y8uas4        2015-01-09
10:37:45.000000000 +0100
    @@ -1 +1,4 @@
    +    10.0.0.10
    +    10.0.0.11
    +    10.0.0.12
...TRUNCATED OUTPUT...
```

5.  Validate the content of the generated file:

    **user@server:~$ cat /tmp/backends.conf**

    ```
    10.0.0.10
    10.0.0.11
    10.0.0.12
    ```

## How it works...

You can use plain Ruby in your templates. We will mix two concepts in our example. First, we use an `if-else` block to decide whether we should print a list of IP addresses or just a message. If we are going to print the list of IP addresses, we will use a loop to go through all of them.

Let's have a look at the conditional:

```
<%- if @enabled %>
...
<%- else %>
  No backends defined!
<%- end %>
```

We either pass `true` or `false` as the value of the variable called `enabled`. You can access the given variables directly in your template. If we pass `true`, the first block of Ruby code will be executed while rendering the template. If we pass `false`, Chef will render the string `"No backends defined!"` as the content of the file.

 You can use `<%- %>` if you want to embed Ruby logic into your template file.

Now, let's see how we loop through the list of IPs:

```
<%- @backends.each do |backend| %>
  <%= backend %>
<%- end %>
```

We pass an array of strings as the value of the `backend` variable. In the template, we use the `each` iterator to loop through the array. While looping, Ruby assigns each value to the variable that we define as the looping variable between the | characters. Inside the loop, we simply print the value of each array element.

While it is possible to use the full power of Ruby inside your templates, it is a good idea to keep them as simple as possible. It is better to put more involved logic into your recipes and pass pre-calculated values to the template. You should limit yourself to simple conditionals and loops to keep templates simple.

## There's more...

You can use conditionals to print strings, as shown in the following code:

```
<%= "Hello world!" if @enabled -%>
```

If you use this in your template, the string `Hello world!` will be printed only if the variable `enabled` is set to `true`.

## See also

▶ Read more about templates in the *Using templates* recipe in *Chapter 3*, *Chef Language and Style*

▶ Find more explanations and examples of templates at `https://docs.chef.io/templates.html`

# Installing packages from a third-party repository

Even though the Ubuntu package repository contains many up-to-date packages, you might bump into situations in which either the package you need is missing or outdated. In such cases, you can either use third-party repositories or your own repositories (containing self-made packages). Chef makes it simple to use additional **APT** repositories with the `apt` cookbook.

## Getting ready

Make sure that you have a cookbook called `my_cookbook` and that the `run_list` of your node includes `my_cookbook`, as described in the *Creating and using cookbooks* recipe in *Chapter 1, Chef Infrastructure*.

Let's retrieve the required `apt` cookbook:

1. Add it to `Berksfile`:

   **mma@laptop:~/chef-repo $ subl Berksfile**

   ```
   source 'https://supermarket.getchef.com'

   cookbook 'apt'
   ```

2. Install it to your local workstation:

   **mma@laptop:~/chef-repo $ berks install**

   ```
   Resolving cookbook dependencies...
   Fetching cookbook index from https://supermarket.getchef.com...
   Installing apt (2.6.1)
   ```

3. Upload it to your Chef server:

   **mma@laptop:~/chef-repo $ berks upload**

   ```
   Uploaded apt (2.6.1) to: 'https://api.opscode.com:443/
   organizations/awo'
   ```

 Remember that if you're using Vagrant and have installed the Berkshelf plugin, all you need to run is `vagrant provision` to get the `apt` cookbook installed on your node.

## How to do it...

Let's take a look at how you can install the `s3cmd` tool from the repository available at `www.s3tools.org` on a Ubuntu Lucid 12.04 LTS node:

 Ubuntu Utopic 14.04 LTS already comes with `s3cmd` version 1.5.0-rc1-2 installed, and therefore, the following recipe isn't necessary to get the latest version of `s3cmd` installed.

1. Edit your cookbook's default recipe:

   **mma@laptop:~/chef-repo $ subl cookbooks/my_cookbook/recipes/default.rb**

```
include_recipe "apt"
apt_repository "s3tools" do
  uri "http://s3tools.org/repo/deb-all"
  components ["stable/"]
  key "http://s3tools.org/repo/deb-all/stable/s3tools.key"
  action :add
end
package "s3cmd"
```

2. Edit your cookbook's metadata to add a dependency on the `apt` cookbook:

   **mma@laptop:~/chef-repo $ subl cookbooks/my_cookbook/metadata.rb**

   ```
   ...
   depends "apt"
   ```

3. Upload the modified `my_cookbook` to the Chef server:

   **mma@laptop:~/chef-repo $ knife cookbook upload my_cookbook**

   ```
   Uploading my_cookbook    [0.1.0]
   ```

4. Validate that the `s3cmd` package is not yet installed:

   **user@server:~$ dpkg -l s3cmd**

   ```
   No packages found matching s3cmd.
   ```

5. Validate that the default repository will install an older version of `s3cmd` (`1.0.0-1`):

   **user@server:~$ apt-cache showpkg s3cmd**

   ```
   Package: s3cmd
   Versions:
   1.0.0-1 (/var/lib/apt/lists/us.archive.ubuntu.com_ubuntu_dists_
   precise_universe_binary-amd64_Packages)
   ```

6. Run the Chef client on your node:

   **user@server:~$ sudo chef-client**

   ```
   ...TRUNCATED OUTPUT...
   [2015-01-12T19:59:04+00:00] INFO: execute[apt-get update] ran
   successfully

       - execute apt-get update -o Dir::Etc::sourcelist='sources.
   list.d/s3tools.list' -o Dir::Etc::sourceparts='-' -o
   APT::Get::List-Cleanup='0'
   [2015-01-12T19:59:04+00:00] INFO: execute[apt-get update] sending
   run action to execute[apt-cache gencaches] (immediate)
       * execute[apt-cache gencaches] action runReading package
   lists...
   ```

```
[2015-01-12T19:59:07+00:00] INFO: execute[apt-cache gencaches] ran
successfully

    - execute apt-cache gencaches

  * apt_package[s3cmd] action install
    - install version 1.0.0-4 of package s3cmd
...TRUNCATED OUTPUT...
```

7.  Ensure that the `s3tools` repository will install a newer version (`1.0.0-4` instead of `1.0.0-1`):

    **user@server:~$ apt-cache showpkg s3cmd**

    ```
    Package: s3cmd
    Versions:
    1.0.0-4 (/var/lib/apt/lists/s3tools.org_repo_deb-all_stable_
    Packages) (/var/lib/dpkg/status)
    ```

8.  Ensure that the `s3cmd` package is installed:

    **user@server:~$ dpkg -l**

    ```
    ...TRUNCATED OUTPUT...
    ii  s3cmd                                    1.0.0-4  The ultimate
    Amazon S3 and CloudFront command line client
    ```

## How it works...

The `apt` cookbook provides an easy way to deal with additional APT repositories.

 If you don't use Berkshelf, as described in the *Managing cookbook dependencies with Berkshelf* recipe in *Chapter 1, Chef Infrastructure*, you need to use `knife cookbook site install` to download the `apt` cookbook to your workstation and `knife cookbook upload apt` to install it on your Chef server.

We need to tell Chef that we want to use the `apt` cookbook by adding the `depends` call to our cookbook's `metadata.rb` file.

The `apt` cookbook defines the `apt_repository` resource. To be able to use it, we need to include the `apt` recipe in our default recipe:

```
include_recipe "apt"
```

As soon as the `apt` cookbook is available, we can add the third-party repository by using the `apt_repository` resource:

```
apt_repository "s3tools" do
  uri "http://s3tools.org/repo/deb-all"
  components ["stable/"]
  key "http://s3tools.org/repo/deb-all/stable/s3tools.key"
  action :add
end
```

After adding the third-party repository, we can install the desired package from there:

```
package "s3cmd"
```

## See also

▶ Learn more about the `s3cmd` package at `http://s3tools.org/debian-ubun3tu-repository-for-s3cmd`

# Installing software from source

If you need to install a piece of software that is not available as a package for your platform, you will need to compile it yourself.

In Chef, you can easily do this by using the `script` resource. What is more challenging is to make such a `script` resource idempotent.

In the following recipe, we will see how to do both.

## Getting ready

Make sure that you have a cookbook called `my_cookbook` and that the `run_list` of your node includes `my_cookbook`, as described in the *Creating and using cookbooks* recipe in *Chapter 1, Chef Infrastructure*.

Retrieve the required cookbooks:

1. Add them to your `Berksfile`:

   **mma@laptop:~/chef-repo $ subl Berksfile**

   ```
   source 'https://supermarket.getchef.com'
   cookbook 'apt'
   cookbook 'build-essential'
   ```

2. Install it on your local workstation:

**`mma@laptop:~/chef-repo $ berks install`**

```
Resolving cookbook dependencies...
Fetching cookbook index from https://supermarket.getchef.com...
Installing build-essential (2.1.3)
Installing apt (2.6.1)
```

3. Upload it to your Chef server:

**`mma@laptop:~/chef-repo $ berks upload`**

```
Uploaded apt (2.6.1) to: 'https://api.opscode.com:443/
organizations/awo'
Uploaded build-essential (2.1.3) to: 'https://api.opscode.com:443/
organizations/awo'
```

> Remember that if you're using Vagrant and have installed the Berkshelf plugin, all you need to run is the Vagrant provision to get the required cookbooks installed on your node.

## How to do it...

Let's take `nginx` as a well-known example for installing it from source:

1. Edit your cookbook's default recipe:

**`mma@laptop:~/chef-repo $ subl cookbooks/my_cookbook/recipes/default.rb`**

```
include_recipe "apt"
include_recipe "build-essential"
version = "1.7.9"
bash "install_nginx_from_source" do
  cwd Chef::Config['file_cache_path']
  code <<-EOH
    wget http://nginx.org/download/nginx-#{version}.tar.gz
    tar zxf nginx-#{version}.tar.gz &&
    cd nginx-#{version} &&
    ./configure --without-http_rewrite_module && make && make
install
  EOH
  not_if "test -f /usr/local/nginx/sbin/nginx"
end
```

2. Edit your cookbook's metadata to add a dependency on the `apt` cookbook:

   **mma@laptop:~/chef-repo $ subl cookbooks/my_cookbook/metadata.rb**

   ```
   ...
   depends "apt"
   depends "build-essential"
   ```

3. Upload the modified cookbook to the Chef server:

   **mma@laptop:~/chef-repo $ knife cookbook upload my_cookbook**

   ```
   Uploading my_cookbook    [0.1.0]
   ```

4. Run the Chef client on your node:

   **user@server:~$ sudo chef-client**

   ```
   ...TRUNCATED OUTPUT...
   make[1]: Leaving directory '/var/chef/cache/nginx-1.7.9'
   [2015-01-12T20:45:20+00:00] INFO: bash[install_nginx_from_source]
   ran successfully

       - execute "bash"  "/tmp/chef-script20150112-13681-1m0wt4u"
   ...TRUNCATED OUTPUT...
   ```

5. Validate that `nginx` is installed:

   **user@server:~$ /usr/local/nginx/sbin/nginx -v**

   ```
   nginx version: nginx/1.7.9
   ```

 The `nginx` community cookbook has a recipe to install `nginx` from source. The following example only illustrates how you can install any software from source.

## How it works...

The `bash` resource executes only if the `nginx` executable is not yet there. Our `not_if` block tests for this.

To be able to compile code on your node, you'll need to have the build essentials installed. That's why you need to include the `build-essential` cookbook before you run your script to make sure you have a compiler installed.

Before Chef runs the script given as `code`, it changes into the working directory that is given as `cwd`. We use Chef's file cache directory instead of `/tmp` because the contents of `/tmp` might get deleted during reboot. In order to avoid downloading the source tarball again, we need to keep it at a permanent location.

> Usually, you would retrieve the value for the version variable from an attribute defined in `my_cookbook/attributes/default.rb`.

The script itself simply unpacks the tarball, configures, prepares, and installs `nginx`. We chain the commands using `&&` to avoid running the following commands if an earlier one fails.

> ```
> <<-EOH
> ...
> EOH
> ```
> The preceding code is a Ruby construct that denotes multiline strings.

## There's more...

Right now, this recipe will download the source tarball repeatedly, even if it is already there (at least as long as the `nginx` binary is not found). You can use the `remote_file` resource instead of calling `wget` in your `bash` script. The `remote_file` resource is idempotent—it will only download the file if it needs to.

Change your default recipe in the following way to use the `remote_file` resource:

```
include_recipe 'apt'
include_recipe 'build-essential'

version = "1.7.9"

remote_file "fetch_nginx_source" do
  source "http://nginx.org/download/nginx-#{version}.tar.gz"
  path "#{Chef::Config['file_cache_path']}/nginx-#{version}.tar.gz"
end

bash "install_nginx_from_source" do
  cwd Chef::Config['file_cache_path']
  code <<-EOH
    tar zxf nginx-#{version}.tar.gz &&
    cd nginx-#{version} &&
    ./configure --without-http_rewrite_module &&
    make && make install
  EOH
  not_if "test -f /usr/local/nginx/sbin/nginx"
end
```

## See also

▶ Find the full `nginx` source recipe of GitHub at `https://github.com/opscode-cookbooks/nginx/blob/master/recipes/source.rb`

▶ Read more about this at `http://stackoverflow.com/questions/8530593/chef-install-and-update-programs-from-source`

# Running a command when a file is updated

If your node is not under complete Chef control, it might be necessary to trigger commands when Chef changes a file. For example, you might want to restart a service that is not managed by Chef when its configuration file (which *is* managed by Chef) changes. Let's see how you can achieve this with Chef.

## Getting ready

Make sure that you have a cookbook called `my_cookbook` and that the `run_list` of your node includes `my_cookbook`, as described in the *Creating and using cookbooks* recipe in *Chapter 1, Chef Infrastructure*.

## How to do it...

Let's create an empty file as a trigger and run a `bash` command, if that file changes:

1. Edit your cookbook's default recipe:

   **mma@laptop:~/chef-repo $ subl cookbooks/my_cookbook/recipes/default.rb**

   ```
   template "/tmp/trigger" do
     notifies :run, "bash[run_on_trigger]", :immediately
   end

   bash "run_on_trigger" do
     user "root"
     cwd "/tmp"
     code "echo 'Triggered'"
     action :nothing
   end
   ```

2. Create an empty template:

   **mma@laptop:~/chef-repo $ touch cookbooks/my_cookbook/templates/default/trigger.erb**

3. Upload the modified cookbook to the Chef server:

   `mma@laptop:~/chef-repo $ knife cookbook upload my_cookbook`

   ```
   Uploading my_cookbook    [0.1.0]
   ```

4. Run the Chef client on your node:

   `user@server:~$ sudo chef-client`

   ```
   ...TRUNCATED OUTPUT...
     * template[/tmp/trigger] action create[2015-01-
   12T20:52:19+00:00] INFO: template[/tmp/trigger] created file /tmp/
   trigger

       - create new file /tmp/trigger[2015-01-12T20:52:19+00:00]
   INFO: template[/tmp/trigger] updated file contents /tmp/trigger

       - update content in file /tmp/trigger from none to e3b0c4
       (no diff)
   [2015-01-12T20:52:19+00:00] INFO: template[/tmp/trigger] sending
   run action to bash[run_on_trigger] (immediate)
     * bash[run_on_trigger] action runTriggered
   [2015-01-12T20:52:19+00:00] INFO: bash[run_on_trigger] ran
   successfully

       - execute "bash"  "/tmp/chef-script20150112-16221-1q4r38y"
   ...TRUNCATED OUTPUT...
   ```

5. Run the Chef client again to verify that the `run_on_trigger` script does not get executed again:

   `user@server:~$ sudo chef-client`

   ```
   ...TRUNCATED OUTPUT...
   Recipe: my_cookbook::default
     * template[/tmp/trigger] action create (up to date)
   ...TRUNCATED OUTPUT...
   ```

## How it works...

We define a `template` resource and tell it to notify our `bash` resource immediately. Chef will notify the `bash` resource only if the `template` resource changes the file. To make sure that the `bash` script runs only when notified, we define its action as `nothing`.

We see in the output of the first Chef client run (which created the trigger file) that the bash script was executed:

```
bash[run_on_trigger] ran successfully
```

We see in the output of the second Chef client run that this message is missing. Chef did not execute the script because it did not modify the trigger file.

## There's more...

Instead of a template, you can let a file or remote_file resource trigger a bash script. When compiling programs from source, you will download the source tarball using a remote_file resource. This resource will trigger a bash resource to extract and compile the program.

## See also

▸   The *Installing software from source* recipe in this chapter

# Distributing directory trees

You need to seed a directory tree on your nodes. It might be a static website or some backup data, which is needed on your nodes. You want Chef to make sure that all the files and directories are there on your nodes. Chef offers the remote_directory resource to handle this case. Let's see how you can use it.

## Getting ready

Make sure you have a cookbook called my_cookbook, and that the run_list of your node includes my_cookbook, as described in the *Creating and using cookbooks* recipe in *Chapter 1, Chef Infrastructure*.

## How to do it...

Let's upload a directory with some files to our node:

1.   Edit your cookbook's default recipe:

```
mma@laptop:~/chef-repo $ subl cookbooks/my_cookbook/recipes/
default.rb
```

```
remote_directory "/tmp/chef.github.com" do
  files_backup 10
  files_owner "root"
```

```
      files_group "root"
      files_mode 00644
      owner "root"
      group "root"
      mode 00755
   end
```

2. Create a directory structure on your workstation with files that you want to upload to your node. In this example, I am using a plain GitHub pages directory, which contains a static website. To follow along, you can use whatever directory structure you want—just be careful that it doesn't get too big so that it doesn't take hours to upload. Just move the directory to the `files/default` directory inside your cookbook:

   **mma@laptop:~/chef-repo $ mv chef.github.com cookbooks/my_cookbook/files/default**

 Chef will not upload empty directories.

3. Upload the modified cookbook on the Chef server:

   **mma@laptop:~/chef-repo $ knife cookbook upload my_cookbook**

   ```
   Uploading my_cookbook    [0.1.0]
   ```

4. Run the Chef client on your node:

   **user@server:~$ sudo chef-client**

   ```
   ...TRUNCATED OUTPUT...
   [2015-01-15T08:48:25+01:00] INFO: remote_directory[/tmp/chef.
   github.com] created directory /tmp/chef.github.com

       - create new directory /tmp/chef.github.com
     Recipe: <Dynamically Defined Resource>
       * directory[/tmp/chef.github.com/images] action create
   [2015-01-15T08:48:25+01:00] INFO: Processing directory[/tmp/chef.
   github.com/images] action create (dynamically defined)
   [2015-01-15T08:48:25+01:00] INFO: directory[/tmp/chef.github.com/
   images] created directory /tmp/chef.github.com/images

         - create new directory /tmp/chef.github.com/images
   [2015-01-15T08:48:25+01:00] INFO: directory[/tmp/chef.github.com/
   images] owner changed to 0
   [2015-01-15T08:48:25+01:00] INFO: directory[/tmp/chef.github.com/
   images] group changed to 0
   ```

```
[2015-01-15T08:48:25+01:00] INFO: directory[/tmp/chef.github.com/
images] mode changed to 644

    - change mode from '' to '0644'
    - change owner from '' to 'root'
    - change group from '' to 'root'
...TRUNCATED OUTPUT...
```

5.  Validate that the directory and its files are there on the node:

    **user@server:~$ ls -l /tmp/chef.github.com**

    ```
    total 16
    4 drwxr-xr-x 2 root root 4096 Mar 22 08:36 images
    4 -rw-r--r-- 1 root root 3383 Mar 22 08:36 index.html
    4 drwxr-xr-x 2 root root 4096 Mar 22 08:36 javascripts
    4 drwxr-xr-x 2 root root 4096 Mar 22 08:36 stylesheets
    ```

## How it works...

You need to put the directory that you want to distribute to your nodes into your cookbook under the `default` folder of `files`. The `remote_directory` resource picks it up from there and uploads it to your nodes. By default, the name of the resource (in our example, `/tmp/chef.github.com`) will act as the target directory.

 Be careful not to put very heavy directory structures into your cookbooks. You will not only need to distribute them to every node but also to your Chef server.

## There's more...

While you could use the `remote_directory` resource to deploy your applications, there are better ways to do the same. Either you could use any of Chef's application cookbooks that are available, for example, for Ruby (`application_ruby`) or PHP (`application_php`) applications, or you could use tools such as Capistrano or Mina for deployment.

## See also

▶   The *Distributing different files based on the target platform* recipe in this chapter

▶   Find out more about GitHub Pages at `http://pages.github.com/`

▶   The documentation for the `remote_directory` resource can be found at `https://docs.chef.io/chef/resources.html#remote-directory`

- ▶ Find the `application_ruby` cookbook at `https://supermarket.chef.io/cookbooks/application_ruby`
- ▶ Find the `application_php` cookbook at `https://supermarket.chef.io/cookbooks/application_php`
- ▶ Find more about Capistrano at `http://www.capistranorb.com/`
- ▶ Find more about Mina at `http://nadarei.co/mina/`

# Cleaning up old files

What happens if you want to remove a software package from your node? You should be aware that Chef does not undo its changes. Removing a resource from your cookbook does not mean that Chef will remove the resource from your nodes. You need to do this by yourself.

 In today's infrastructure, it's far better to replace a node than try to clean things up with Chef.

## Getting ready

Make sure that you have a cookbook called `my_cookbook` and that the `run_list` of your node includes `my_cookbook`, as described in the *Creating and using cookbooks* recipe in *Chapter 1, Chef Infrastructure*.

Make sure that you have a `remote_directory` resource in `my_cookbook`, as described in the *Distributing directory trees* recipe.

## How to do it...

Let's remove the `remote_directory` resource from `my_cookbook` and see what happens:

1. Edit your cookbook's default recipe and remove the `remote_directory` resource:

   **mma@laptop:~/chef-repo $ subl cookbooks/my_cookbook/recipes/default.rb**

   ```
   # there used to be the remote_directory resource
   ```

2. Upload the modified cookbook to the Chef server:

   **mma@laptop:~/chef-repo $ knife cookbook upload my_cookbook**

   ```
   Uploading my_cookbook     [0.1.0]
   ```

3. Run the Chef client on your node:

   **user@server:~$ sudo chef-client**

   ...TRUNCATED OUTPUT...

   ...TRUNCATED OUTPUT...

4. Validate that the directory and its files are still there on the node:

   **user@server:~$ ls -l /tmp/chef.github.com**

   ```
   total 16
   4 drwxr-xr-x 2 root root 4096 Mar 22 08:36 images
   4 -rw-r--r-- 1 root root 3383 Mar 22 08:36 index.html
   4 drwxr-xr-x 2 root root 4096 Mar 22 08:36 javascripts
   4 drwxr-xr-x 2 root root 4096 Mar 22 08:36 stylesheets
   ```

Now, let's explicitly remove the directory structure:

1. Edit your cookbook's default recipe:

   **mma@laptop:~/chef-repo $ subl cookbooks/my_cookbook/recipes/ default.rb**

   ```
   directory "/tmp/chef.github.com" do
     action :delete
     recursive true
   end
   ```

2. Upload the modified cookbook to the Chef server:

   **mma@laptop:~/chef-repo $ knife cookbook upload my_cookbook**

   ```
   Uploading my_cookbook     [0.1.0]
   ```

3. Run the Chef client on your node:

   **user@server:~$ sudo chef-client**

   ```
   ...TRUNCATED OUTPUT...
   [2015-01-15T08:58:24+01:00] INFO: remote_directory[/tmp/chef.
   github.com] deleted /tmp/chef.github.com recursively

        - delete existing directory /tmp/chef.github.com
   ...TRUNCATED OUTPUT...
   ```

4. Validate that the directory and its files are deleted from the node:

   **user@server:~$ ls -l /tmp/chef.github.com**

   ```
   ls: cannot access /tmp/chef.github.com: No such file or directory
   ```

## How it works...

Removing a resource from your cookbook will lead to Chef not knowing anything about it anymore. Chef does not touch things that are not defined in cookbooks, even if it might have created them once.

To clean up stuff you created using Chef, you need to put the reverse actions into your cookbooks. If you created a directory using Chef, you need to explicitly delete it by using the `directory` resource with `action :delete` in your cookbook.

The directory resource is idempotent. Even if the directory is already deleted, it will run fine and simply do nothing.

## There's more...

If you upload a directory structure by using the `remote_directory` resource, you can use the `purge` parameter to delete files within that directory structure if they are no longer in your cookbook. In this case, you do not need to delete each file by using a file resource with the delete action:

```
remote_directory "/tmp/chef.github.com" do
  ...
  purge true
end
```

## See also

- ▸  The *Distributing directory trees* recipe in this chapter
- ▸  Learn more about the `directory` resource at `https://docs.chef.io/resource_directory.html`
- ▸  Learn more about the `remote_directory` resource at `https://docs.chef.io/chef/resources.html#remote-directory`

# Distributing different files based on the target platform

If you have nodes with different operating systems, such as Ubuntu and CentOS, you might want to deliver different files to each of them. There might be differences in the necessary configuration options and the like. Chef offers a way for files and templates to differentiate which version to use, based on a node's platform.

## Getting ready

Make sure that you have a cookbook called `my_cookbook` and that the `run_list` of your node includes `my_cookbook`, as described in the *Creating and using cookbooks* recipe in *Chapter 1, Chef Infrastructure*.

## How to do it...

Let's add two templates to our cookbook and see which one gets used:

1. Edit your cookbook's default recipe:

   **mma@laptop:~/chef-repo $ subl cookbooks/my_cookbook/recipes/default.rb**

   ```
   template "/tmp/message" do
     source "message.erb"
   end
   ```

2. Create a template as a default:

   **mma@laptop:~/chef-repo $ subl cookbooks/my_cookbook/templates/default/message.erb**

   ```
   Hello from default template!
   ```

3. Create a template only for Ubuntu 14.04 nodes:

   **mma@laptop:~/chef-repo $ subl cookbooks/my_cookbook/templates/ubuntu-14.04/message.erb**

   ```
   Hello from Ubuntu 14.04!
   ```

4. Upload the modified cookbook to the Chef server:

   **mma@laptop:~/chef-repo $ knife cookbook upload my_cookbook**

   ```
   Uploading my_cookbook    [0.1.0]
   ```

5. Run the Chef client on your node:

   **user@server:~$ sudo chef-client**

   ```
   ...TRUNCATED OUTPUT...
   [2015-01-16T18:19:16+01:00] INFO: template[/tmp/message] created
   file /tmp/message

      - create new file /tmp/message
   [2015-01-16T18:19:16+01:00] WARN: Could not set gid = 0 on /
   var/folders/fz/dcb5y3qs4m5g1hk8zrxd948m0000gn/T/chef-rendered-
   template20150115-74876-coftw0, file modes not preserved
   ```

```
[2015-01-16T18:19:16+01:00] INFO: template[/tmp/message] updated
file contents /tmp/message

    - update content in file /tmp/message from none to 01666e
...TRUNCATED OUTPUT...
```

6. Validate that the Ubuntu specific template has been used:

**user@server:~$ sudo cat /tmp/message**

```
Hello from Ubuntu 14.04!
```

## How it works...

Chef tries to use the most specific template for a given platform by looking for templates in the following order, if the given platform is Ubuntu 14.04:

```
my_cookbook/templates/my_node.example.com/message.erb
my_cookbook/templates/ubuntu-14.04/message.erb
my_cookbook/templates/ubuntu-14/message.erb
my_cookbook/templates/ubuntu/message.erb
my_cookbook/templates/default/message.erb
```

Chef takes the first hit. If there is a file in a directory with the same name as the **fully qualified domain name** (**FQDN**) of the node, it will take that one.

If not, it will look through the other directories (if they exist), such as `ubuntu-14.04` or `ubuntu-14`, and so on.

The only directory, which is mandatory, is the `default` directory.

## See also

  ▶ Learn more about this in the *Using templates* recipe in *Chapter 4, Writing Better Cookbooks*

  ▶ Find more details about file specificity at `https://docs.chef.io/resource_template.html#file-specificity`

# 6
# Users and Applications

*"The system should treat all user input as sacred."*

*Jef Raskin*

In this chapter, we will cover the following recipes:

- ▸ Creating users from data bags
- ▸ Securing the Secure Shell Daemon (SSHD)
- ▸ Enabling passwordless sudo
- ▸ Managing NTP
- ▸ Managing nginx
- ▸ Creating nginx virtual hosts
- ▸ Creating MySQL databases and users
- ▸ Managing WordPress sites
- ▸ Managing Ruby on Rails applications
- ▸ Managing Varnish
- ▸ Managing your local workstation

## Introduction

In this chapter, we'll see how to manage the user accounts on your nodes with Chef. This is one of the fundamental things you can start your infrastructure automation efforts with.

After dealing with users, we'll take a look at how to install and manage more advanced applications. Our examples mainly cover a web application stack using nginx as a web server, MySQL as a database, and WordPress or Ruby on Rails for the web application.

We'll close the chapter with showing you how to manage your local workstation with Chef.

# Creating users from data bags

When managing a set of servers, it's important to make sure that the right people (and only they) have access. You definitely don't want a shared account whose password is known by everyone. You don't want to hardcode any users into your recipes either, because you want to separate logic and data.

Chef helps you to manage users on your nodes using data bags for your users and let a recipe create and remove the users, accordingly.

Let's take a look at how you can do that.

## Getting ready

Make sure the you have a cookbook named my_cookbook and that the run_list of your node includes my_cookbook, as described in the *Creating and using cookbooks* section in *Chapter 1, Chef Infrastructure*.

Create Berksfile in your Chef repository which includes my_cookbook:

**mma@laptop:~/chef-repo $ subl Berksfile**

```
source 'https://supermarket.chef.io'

cookbook 'my_cookbook', path: './cookbooks/my_cookbook'
```

Make sure that you have a public SSH key available for your user by following the instructions at http://git-scm.com/book/en/v2/Git-on-the-Server-Generating-Your-SSH-Public-Key

## How to do it...

First, we need to set up the data bag and at least one data bag item for our first user:

1. Create a data bag for your users:

    **mma@laptop:~/chef-repo $ knife data bag create users**

    ```
    Created data_bag[users]
    ```

2. Create a directory for your data bag item's JSON files:

```
mma@laptop:~/chef-repo $ mkdir -p data_bags/users
```

3. Create a data bag item for your first user. Keep the username as the filename (here, mma). You need to replace `ssh-rsa AAA345...bla==` `mma@laptop` with the contents of your public key file:

```
mma@laptop:~/chef-repo $ subl data_bags/users/mma.json
```

```
{
  "id": "mma",
  "ssh_keys": [
    "ssh-rsa AAA345...bla== mma@laptop"
  ],
  "groups": [ "staff"],
  "shell": "\/bin\/bash"
}
```

4. Upload the data bag item to the Chef server:

```
mma@laptop:~/chef-repo $ knife data bag from file users mma.json
```

```
Updated data_bag_item[users::mma]
```

 Because the Chef server indexes data bags, it can take a few minutes until a new data bag is available for use. If you encounter an error, please wait a few minutes and then try again.

Now it's time to set up the recipe to manage our users:

1. Edit your cookbook's `metadata.rb` to include the dependency on the `users` cookbook:

```
mma@laptop:~/chef-repo $ subl cookbooks/my_cookbook/metadata.rb
```

```
depends "users"
```

2. Install your cookbook's dependencies:

```
mma@laptop:~/chef-repo $ berks install
```

```
...TRUNCATED OUTPUT...
Installing users (1.7.0)
Using my_cookbook (0.1.0) from source at cookbooks/my_cookbook
```

3. Edit your cookbook's default recipe:

```
mma@laptop:~/chef-repo $ subl cookbooks/my_cookbook/recipes/
default.rb
```

```
        include_recipe "users"

        users_manage "staff" do
          group_id 50
          action [ :remove, :create ]
        end
```

4. Upload the modified cookbook to the Chef server:

   ```
   mma@laptop:~/chef-repo $ berks upload
   ```

   ```
   ...TRUNCATED OUTPUT...
   Uploading my_cookbook (0.1.0) to: 'https://api.chef.io:443/
   organizations/awo'
   ...TRUNCATED OUTPUT...
   ```

5. Run the Chef client on your node:

   **user@server:~$ sudo chef-client**

   ```
   ...TRUNCATED OUTPUT...
     * users_manage[staff] action remove (up to date)
     * users_manage[staff] action create
   ...TRUNCATED OUTPUT...
   ```

6. Validate that the user, mma, exists:

   **user@server:~$ fgrep mma /etc/passwd**

   ```
   mma:x:1000:1000::/home/mma:/bin/bash
   ```

7. Validate that the user, mma, belongs to the group staff now:

   **user@server:~$ fgrep staff /etc/group**

   ```
   staff:x:50:mma
   ```

## How it works...

The users cookbook requires that you create a users data bag and one data bag item for each user. In that data bag item, you define the attributes of the user: groups, shell, and so on. You even can include an action attribute, which defaults to create, but could be remove as well.

To be able to manage users with my_cookbook, you need to include the users cookbook as a dependency. In your recipe, you can include the users cookbook's default recipe in order to be able to use the manage_users **Light Weight Resource Provider** (**LWRP**), provided by the users cookbook.

The `manage_users` LWRP takes its name attribute `"staff"` as the group name it should manage. It searches for data bag items, which have this group in their `groups` entry, and uses every entry found to create those users and groups.

 The `manage_users` LWRP replaces group members—existing (non-Chef managed) users will get thrown out of the given group (bad, if you manage the `sudo` group on Vagrant).

By passing both actions, `:create` and `:remove`, into the LWRP, we make sure that it searches for both: users to remove and users to add.

## There's more...

Let's take a look at how you can remove a user:

1.  Edit the data bag item for your first user, setting `action` to `remove`:

    **mma@laptop:~/chef-repo $ subl data_bags/users/mma.json**

    ```
    {
      "id": "mma",
      "ssh_keys": [
        "ssh-rsa AAA345...bla== mma@laptop"
      ],
      "groups": [ "staff"],
      "shell": "\/bin\/bash",
      "action": "remove"
    }
    ```

2.  Upload the data bag item to the Chef server:

    **mma@laptop:~/chef-repo $ knife data bag from file users mma.json**

    ```
    Updated data_bag_item[users::mma]
    ```

3.  Run the Chef client on your node:

    **user@server:~$ sudo chef-client**

    ```
    ...TRUNCATED OUTPUT...
    - remove user user[mma]
    ...TRUNCATED OUTPUT...
    ```

4.  Validate that the user `mma` does not exist anymore:

    **user@server:~$ fgrep mma /etc/passwd**

    ```
    ...NO OUTPUT...
    ```

If the user you want to remove is currently logged on, you will get an error. This happens because the underlying operating system command `userdel` cannot remove the user (and exits with return code 8):

```
Chef::Exceptions::Exec
----------------------
userdel mma returned 8, expected 0
```

## See also

▸ Find the `users` cookbook on GitHub at `https://github.com/opscode-cookbooks/users`

▸ The *Using data Bags* recipe in *Chapter 4, Writing Better Cookbooks*

# Securing the Secure Shell Daemon (SSHD)

Depending on your Linux flavor, the `ssh` daemon might listen on all network interfaces on the default port, and allow root and password logins.

This default configuration is not very safe. Automated scripts can try to guess the root password. You're at the mercy of the strength of your root password.

It's a good idea to make things stricter. Let's see how you can do this.

## Getting ready

Create a user who can log in using his `ssh` key instead of a password. Doing this with Chef is described in the *Creating users from data bags* recipe in this chapter.

Make sure that you have a cookbook named `my_cookbook` and that the `run_list` of your node includes `my_cookbook`, as described in the *Creating and using cookbooks* recipe in *Chapter 1, Chef Infrastructure*.

Create `Berksfile` in your Chef repository including `my_cookbook`:

**mma@laptop:~/chef-repo $ subl Berksfile**

```
cookbook 'my_cookbook', path: './cookbooks/my_cookbook'
```

Note that configuring sshd might lock you out of your system. Make sure you have an open `ssh` connection with root access to fix what an error in your cookbook might have broken!

## How to do it...

We'll secure `sshd` by disabling the root login (you should use `sudo` instead) and by disabling password logins. Users should only be able to log in using their `ssh` key.

1. Edit your cookbook's `metadata.rb` and add a dependency on the `openssh` cookbook:

   ```
   mma@laptop:~/chef-repo $ subl cookbooks/my_cookbook/metadata.rb

   ...
   depends "openssh"
   ```

2. Install your cookbook's dependencies:

   ```
   mma@laptop:~/chef-repo $ berks install

   Resolving cookbook dependencies...
   ...TRUNCATED OUTPUT...
   Using my_cookbook (0.1.0) at './cookbooks/my_cookbook'
   ```

3. Edit your cookbook's default recipe:

   ```
   mma@laptop:~/chef-repo $ subl cookbooks/my_cookbook/recipes/
   default.rb

   node.default['openssh']['server']['permit_root_login'] = "no"
   node.default['openssh']['server']['password_authentication'] =
   "no"

   include_recipe 'openssh'
   ```

4. Upload the modified cookbook to the Chef server:

   ```
   mma@laptop:~/chef-repo $ berks upload

   ...TRUNCATED OUTPUT...
   Uploading my_cookbook (0.1.0) to: 'https://api.opscode.com:443/
   organizations/awo'
   ...TRUNCATED OUTPUT...
   ```

5. Run the Chef client on your node:

   ```
   user@server:~$ sudo chef-client

   ...TRUNCATED OUTPUT...
   [2015-02-09T20:15:22+00:00] INFO: template[/etc/ssh/sshd_config]
   sending restart action to service[ssh] (delayed)
      * service[ssh] action restart[2015-02-09T20:15:22+00:00] INFO:
   service[ssh] restarted

        - restart service service[ssh]
   ...TRUNCATED OUTPUT...
   ```

6. Validate the content of the generated file:

```
user@server:~$ cat /etc/ssh/sshd_config

# This file was generated by Chef for vagrant.vm
# Do NOT modify this file by hand!

ChallengeResponseAuthentication no
UsePAM yes
PermitRootLogin no
PasswordAuthentication no
```

## How it works...

The openssh cookbook offers attributes for most configuration parameters in ssh_config and sshd_config. We override the default values in our cookbook and include the openssh default recipe.

The order is significant here because this way, the openssh recipe will use our overridden values instead of its default values.

The openssh cookbook writes the /etc/ssh/sshd_config file and restarts the sshd service. After running this recipe, you will no longer be able to SSH into the node using a password.

## There's more...

If your nodes are connected to a **Virtual Private Network** (**VPN**) by using a second network interface, it's a good idea to bind sshd to that secure network only. This way, you block anyone from the public Internet trying to hack into your sshd.

You can override listen_address in your cookbook:

```
node.default['openssh']['server']['listen_address']
```

If your nodes need to be accessible via the Internet, you might want to move sshd to a higher port to avoid automated attacks:

```
node.default['openssh']['server']['port'] = '6222'
```

In this case, you need to use -p 6222 with your ssh commands in order to be able to connect to your nodes.

Moving `sshd` to a non-privileged port adds one layer of security, but comes at the price of moving from a privileged port to a non-privileged port on your node. This presents the risk that someone on your box might highjack that port. Read more about the implications at `http://www.adayinthelifeof.nl/2012/03/12/why-putting-ssh-on-another-port-than-22-is-bad-idea/`

## See also

▸ Find the `openssh` cookbook on GitHub at `https://github.com/opscode-cookbooks/openssh`

▸ Find a detailed list of all attributes the `openssh` cookbook offers to configure `sshd` at `https://github.com/opscode-cookbooks/openssh/blob/master/attributes/default.rb`

# Enabling passwordless sudo

You have secured your `sshd` so that your users can only log in with their own user accounts, instead of root. Additionally, you made sure that your users do not need passwords, but have to use their private keys for authentication.

However, once authenticated, users want to administer the system. That's why it is a good idea to have `sudo` installed on all boxes. Sudo enables non-root users to execute commands as root, if they're allowed to. Sudo will log all such command executions.

To make sure that your users don't need passwords here, you should configure `sudo` for passwordless logins. Let's take a look at how to do this.

## Getting ready

Make sure that you have a cookbook named `my_cookbook` and that the `run_list` of your node includes `my_cookbook`, as described in the *Creating and using cookbooks* recipe in *Chapter 1, Chef Infrastructure*.

Create `Berksfile` in your Chef repository including `my_cookbook`:

```
mma@laptop:~/chef-repo $ subl Berksfile
```

```
cookbook 'my_cookbook', path: './cookbooks/my_cookbook'
```

## How to do it...

Let's make Chef modify the `sudo` configuration to enable passwordless `sudo` for the staff group:

1.  Edit your cookbook's `metadata.rb` and add the dependency on the `sudo` cookbook:

    **mma@laptop:~/chef-repo $ subl cookbooks/my_cookbook/metadata.rb**

    ```
    . . .
    depends "sudo"
    ```

2.  Install your cookbook's dependencies:

    **mma@laptop:~/chef-repo $ berks install**

    ```
    Installing sudo (2.7.1)
    Using my_cookbook (0.1.0) at './cookbooks/my_cookbook'
    ```

3.  Edit your cookbook's default recipe:

    **mma@laptop:~/chef-repo $ subl cookbooks/my_cookbook/recipes/default.rb**

    ```
    node.default['authorization']['sudo']['passwordless'] = true
    node.default['authorization']['sudo']['groups'] = ['staff',
    'vagrant']

    include_recipe 'sudo'
    ```

 **Vagrant users**: If you are working with a vagrant managed VM, make sure to include the `vagrant` group in the `sudo` configuration; otherwise, your `vagrant` user will not be able to `sudo` anymore.

4.  Upload the modified cookbook to the Chef server:

    **mma@laptop:~/chef-repo $ berks upload**

    ```
    ...TRUNCATED OUTPUT...
    Uploading my_cookbook (0.1.0) to: 'https://api.opscode.com:443/
    organizations/awo'
    Uploaded sudo (2.7.1) to: 'https://api.opscode.com:443/
    organizations/awo'
    ```

5. Run the Chef client on your node:

```
user@server:~$ sudo chef-client

...TRUNCATED OUTPUT...
  * template[/etc/sudoers] action create
[2015-02-09T20:22:20+00:00] INFO: template[/etc/sudoers] backed up
to /var/chef/backup/etc/sudoers.chef-20150209202220.755848
[2015-02-09T20:22:20+00:00] INFO: template[/etc/sudoers] updated
file contents /etc/sudoers

    - update content in file /etc/sudoers from d49b83 to cd7842
    --- /etc/sudoers2014-10-27 02:18:28.623220955 +0000
    +++ /tmp/chef-rendered-template20150209-5333-cviwbs2015-02-09
20:22:20.751179595 +0000
...TRUNCATED OUTPUT...
```

6. Validate the content of the generated `sudoers` file:

```
user@server:~$ sudo cat /etc/sudoers

...
# Members of the group 'staff' may gain root privileges
%staff ALL=(ALL) NOPASSWD:ALL
# Members of the group 'vagrant' may gain root privileges
%vagrant ALL=(ALL) NOPASSWD:ALL
```

## How it works...

The `sudo` cookbook rewrites the `/etc/sudoers` file by using the attribute values that we set in the node. In our case, we set the following:

```
node.default['authorization']['sudo']['passwordless'] = true
```

This will tell the `sudo` cookbook that we want to enable our users to `sudo` without passwords.

Then, we tell the `sudo` cookbook which groups should have passwordless `sudo` rights:

```
node.default['authorization']['sudo']['groups'] = ['staff', 'vagrant']
```

The last step is to include the `sudo` cookbook's default recipe to let it install and configure `sudo` on your nodes:

```
include_recipe 'sudo'
```

## There's more...

By using the LWRP from the `sudo` cookbook, you can manage each group or user individually. The LWRP will place configuration fragments inside `/etc/sudoers.d`. You can use this to use your own template for the `sudo` configuration:

```
sudo 'mma' do
  template    'staff_member.erb' # local cookbook template
  variables   :cmds => ['/etc/init.d/ssh restart']
end
```

This snippet assumes that you have `my_cookbook/templates/default/staff_member.erb` in place.

## See also

 ▶  The *Creating users from data bags* recipe in this chapter

 ▶  Find the `sudo` cookbook at GitHub at `https://github.com/opscode-cookbooks/sudo`

# Managing NTP

Your nodes should always have synchronized clocks, if nothing else, because the Chef server requires clients' clocks to be synchronized with it. This is required because the authentication of clients is based on a time window in order to prevent man-in-the-middle attacks.

NTP is there to synchronize your nodes' clocks with its upstream peers. It usually uses a set of trusted upstream peers so that it gets a reliable timing signal.

It's a good idea to put the installation of NTP into a role, which you assign to every node. Bugs caused by clocks, which are out of sync, are not nice to track down. Better avoid them in the first place by using NTP on every node.

## Getting ready

Create `Berksfile` in your Chef repository including the `ntp` cookbook:

**mma@laptop:~/chef-repo $ subl Berksfile**

```
cookbook 'ntp'
```

Install the `ntp` cookbook:

**mma@laptop:~/chef-repo $ berks install**

```
Resolving cookbook dependencies...
Using ntp (1.7.0)
```

Upload the `ntp` cookbook to the Chef server:

**mma@laptop:~/chef-repo $ berks upload**

```
...TRUNCATED OUTPUT...
Uploading ntp (1.7.0) to: 'https://api.opscode.com:443/organizations/
awo'
...TRUNCATED OUTPUT...
```

## How to do it...

Let's create a role called `"base"`, which ensures that your nodes will synchronize their clocks, using NTP:

1. Create a `base.rb` file for your role:

   **mma@laptop:~/chef-repo $ subl roles/base.rb**

   ```
   name "base"

   run_list "recipe[ntp]"

   default_attributes "ntp" => {
     "servers" => ["0.pool.ntp.org", "1.pool.ntp.org", "2.pool.ntp.
   org"]
   }
   ```

2. Upload the new role to the Chef server:

   **mma@laptop:~/chef-repo $ knife role from file base.rb**

   ```
   Updated Role base!
   ```

3. Add the base role to your node's run list:

   **mma@laptop:~/chef-repo $ knife node run_list set server
   'role[base]'**

   ```
   server:
     run_list: role[base]
   ```

4. Run the Chef client on your node:

   **user@server:~$ sudo chef-client**

   ```
   ...TRUNCATED OUTPUT...
   Recipe: ntp::default
   ```

```
     * template[/etc/ntp.conf] action create[2015-02-
10T07:56:03+00:00] INFO: template[/etc/ntp.conf] backed up to /
var/chef/backup/etc/ntp.conf.chef-20150210075603.587108
[2015-02-10T07:56:03+00:00] INFO: template[/etc/ntp.conf] updated
file contents /etc/ntp.conf

     - update content in file /etc/ntp.conf from af9be0 to d933a5
...TRUNCATED OUTPUT...
     * service[ntp] action restart[2015-02-10T07:56:05+00:00] INFO:
service[ntp] restarted

     - restart service service[ntp]
...TRUNCATED OUTPUT...
```

5.  Validate that `ntp` is installed correctly:

    **`user@server:~$ /etc/init.d/ntp status`**

    ```
    * NTP server is running
    ```

## How it works...

The `ntp` cookbook installs the required packages for your node's platform and writes a configuration file. You can influence the configuration by setting default attributes in the `ntp` namespace. In the preceding example, we configured the upstream NTP servers for our node to query.

 If you're on Debian or Ubuntu, the `ntp` cookbook installs `ntpdate` as well. `ntpdate` is there to quickly synchronize and set a node's date and time.

## There's more...

The `ntp` cookbook also contains an `ntp::undo` recipe. You can completely remove NTP from your node by adding `ntp::undo` to your node's run list.

## See also

▸   You can find the `ntp` cookbook on GitHub at `https://github.com/gmiranda23/ntp`

▸   The *Overriding attributes* recipe in *Chapter 4, Writing Better Cookbooks*

# Managing nginx

Say you need to set up a website, which handles a lot of traffic simultaneously. nginx is a web server that is designed to handle many connections and is used by a lot of big web companies such as Facebook, Dropbox, and WordPress.

You'll find nginx packages in most major distributions, but if you want to extend nginx by using modules, you'll need to compile nginx from source.

In this section, we'll configure the `nginx` community cookbook to do just that.

## Getting ready

Let's get ready for set up of nginx:

1. Create `Berksfile` in your Chef repository including the `nginx` cookbook:

   **mma@laptop:~/chef-repo $ subl Berksfile**

   ```
   cookbook 'nginx'
   ```

2. Install the `nginx` cookbook:

   **mma@laptop:~/chef-repo $ berks install**

   ```
   ...TRUNCATED OUTPUT...
   Installing nginx (2.7.4)
   ...TRUNCATED OUTPUT...
   ```

3. Upload the `nginx` cookbook to your Chef server:

   **mma@laptop:~/chef-repo $ berks upload**

   ```
   Using nginx (1.7.0)
   ...TRUNCATED OUTPUT...
   Uploading nginx (1.7.0) to: 'https://api.opscode.com:443/
   organizations/agilewebops'
   ...TRUNCATED OUTPUT...
   ```

## How to do it...

Let's set up a role and configure how we want to build nginx:

1. Create a new role called `web_server` with the following content:

   **mma@laptop:~/chef-repo $ subl roles/web_server.rb**

   ```
   name "web_server"
   ```

```
run_list "recipe[nginx::source]"

default_attributes "nginx" => {
  "version" => "1.7.9",
  "init_style" => "init",
  "enable_default_site" => false,
  "upload_progress" => {
    "url" => "https://github.com/masterzen/nginx-upload-progress-
module/archive/v0.9.1.tar.gz",
    "checksum" =>
"99ec072cca35cd7791e77c40a8ded41a7a8c1111e057be26e55fba2fdf105f43"
  },
  "source" => {
  "checksum" =>
1aafc7f0f530ddaa86d4ba24c14941ce0a584cc896f8261d6218f99625318f8a",
    "modules" => ["nginx::upload_progress_module"]
  }
}
```

To generate the checksum for the `remote_file` resource, you need to run the following command:

```
mma@laptop:~/chef-repo $ shasum -a 256 <PATH_TO_FILE>
```

To generate the checksum for the `upload_progress` module, you can run the following command:

```
mma@laptop:~/chef-repo $ curl -L -s https://github.
com/masterzen/nginx-upload-progress-module/archive/
v0.9.1.tar.gz | shasum -a 256
```

To generate the checksum for the `nginx` source, run the following command:

```
mma@laptop:~/chef-repo $ shasum -a 256 ~/Downloads/
nginx-1.7.9.tar.gz
```

2. Upload the role to the Chef server:

   **mma@laptop:~/chef-repo $ knife role from file web_server.rb**

   ```
   Updated Role web_server!
   ```

3. Add the `web_server` role to your node's run list:

   **mma@laptop:~/chef-repo $ knife node run_list set server 'role[web_server]'**

   ```
   server:
     run_list: role[web_server]
   ```

4.  Run the Chef client on your node:

    **user@server:~$ sudo chef-client**

    ```
    ...TRUNCATED OUTPUT...
    [2015-02-10T19:47:37+00:00] INFO: bash[compile_nginx_source]
    sending restart action to service[nginx] (delayed)
       * service[nginx] action restart[2015-02-10T19:47:39+00:00] INFO:
    service[nginx] restarted

        - restart service service[nginx]
    ...TRUNCATED OUTPUT...
    ```

5.  Validate that `nginx` is installed with `upload_progress_module`:

    **user@server:~$ /opt/nginx-1.7.9/sbin/nginx -V**

    ```
    nginx version: nginx/1.7.9
    built by gcc 4.9.1 (Ubuntu 4.9.1-16ubuntu6)
    TLS SNI support enabled
    configure arguments: --prefix=/opt/nginx-1.7.9 --conf-path=/etc/
    nginx/nginx.conf --sbin-path=/opt/nginx-1.7.9/sbin/nginx --with-
    http_ssl_module --with-http_gzip_static_module --add-module=/var/
    chef/cache/nginx_upload_progress/99ec072cca35cd7791e77c40a8ded41a7
    a8c1111e057be26e55fba2fdf105f43
    ```

## How it works...

We configure `nginx` in our new role `web_server`. First, we decide that we want to install `nginx` from source because we want to add an additional module. We do this by adding the `nginx::source` recipe to the run list:

```
run_list "recipe[nginx::source]"
```

Then, we set the attributes that will be necessary for our source build. They all live in the `nginx` name space:

```
default_attributes "nginx" => {
...
}
```

Since we want to use the default way of starting the `nginx` service on Ubuntu, we set `init_style` to init. This will create start up scripts for `init.d`, as shown in the following code:

```
"init_style" => "init",
```

Other options would have been to use `runit` or `bluepill`, among others.

Next, we have to tell the `nginx` recipe where to find the source code for the `upload_progress` module and provide the SHA checksum for the file, so that the `remote_file` resource can validate that the file it downloads is exactly the one you requested:

```
"upload_progress" => {
    "url" => "https://github.com/masterzen/nginx-upload-progress-
module/archive/v0.9.1.tar.gz ",
"checksum" => "..."
    },
```

Finally, we have to instruct the `nginx` recipe to compile `nginx` with `upload_progress_module` enabled:

```
"source" => {
    "modules" => ["upload_progress_module"]
}
```

After defining the role, we have to upload it to the Chef server and add it to the node's run list. Running the Chef client on the node will now create all the necessary directories, download all the required sources, and build `nginx` with the module enabled.

The `nginx` cookbook will create a default site, which we disabled in our role settings. It installs nginx in `/opt/nginx-1.7.9/sbin`.

## There's more...

If you only want to use your distribution's default `nginx` package, you can use the `nginx` default recipe instead of `nginx::source` in your role's run list:

```
run_list "recipe[nginx]"
```

If you want to disable the default site, you need to set the attributes accordingly:

```
"default_site_enabled" => false
```

You'll find all tunable configuration parameters in the `nginx` cookbook's attributes file. You can modify them according to preceding examples.

> The `nginx` cookbook sets up handling of sites and its configuration in a similar way to Debian's way of configuring `Apache2`. You can use `nxdissite` and `nxensite` to disable and enable your sites, which you will find under `/etc/nginx/sites-available` and `/etc/nginx/sites-enabled`, respectively.

You can set up `nginx` as a reverse proxy using the `application_nginx` cookbook.

## See also

- Find the `nginx` cookbook on GitHub at `https://github.com/miketheman/nginx/blob/master/recipes/source.rb`

- Find the `application_nginx` cookbook on GitHub at `https://github.com/poise/application_nginx`

- Find the HTTP Upload Progress Module at `http://wiki.nginx.org/HttpUploadProgressModule`

- Learn how to calculate checksums for the `remote_file` resource at `https://coderwall.com/p/bbfjrw/calculate-checksum-for-chef-s-remote_file-resource`

- The *Overriding attributes* recipe *Chapter 4, Writing Better Cookbooks*

# Creating nginx virtual hosts

Assuming you have `nginx` installed, you want to manage your websites with Chef. You need to create an `nginx` configuration file for your website and upload your HTML file(s). Let's see how to do this.

## Getting ready

Make sure that you have a cookbook named `my_cookbook`, as described in the *Creating and using cookbooks* recipe in *Chapter 1, Chef Infrastructure*.

1. Create `Berksfile` in your Chef repository including `my_cookbook`:

   **mma@laptop:~/chef-repo $ subl Berksfile**

   ```
   cookbook 'my_cookbook', path: './cookbooks/my_cookbook'
   ```

2. Create or edit a role called `web_server` with the following content:

   **mma@laptop:~/chef-repo $ subl roles/web_server.rb**

   ```
   name "web_server"
   run_list "recipe[my_cookbook]"

   default_attributes "nginx" => {
     "init_style" => "init",
     "enable_default_site" => false
   }
   ```

3. Upload the role to the Chef server:

```
mma@laptop:~/chef-repo $ knife role from file web_server.rb
```

```
Updated Role web_server!
```

4. Add the `web_server` role to your node's run list:

```
mma@laptop:~/chef-repo $ knife node run_list set server 'role[web_server]'
```

```
server:
  run_list: role[web_server]
```

## How to do it...

Let's put together all the code to configure your site in `nginx` and upload a sample `index.html` file:

1. Edit your cookbook's `metadata.rb` file to include the dependency on the `nginx` cookbook:

```
mma@laptop:~/chef-repo $ subl cookbooks/my_cookbook/metadata.rb
```

```
...
depends "nginx"
```

2. Install your cookbook's dependencies:

```
mma@laptop:~/chef-repo $ berks install
```

```
Resolving cookbook dependencies...
Fetching 'my_cookbook' from source at cookbooks/my_cookbook
...TRUNCATED OUTPUT...
```

3. Edit your cookbook's default recipe:

```
mma@laptop:~/chef-repo $ subl cookbooks/my_cookbook/recipes/default.rb
```

```
include_recipe "nginx"

nginx_site "default" do
  enable false
end

app_name = "my_app"
app_home = "/srv/#{app_name}"

template "#{node[:nginx][:dir]}/sites-available/#{app_name}" do
```

```
    source "nginx-site-#{app_name}.erb"
    owner  "root"
    group  "root"
    mode   "0644"
    variables :app_home => app_home
    notifies :restart, resources(:service => "nginx")
  end

  directory "#{app_home}/public" do
    recursive true
  end

  file "#{app_home}/public/index.html" do
    content "<h1>Hello World!</h1>"
  end

  nginx_site "#{app_name}"
```

4. Create a template for your `nginx` configuration:

   **mma@laptop:~/chef-repo $ subl cookbooks/my_cookbook/templates/
   default/nginx-site-my_app.erb**

```
server {
  listen 80;
  server_name _;
  root <%= @app_home %>/public;
}
```

5. Upload the modified cookbook to the Chef server:

   **mma@laptop:~/chef-repo $ berks upload**

```
...TRUNCATED OUTPUT...
Uploading my_cookbook (0.1.0) to: 'https://api.opscode.com:443/
organizations/awo'
...TRUNCATED OUTPUT...
```

6. Run the Chef client on your node:

   **user@server:~$ sudo chef-client**

```
...TRUNCATED OUTPUT...
[2015-02-22T22:59:34+00:00] INFO: execute[nxensite my_app] ran
successfully

    - execute /usr/sbin/nxensite my_app
...TRUNCATED OUTPUT...
```

7. Validate whether the `nginx` site is up and running by requesting `index.html` from the web server:

**user@server:~$ wget localhost**

```
--2015-02-22 23:27:36--  http://localhost/
Resolving localhost (localhost)... ::1, 127.0.0.1
Connecting to localhost (localhost)|::1|:80... failed: Connection
refused.
Connecting to localhost (localhost)|127.0.0.1|:80... connected.
HTTP request sent, awaiting response... 200 OK
Length: 21 [text/html]
Saving to: 'index.html'


100%[============================================================
==============================>] 21              --.-K/s    in 0s

2015-02-22 23:27:36 (2.00 MB/s) - 'index.html' saved [21/21]
```

8. Validate whether the downloaded `index.html` file contains the text we set:

**user@server:~$ cat index.html**

```
<h1>Hello World!</h1>+
```

## How it works...

After setting two variables, the recipe installs a template for the `nginx` configuration file. The template ends up as `/etc/nginx/sites-available/my_app` and gets symlinked to `/etc/nginx/sites-enabled/my_app`.

Next, we create the directory and the `index.html` file in `/srv/my_app/public`. This is the directory that our `nginx` configuration template uses as its `root` location.

Finally, we enable the site that we just created using the `nginx_site` resource, which is defined by the `nginx` cookbook.

The configuration file template `nginx-site-my_app.erb` makes `nginx` listen on `port 80` and defines the root location as `/srv/my_app/public`.

## There's more...

If you want to disable your site, consider the following line:

```
nginx_site "#{app_name}"
```

Replace the preceding line with the folllowing:

```
nginx_site "#{app_name}"  do
  enable false
end
```

After uploading the modified cookbook and running the Chef client again, you should not be able to retrieve `index.html` file anymore:

**user@server:~$ wget localhost**

```
--2015-02-22 23:29:47--  http://localhost/
Resolving localhost (localhost)... 127.0.0.1
Connecting to localhost (localhost)|127.0.0.1|:80... failed:
Connection refused.
```

## See also

▸ Learn how to install `nginx` in the *Managing nginx* recipe in this chapter

▸ Read more about the `nginx_site` resource at `https://github.com/opscode-cookbooks/nginx/blob/master/definitions/nginx_site.rb`

# Creating MySQL databases and users

You need to use two different cookbooks to manage MySQL (or any other database) on your nodes: the generic `database` cookbook and the `mysql` cookbook.

The `database` cookbook provides resources for managing databases and database users for MySQL, PostgreSQL, and Microsoft SQL Server. The `mysql` cookbook installs MySQL client and server.

Let's see how we can install MySQL server and create a database and a database user.

## Getting ready

Make sure that you have a cookbook called `my_cookbook` and that the `run_list` of your node includes `my_cookbook`, as described in the *Creating and using cookbooks* recipe in *Chapter 1, Chef Infrastructure*.

Make sure `Berksfile` in your Chef repository includes `my_cookbook`:

**mma@laptop:~/chef-repo $ subl Berksfile**

```
cookbook 'my_cookbook', path: './cookbooks/my_cookbook'
```

## How to do it...

We'll install the MySQL server with a database and user:

1. Edit your cookbook's `metadata.rb` file to include the dependencies on the `database` and `mysql` cookbooks:

   **mma@laptop:~/chef-repo $ subl cookbooks/my_cookbook/metadata.rb**

   ```
   ...
   depends "mysql2_chef_gem"
   depends "database"
   depends "mysql"
   ```

2. Install your cookbook's dependencies:

   **mma@laptop:~/chef-repo $ berks install**

   ```
   Using my_cookbook (0.1.0) at './cookbooks/my_cookbook'
   ...TRUNCATED OUTPUT...
   ```

3. Edit your cookbook's default recipe:

   **mma@laptop:~/chef-repo $ subl cookbooks/my_cookbook/recipes/default.rb**

   ```
   mysql2_chef_gem 'default' do
     action :install
   end

   connection_params = {
     :username => 'root',
     :password => 'root_password_15',
     :host => '127.0.0.1'
   }

   mysql_service 'default' do
     port '3306'
     version '5.5'
     initial_root_password connection_params[:password]
     action [:create, :start]
   end

   mysql_database 'my_db' do
   ```

```
    connection connection_params
    action :create
end

mysql_database_user 'me' do
    connection connection_params
    password 'my_password_11'
    privileges [:all]
    action [:create, :grant]
end
```

4. Upload the modified cookbook to the Chef server:

   **mma@laptop:~/chef-repo $ berks upload**

   ```
   ...TRUNCATED OUTPUT...
   Uploading my_cookbook (0.1.0) to: 'https://api.opscode.com:443/
   organizations/awo'
   ...TRUNCATED OUTPUT...
   ```

5. Run the Chef client on your node:

   **user@server:~$ sudo chef-client**

   ```
   ...TRUNCATED OUTPUT...
          - start service service[default :start mysql-default]

      * mysql_database[my_db] action create
        - Creating schema 'my_db'
      * mysql_database_user[me] action create
        - Creating user 'me'@'localhost'
   ...TRUNCATED OUTPUT...
   ```

6. Validate that we can log in to our MySQL server with the user that we have just created and see the database `my_db`:

   **user@server:~$ mysql -h 127.0.0.1 -u me -p**

   ```
   mysql> show databases;
   +--------------------+
   | Database           |
   +--------------------+
   | information_schema |
   | my_db              |
   ...
   ```

## How it works...

First, we install the `mysql2` Ruby gem so that Chef can access MySQL:

```
mysql2_chef_gem 'default' do
  action :install
end
```

Since we want to connect to our MySQL server multiple times, we define the connection parameters as a variable called `connection_params` in our recipe:

```
connection_params = {
  :username => 'root',
  :password => 'root_password_15',
  :host => '127.0.0.1'
}
```

Now, it's time to install MySQL Server 5.5 listening to `port 3306` and start it:

```
mysql_service 'default' do
  port '3306'
  version '5.5'
  initial_root_password connection_params[:password]
  action [:create, :start]
end
```

Then, we use the `mysql_database` resource from the database cookbook to create a database called `my_db`:

```
mysql_database 'my_db' do
  connection connection_params
  action :create
end
```

Finally, we use the `mysql_database_user` resource to create a user called `me` and grant them all privileges:

```
mysql_database_user 'me' do
  connection connection_params
  password 'my_password_11'
  privileges [:all]
  action [:create, :grant]
end
```

## There's more...

It's quite common to have things such as a database name or users with their privileges stored in data bags. You can find out how to do this in the *Using search to find data bag items* recipe in *Chapter 4, Writing Better Cookbooks*.

## See also

- ▶ The *Using data bags* recipe in *Chapter 4, Writing Better Cookbooks*
- ▶ Find the `database` cookbook on GitHub at `https://github.com/opscode-cookbooks/database`.
- ▶ Find the `mysql` cookbook on GitHub at `https://github.com/chef-cookbooks/mysql`.

# Managing WordPress sites

You need to enable your business users to manage their own website. Fast. WordPress has come a long way. You might have seen it as a simple blogging tool, however, in recent years, it has grown into a fully featured content management system. Fortunately, managing WordPress with Chef is pretty straightforward.

Let's take a look at how to do it.

## Getting ready

Make sure that you have a cookbook called `my_cookbook` and that the `run_list` of your node includes `my_cookbook`, as described in the *Creating and using cookbooks* recipe in *Chapter 1, Chef Infrastructure*.

Create `Berksfile` in your Chef repository including `my_cookbook`:

**mma@laptop:~/chef-repo $ subl Berksfile**

```
cookbook 'my_cookbook', path: './cookbooks/my_cookbook'
```

If you're using Vagrant for your node, you need to configure a bridged network to be able to browse to your WordPress installation from your local workstation:

```
Vagrant::Config.run do |config|
  config.vm.network :bridged
end
```

## How to do it...

We'll install WordPress by using the community cookbook:

1.  Edit your cookbook's metadata to make sure it depends on the `wordpress` cookbook:

    **`mma@laptop:~/chef-repo $ subl cookbooks/my_cookbook/metadata.rb`**

    ```
    ...
    depends "wordpress"
    ```

2.  Install your cookbook's dependencies:

    **`mma@laptop:~/chef-repo $ berks install`**

    ```
    Using my_cookbook (0.1.0) at './cookbooks/my_cookbook'
    ...TRUNCATED OUTPUT...
    ```

3.  Edit your cookbook's default recipe to set some attributes and include the `wordpress` cookbook:

    **`mma@laptop:~/chef-repo $ subl cookbooks/my_cookbook/recipes/`**
    **`default.rb`**

    ```
    node.default['apache']['mpm'] = 'prefork'
    node.default['wordpress']['db']['database'] = "my_wordpress"
    node.default['wordpress']['db']['user'] = "me"
    node.default['wordpress']['db']['password'] = "my_password_11"

    include_recipe 'wordpress'
    ```

4.  Upload the modified cookbook to the Chef server:

    **`mma@laptop:~/chef-repo $ berks upload`**

    ```
    ...TRUNCATED OUTPUT...
    Uploading my_cookbook (0.1.0) to: 'https://api.opscode.com:443/
    organizations/awo'
    ...TRUNCATED OUTPUT...
    ```

5.  Run the Chef client on your node:

    **`user@server:~$ sudo chef-client`**

    ```
    ...TRUNCATED OUTPUT...
    [2015-02-25T21:55:03+00:00] INFO: execute[a2ensite wordpress.conf]
    ran successfully

        - execute /usr/sbin/a2ensite wordpress.conf

    ...TRUNCATED OUTPUT...
    ```

6. Validate whether WordPress is installed on your host by firing up your browser and navigating to the WordPress installation page:

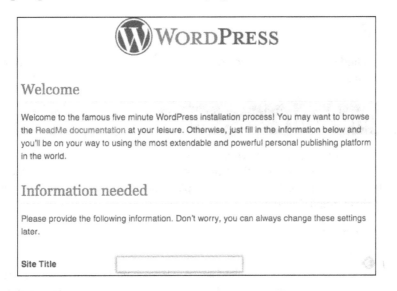

## How it works...

The `wordpress` cookbook installs a full Apache-MySQL-PHP-stack. That's why, when you're installing it in your repository, it will install quite a few supporting cookbooks as well.

To use the `wordpress` cookbook, you simply include it in your own cookbook's recipe:

```
include_recipe 'wordpress'
```

Because we do not like the default values for the database name, database user, and the password for the database user, we override those attributes at the beginning of our default recipe:

```
node.default['wordpress']['db']['database'] = 'my_wordpress'
node.default['wordpress']['db']['user'] = 'me'
node.default['wordpress']['db']['password'] = 'my_password_11'
```

You can lookup the default values in `cookbooks/wordpress/attributes/default.rb`.

## There's more...

The `wordpress` cookbook installs the complete stack but does not set up your first blog. It asks you to call the WordPress installation page with your browser to set up your first blog.

If you already have a tarball of your blog available, you could deliver it to your node, as described in the *Distributing directory trees* recipe in *Chapter 5, Working with Files and Packages*.

## See also

> ▶ You can find the `wordpress` cookbook on GitHub at `https://github.com/brint/wordpress-cookbook`.

# Managing Ruby on Rails applications

Ruby on Rails helps you to quickly get your web applications up and running. However, deployment is not an issue solved by the framework. In this section, we'll see how to write the simplest possible recipe to deploy a Rails application, using unicorn as the application server and SQLite as the database.

## Getting ready

Make sure that you have a cookbook called `my_cookbook` and that the `run_list` of your node includes `my_cookbook`, as described in the *Creating and using cookbooks* recipe in *Chapter 1, Chef Infrastructure*.

Create `Berksfile` in your Chef repository including `my_cookbook`:

```
mma@laptop:~/chef-repo $ subl Berksfile
```

```
cookbook 'my_cookbook', path: './cookbooks/my_cookbook'
```

## How to do it...

Let's get our Ruby on Rails application up and running on our node:

1. Edit your cookbook's `metadata.rb` file to make it depend on the `application_ruby` cookbook:

   ```
   mma@laptop:~/chef-repo $ subl cookbooks/my_cookbook/metadata.rb
   ```

   ```
   ...
   depends "application_ruby"
   ```

2. Install your cookbook's dependencies:

   ```
   mma@laptop:~/chef-repo $ berks install
   ```

   ```
   Using my_cookbook (0.1.0) at './cookbooks/my_cookbook'
   ...TRUNCATED OUTPUT...
   ```

3. Edit your cookbook's default recipe:

   **mma@laptop:~/chef-repo $ subl cookbooks/my_cookbook/recipes/
   default.rb**

   ```
   application "rails-app" do
     packages %w[build-essential ruby2.1-dev runit git libsqlite3-dev
   libssl-dev]

       path "/usr/local/www/rails-app"
       owner "www-data"
       group "www-data"

       environment_name "development"

       repository "https://github.com/mmarschall/rails-app.git"

       rails do
         gems %w[bundler]

         database_template "sqlite3_database.yml.erb"

         database do
           adapter "sqlite3"
           database "db/rails-app.sqlite3"
         end
       end

       unicorn do
       end
   end
   ```

4. Add your own template file to your `database.yml` file:

   **mma@laptop:~/chef-repo $ subl cookbooks/my_cookbook/templates/
   default/sqlite3_database.yml.erb**

   ```
   <%= @rails_env %>:
     adapter: <%= @database['adapter'] %>
     host: <%= @host %>
     database: <%= @database['database'] %>
     pool: 5
     timeout: 5000
   ```

5. Upload the modified cookbook to the Chef server:

```
mma@laptop:~/chef-repo $ berks upload
...TRUNCATED OUTPUT...
Uploading my_cookbook (0.1.0) to: 'https://api.opscode.com:443/
organizations/awo'
...TRUNCATED OUTPUT...
```

6. Run the Chef client on your node:

```
user@server:~$ sudo chef-client

...TRUNCATED OUTPUT...
  - update release history data[2015-02-27T20:45:06+00:00] INFO:
deploy_revision[rails-app] deployed to /usr/local/www/rails-app

* execute[/etc/init.d/rails-app hup] action run
[2015-02-27T20:45:06+00:00] INFO: execute[/etc/init.d/rails-app
hup] ran successfully

  - execute /etc/init.d/rails-app hup
...TRUNCATED OUTPUT...
```

7. Validate whether your Rails application is up and running by hitting your node at port `8080`:

```
user@server:~$ wget localhost:8080

2015-02-27 21:35:37 (346 MB/s) - 'index.html' saved [14935]
```

8. Then, you can have a look at the downloaded file to verify whether the **Welcome page** of your Rails app shows up:

```
user@server:~$ cat index.html

<!DOCTYPE html>
<html>
  <head>
    <title>Ruby on Rails: Welcome aboard</title>
  ...
```

## How it works...

Chef provides an abstract `application` cookbook to deploy web applications. We call our application `rails-app`:

```
application "rails-app" do
...
end
```

Inside the application block, we define the details of our web app. First, we need to install a few operating system packages as follows:

```
packages %w[build-essential ruby2.1-dev runit git libsqlite3-dev
libssl-dev]
```

The `ruby2.1-dev` package will make sure that we have Ruby runtime and headers to build native gems installed. If you installed your Chef client by using the Omnibus installer, it comes with an embedded Ruby, which you might not want to use to run your Rails application.

Since we're going to use unicorn to run our Rails application, we need to install `runit` because that's the way that unicorn is installed at the time of writing this book.

Git is required to be able to check out our repository from `www.github.com`.

Finally, we're using SQLite for our Rails application and need to install it first.

The next step is to configure the deployment details—where our app should go (`path`), which user and group should own the application (`owner`, `group`), and where our app should find the source code of our app (`repository`):

```
path "/usr/local/www/rails-app"
  owner "www-data"
  group "www-data"
...
repository "https://github.com/mmarschall/rails-app.git"
```

Make sure you enabled the `unicorn` gem in your Rails application's `Gemfile`:

```
gem 'unicorn'
```

If you don't want to run your application in the production environment, you can specify the desired `environment_name` in your cookbook, just as we did:

```
environment_name "development"
```

Your application will be fetched from `www.github.com` and the cookbook will install it in a directory structure similar to a directory structure that is maintained by **Capistrano**. It will put the current revision of your app into the `releases` directory and create a **symlink** to it as `current`.

Now, it's time to define the Rails-specific things. First of all, we want to install the `bundler` gem because our Rails application uses `Gemfile` for its dependencies:

```
rails do
    gems %w[bundler]
    ...
end
```

The `%w[]` syntax creates an array of strings. You could write `["bundler"]` instead. It doesn't make any difference for one element, but when placing multiple elements into your array, you save a lot of double quotes and commas with the `%w` syntax.

Since our Rails application uses SQLite as its persistence store, we need to use our own template for the `database.yml` file:

```
database_template "sqlite3_database.yml.erb"
```

Then, we can use a database block to populate it with the values we need:

```
database do
  adapter "sqlite3"
  database "db/rails-app.sqlite3"
end
```

We need to tell our Rails application that we're using a SQLite database and want it to store its data in a file called `db/rails-app.sqlite3`.

Finally, we need to tell our cookbook that we want to run our Rails application by using unicorn. An empty block will suffice, as long as we don't want to change any default attributes such as port number or number of workers:

```
unicorn do
end
```

## There's more...

Usually, the application cookbook's `deploy` resource will only deploy new revisions of your Rails app. If you want to ensure that it grabs the same revision again and again, you need to call the `force_deploy` action on your application resource:

```
application "rails-app" do
  ...
  action :force_deploy
end
```

If you want to use a new or existing MySQL server, you can assign it a role, for example, `rails_database_master`, and pass that role name to the `application` resource. It will then search for the node and use its IP address in `database.yml`:

```
application "rails-app" do
  ...
```

```
    database_master_role " rails_database_master"
  end
```

In this case, you don't need to use your own `database.yml` template.

If you want to run a cluster of nodes, each one installed with your Rails application, you can use the `application_nginx` cookbook to install an `nginx` load balancer in front of your application server cluster and the database cookbook to set up a networked database instead of SQLite.

## See also

▸ Find the `application` cookbook on GitHub at `https://github.com/poise/application`

▸ Find the `application_ruby` cookbook on GitHub at `https://github.com/poise/application_ruby`

▸ The *Using search to find nodes* recipe in *Chapter 4, Writing Better Cookbooks*

# Managing Varnish

Varnish is a web application accelerator. You install it in front of your web application to cache generated HTML files and serve them faster. It will take a lot of burden from your web application and can even provide you with extended uptime—covering up for application failures through its cache while you are fixing your application.

Let's see how to install Varnish.

## Getting ready

You need a web server running on your node at port `8080`. We'll set up Varnish to use `localhost:8080` as its backend host and port. You can achieve this by installing a Ruby on Rails application on your node as described in the *Managing Ruby on Rails applications* recipe.

Make sure that you have a cookbook called `my_cookbook` and that the `run_list` of your node includes `my_cookbook` as described in the *Creating and using cookbooks* recipe in *Chapter 1, Chef Infrastructure*.

Create `Berksfile` in your Chef repository including `my_cookbook`:

**mma@laptop:~/chef-repo $ subl Berksfile**

```
  cookbook 'my_cookbook', path: './cookbooks/my_cookbook'
```

## How to do it...

Let's install Varnish with its default parameters. We will use the Varnish-provided apt repository to have access to the latest versions of Varnish:

1. Edit your cookbook's metadata to add the dependency on the `varnish` cookbook:

   **mma@laptop:~/chef-repo $ subl cookbooks/my_cookbook/metadata.rb**

   ```
   ...
   depends "varnish"
   ```

 If you don't have the `apt` cookbook in your node's run list (which you should), you need `include_recipe "apt"` in your cookbook's default recipe.

2. Install your cookbook's dependencies:

   **mma@laptop:~/chef-repo $ berks install**

   ```
   Using my_cookbook (0.1.0) at './cookbooks/my_cookbook'
   ...TRUNCATED OUTPUT...
   ```

3. Edit your cookbook's default recipe:

   **mma@laptop:~/chef-repo $ subl cookbooks/my_cookbook/recipes/default.rb**

   ```
   include_recipe 'apt'

   varnish_install "webapp" do
     vendor_repo true
   end
   ```

4. Upload the modified cookbook to the Chef server:

   **mma@laptop:~/chef-repo $ berks upload**

   ```
   ...TRUNCATED OUTPUT...
   Uploading my_cookbook (0.1.0) to: 'https://api.opscode.com:443/
   organizations/awo'
   ...TRUNCATED OUTPUT...
   ```

5. Run the Chef client on your node:

   **user@server:~$ sudo chef-client**

   ```
   ...TRUNCATED OUTPUT...
     * apt_package[varnish] action install
   ```

```
        - install version 4.0.1-1 of package varnish
     * service[varnish] action enable (up to date)
     * service[varnish] action restart[2015-02-27T23:38:54+00:00]
  INFO: service[varnish] restarted

        - restart service service[varnish]
  ...TRUNCATED OUTPUT...
```

6.  Validate whether your Varnish cache is up and running by hitting your node at port 6081:

    **user@server:~$ wget localhost:6081**

    ```
    2015-02-27 23:39:41 (16.4 MB/s) - `index.html' saved [14900]
    ```

## How it works...

As we want to use the latest version of Varnish (and not the usually outdated one from the default Ubuntu package repository), we ask the `varnish_install` resource to use the original apt repository provided by Varnish by setting `vendor_repo` to `true`:

```
varnish_install "webapp" do
  vendor_repo true
end
```

This call will install, configure, and start the Varnish server listening to its default port 6081.

## There's more...

If you want to build your own configuration file instead of the default one provided by the apt package, you can use `varnish_default_config` in your recipe.

You can change the backend host Varnish uses, as shown in the following code:

```
varnish_default_vcl do
  backend_host 'webapp.example.com'
  backend_port 8000
end
```

Use `varnish_log` to change varnish's log settings.

You can connect to the Varnish admin interface by logging in to your node and running telnet:

**user@server:~$ sudo telnet localhost 6082**

See also

▶ Find out more about Varnish at `https://www.varnish-cache.org/`

▶ You can find the `varnish` cookbook on GitHub at `https://github.com/rackspace-cookbooks/varnish`

▶ The *Managing Ruby on Rails applications* recipe in this chapter

# Managing your local workstation

You know the drill. You get a brand new MacBook and need to set up all your software—again. Chef can help here, too.

We will take a look at how to install applications and tweak settings on your local development box with Chef.

This example is based on recipes for OS X only, but you can tweak it to run on Windows or Linux, too.

## Getting ready

First, we need to prepare our own repository for our individual setup:

1.  Fork the `github.com/mmarschall/kitchenplan-config` repository:

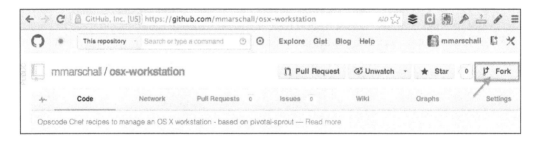

2.  Clone it to your local development box, replacing `<YOUR GITHUB USER>` with the name of your GitHub account:

    ```
    mma@laptop:~/ $ git clone https://github.com/<YOUR GITHUB USER>/
    kitchenplan-config.git
    ```

3. Go into your clone of the `kitchenplan-config` repository:

   **mma@laptop:~/ $ cd kitchenplan-config**

4. Make sure you have the `kitchenplan` gem installed by running the following code:

   **mma@laptop:~/kitchenplan-config $ gem install kitchenplan**

   ```
   ...TRUNCATED OUTPUT...
   Installing kitchenplan (2.1.18)
   ...TRUNCATED OUTPUT...
   ```

## How to do it...

Let's set up Kitchenplan to use a few readymade recipes:

1. Make sure you have a configuration for your user that tells Kitchenplan what to install on your box:

   **mma@laptop:~/kitchenplan-config $ subl config/people/<YOUR OSX USER>.yml**

   ```
   recipes:
       global:
       mac_os_x:
           - osxdefaults::dock_position_the_dock_on_the_left_side
   attributes:
       homebrewalt:
           cask_apps:
               - free-ruler
   ```

2. Commit and push your changes to your `kitchenplan-config` repository:

   **mma@laptop:~/kitchenplan-config $ git add config/people/<YOUR OSX USER>.yml**

   **mma@laptop:~/kitchenplan-config $ git commit -a -m "initial config"**

   **mma@laptop:~/kitchenplan-config $ git push origin master**

3. Set up `Kitchenplan` on your development box. Choose `y` when asked whether you have a `config` repository and provide the GitHub URL of your `kitchenplan-config` repository:

   **mma@laptop:~/kitchenplan-config $ kitchenplan setup**

   ```
   Do you have a config repository? [y,n] y
   Please enter the clone URL of your git config repository: git@
   github.com:mmarschall/kitchenplan-config.git
   ```

```
-> Making sure /opt exists and I can write to it
        run   sudo mkdir -p /opt from "."
Password:
        run   sudo chown -R mma /opt from "."
sh: line 0: cd: /opt/kitchenplan: No such file or directory
-> Fetching git@github.com:mmarschall/kitchenplan-config.git to /
opt/kitchenplan.
        run   git clone -q git@github.com:mmarschall/kitchenplan-
config.git kitchenplan from "/opt"
        run   git submodule init from "/opt/kitchenplan"
        run   git submodule update from "/opt/kitchenplan"
  ...TRUNCATED OUTPUT...
```

4.  Let `Kitchenplan` provision your box:

    **mma@laptop:~/kitchenplan-config $ kitchenplan provision**

    ```
    ...TRUNCATED OUTPUT...
      * homebrewalt_cask[free-ruler] action cask

      * execute[installing cask free-ruler] action run
        - execute sudo -u mma /usr/local/bin/brew cask install
    --appdir=/Applications free-ruler
    ...TRUNCATED OUTPUT...
    Recipe: osxdefaults::dock_position_the_dock_on_the_left_side
      * osxdefaults_defaults[Move the Dock to the left side of the
    screen] action write

      * execute[Move the Dock to the left side of the screen - com.
    apple.dock - orientation] action run
        - execute defaults write "com.apple.dock" "orientation"
    -string left
    ...TRUNCATED OUTPUT...
    => Installation complete!
    ```

5.  Now, your dock should be located at the left-hand side of the screen and the application **Free Ruler** should show up in your `Applications` folder.

## How it works...

Kitchenplan is a quick and easy way to configure your box. It uses **Librarian** and Chef solo to manage cookbooks. That's why Kitchenplan still uses Chef 11 at the time of writing this book.

Kitchenplan setup puts everything it needs into the `/opt/kitchenplan` directory. It will check out your `kitchenplan-config` repository and run Chef solo from there.

You can configure what to install in YAML files that are placed in the config directory of your kitchenplan-config repository. You can configure OS X using the mac_os_x recipe and you can install applications using homebrew by listing them in the attributes section of your config file:

```
recipes:
    global:
    mac_os_x:
        - osxdefaults::dock_position_the_dock_on_the_left_side
attributes:
    homebrewalt:
        cask_apps:
            - free-ruler
```

Kitchenplan will use Librarian to install all cookbooks defined in Cheffile which is located in your kitchenplan-config repository and then converge all recipes listed in your YAML files. Before converging, it will set all the given node attributes that will be used by the recipes.

## There's more...

You can create various config files for your users and groups, and a default.yml. Kitchenplan will merge all YAML files before provisioning your box using the currently logged in username to find the correct file in the config/people directory.

## See also

- Find Kitchenplan at https://github.com/kitchenplan/kitchenplan.
- You can find more configuration examples here: https://github.com/kitchenplan/kitchenplan-config-test and here https://github.com/roderik/kitchenplan-config.

# 7
# Servers and Cloud Infrastructure

*"The interesting thing about cloud computing is that we've redefined cloud computing to include everything that we already do."*

*Richard Stallman*

In this chapter, we will cover the following recipes:

- ▶ Creating your infrastructure using Chef Provisioning
- ▶ Creating cookbooks from a running system with Blueprint
- ▶ Running the same command on many machines at once
- ▶ Setting up SNMP for external monitoring services
- ▶ Deploying a Nagios monitoring server
- ▶ Building high-availability services using heartbeat
- ▶ Using HAProxy to load-balance multiple web servers
- ▶ Using custom bootstrap scripts
- ▶ Managing firewalls with iptables
- ▶ Managing fail2ban to ban malicious IP addresses
- ▶ Managing Amazon EC2 instances
- ▶ Loading your Chef infrastructure from a file with spiceweasel and knife

# Introduction

In the preceding chapters, we mostly looked at individual nodes. Now, it's time to consider your infrastructure as a whole. We'll see how to manage services spanning multiple machines, such as load balancers, and how to manage the networking aspects of your infrastructure.

# Creating your infrastructure using Chef Provisioning

You know how to use Chef to manage the software on individual machines and you know how to use knife to bootstrap individual nodes. Chef Provisioning helps you to use the power of Chef to create your whole infrastructure for you.

No matter whether you want to create a cluster of Vagrant boxes, Docker instances, or Cloud servers, Chef Provisioning lets you define your infrastructure in a simple recipe and run it idempotently.

Let's see how to create a Vagrant machine using a Chef recipe.

## Getting ready

Make sure that you have your `Berksfile`, `my_cookbook` and `web_server` roles ready to create an nginx site, as described in *Creating nginx virtual hosts* section in *chapter 6, Users and Applications*.

## How to do it...

Let's see how to create a Vagrant machine and install nginx on it:

1. Describe your Vagrant machine in a recipe called `mycluster.rb`:

   **mma@laptop:~/chef-repo $ subl mycluster.rb**

   ```
   require 'chef/provisioning'

   with_driver 'vagrant'
   with_machine_options :vagrant_options => { 'vm.box' => 'opscode-
   ubuntu-14.04' }

   machine 'web01' do
     role 'web_server'
   end
   ```

2.  Install all required cookbooks in your local chef-repo:

    **mma@laptop:~/chef-repo $ berks install**

    **mma@laptop:~/chef-repo $ berks vendor cookbooks**

    ```
    Resolving cookbook dependencies...
    Using apt (2.6.1)
    ...TRUNCATED OUTPUT...
    Vendoring yum-epel (0.6.0) to cookbooks/yum-epel
    ```

3.  Run the Chef client in local mode to bring up the Vagrant machine and execute a Chef run on it:

    **mma@laptop:~/chef-repo $ chef-client -z mycluster.rb**

    ```
    [2015-03-08T21:09:39+01:00] INFO: Starting chef-zero on host
    localhost, port 8889 with repository at repository at /Users/mma/
    work/chef-repo
    ...TRUNCATED OUTPUT...
    Recipe: @recipe_files::/Users/mma/work/chef-repo/mycluster.rb
       * machine[webserver] action converge[2015-03-08T21:09:43+01:00]
    INFO: Processing machine[web01] action converge (@recipe_files::/
    Users/mma/work/chef-repo/mycluster.rb line 6)
    ...TRUNCATED OUTPUT...
    [2015-03-08T21:09:47+01:00] INFO: Executing sudo chef-client -l
    info on vagrant@127.0.0.1

          [web01] [2015-03-08T20:09:21+00:00] INFO: Forking chef
    instance to converge...
                         Starting Chef Client, version 12.1.0
                         ...TRUNCATED OUTPUT...
                         Chef Client finished, 18/25 resources updated in
    73.839065458 seconds
    ...TRUNCATED OUTPUT...
    [2015-03-08T21:11:05+01:00] INFO: Completed chef-client -l info on
    vagrant@127.0.0.1: exit status 0
          - run 'chef-client -l info' on web01
    [2015-03-08T21:11:05+01:00] INFO: Chef Run complete in 82.948293
    seconds
    ...TRUNCATED OUTPUT...
    Chef Client finished, 1/1 resources updated in 85.914979 seconds
    ```

4.  Change into the directory where Chef put the Vagrant configuration:

    **mma@laptop:~/chef-repo $ cd ~/.chef/vms**

5.  Validate that there is a Vagrant machine named `web01` running:

```
mma@laptop:~/.chef/vms $ vagrant status

Current machine states:

web01                      running (virtualbox)
```

6.  Validate that nginx is installed and running on the Vagrant machine:

```
mma@laptop:~/.chef/vms $ vagrant ssh
vagrant@web01:~$ wget localhost:80

...TRUNCATED OUTPUT...
2015-03-08 22:14:45 (2.80 MB/s) - 'index.html' saved [21/21]
```

## How it works...

Chef Provisioning comes with a selection of drivers for all kinds of infrastructures, including Fog (supporting Amazon EC2, OpenStack, and others), VMware VSphere, Vagrant (supporting Virtualbox and VMware Fusion), various Containers, such as LXC Docker and Secure Shell (SSH).

In this recipe, we make sure that we can use the directives provided by Chef Provisioning by requiring `chef/provisioning` library.

Then, we configure the driver that we want to use. We use Vagrant and tell Chef to use the `opscode-ubuntu-14.04` Vagrant box to spin up our machine.

Using the machine resource, we ask Chef to spin up a Vagrant machine and configure it using Chef by applying the role `web_server`.

The `web_server` role uses the cookbook `my_cookbook` to configure the newly created Vagrant machine. To make sure that all the required cookbooks are available to Chef, we use `berks install` and `berks vendor cookbooks`. The `berks vendor cookbooks` installs all the required cookbooks in the local cookbooks directory. The Chef client can access the cookbooks here, without the need for a Chef server.

Finally, we use the Chef client to execute our Chef Provisioning recipe. It will spin up the defined Vagrant machine and execute a Chef client run on it.

Chef Provisioning will put the Vagrant Virtual Machine (VM) definition into the directory `~/.chef/vms`. To manage the Vagrant VM, you need to change to this directory.

## There's more...

Instead of using the `with_driver` directive, you can use the `CHEF_DRIVER` environment variable:

```
mma@laptop:~/chef-repo $ CHEF_DRIVER=vagrant chef-client -z
mycluster.rb
```

You can create multiple instances of a machine by using the `machine_image` directive in your recipe:

```
machine_image 'web_server' do
  role 'web_server'
end
1.upto(2) do |i|
  machine "web0#{i}" do
    from_image 'web_server'
  end
end
```

## See also

▸ Find the source code of the Chef Provisioning library at GitHub: `https://github.com/chef/chef-provisioning`

▸ Find the Chef Provisioning documentation at `https://docs.chef.io/provisioning.html`

▸ Learn how to set up a Chef server using Chef Provisioning: `https://www.chef.io/blog/2014/12/15/sysadvent-day-14-using-chef-provisioning-to-build-chef-server/`

# Creating cookbooks from a running system with Blueprint

Everyone has it: that one server in the corner of the data center, which no one dares to touch anymore. It's like a precious snowflake: unique and infinitely fragile. How do you get such a server under configuration management?

**Blueprint** is a tool that can find out exactly what's on your server. It records all directories, packages, configuration files, and so on.

Blueprint can spit out that information about your server in various formats; one of them is a Chef recipe. You can use such a generated Chef recipe as a basis to rebuild that one unique snowflake server.

Let's see how to do that.

## Getting ready

Make sure that you have Python and Git installed on the node that you want to run Blueprint on. Install Python and Git by running the following command:

```
user@server:~$ sudo apt-get install git python python-pip
```

## How to do it...

Let's see how to install Blueprint and create a Chef cookbook for our node:

1. Install Blueprint using the following command:

    ```
    user@server:~$ sudo pip install blueprint
    ```

2. Configure Git:

    ```
    user@server:~$ git config --global user.email "YOUR EMAIL"
    user@server:~$ git config --global user.name "YOUR NAME"
    ```

3. Run Blueprint. Replace my-server with any name you want to use for your Blueprint. This name will become the name of the cookbook in the following step:

    ```
    user@server:~$ sudo blueprint create my-server
    # [blueprint] caching excluded APT packages
    # [blueprint] searching for Yum packages to exclude
    # [blueprint] parsing blueprintignore(5) rules
    # [blueprint] searching for Python packages
    # [blueprint] searching for Yum packages
    # [blueprint] searching for configuration files
    ...TRUNCATED OUTPUT...
    # [blueprint] searching for APT packages
    # [blueprint] searching for PEAR/PECL packages
    # [blueprint] searching for Ruby gems
    # [blueprint] searching for npm packages
    # [blueprint] searching for software built from source
    # [blueprint] searching for service dependencies
    ```

4. Create a Chef cookbook from your blueprint:

   **user@server:~$ blueprint show -C my-server**

   ```
   my-server/recipes/default.rb
   ```

5. Validate the content of the generated file:

   **user@server:~$ cat my-server/recipes/default.rb**

   ```
   #
   # Automatically generated by blueprint(7).  Edit at your own risk.
   #
   directory('/etc/apt/apt.conf.d') do
     group 'root'
     mode '0755'
     owner 'root'
     recursive true
   end
   ...TRUNCATED OUTPUT...
   service('ssh') do
     action [:enable, :start]
     provider Chef::Provider::Service::Upstart
     subscribes :restart, resources('cookbook_file[/etc/default/nfs-
   common]', 'cookbook_file[/etc/default/ntfs-3g]', 'cookbook_file[/
   etc/default/keyboard]', 'cookbook_file[/etc/pam.d/common-session-
   noninteractive]', 'cookbook_file[/etc/default/console-setup]',
   'cookbook_file[/etc/pam.d/common-auth]', 'cookbook_file[/etc/
   pam.d/common-session]', 'package[openssh-server]')
   end
   ```

## How it works...

Blueprint is a Python package, which finds out all the relevant configuration data of your node and stores it in a Git repository. Each Blueprint has its own name.

You can ask Blueprint to show the contents of its Git repository in various formats. Using the -C flag to the blueprint show command creates a Chef cookbook containing everything you need in that cookbook's default recipe. It stores the cookbook in the directory from where you run Blueprint and uses the Blueprint name as the cookbook name, as shown in the following code:

**user@server:~$ ls -l my-server/**

```
total 8
drwxrwxr-x 3 vagrant vagrant 4096 Mar  5 06:01 files
-rw-rw-r-- 1 vagrant vagrant    0 Mar  5 06:01 metadata.rb
drwxrwxr-x 2 vagrant vagrant 4096 Mar  5 06:01 recipes
```

## There's more...

You can inspect your Blueprints using specialized show commands in the following way:

```
user@server:~$ blueprint show-packages my-server

    ...TRUNCATED OUTPUT...
    apt watershed 7
    apt wireless-regdb 2013.02.13-1ubuntu1
    apt zlib1g-dev 1:1.2.8.dfsg-1ubuntu1
    python-pip blueprint 3.4.2
```

The preceding command shows all kinds of installed packages. Other show commands are as follows:

 ▸ show-files

 ▸ show-services

 ▸ show-sources

Blueprint can output your server configuration as a **shell script**, as shown in the following command line:

```
user@server:~$ blueprint show -S my-server
```

You can use this script as a basis for a knife bootstrap as described in the *Using custom bootstrap scripts* recipe in this chapter.

## See also

 ▸ Read about all you can do with Blueprint at http://devstructure.com/blueprint/

 ▸ You find the source code of Blueprint at https://github.com/devstructure/blueprint

# Running the same command on many machines at once

A simple problem with so many self-scripted solutions is logging in to multiple boxes in parallel, executing the same command on every box at once. No matter whether you want to check the status of a certain service or look at some critical system data on all boxes, being able to log in to many servers in parallel can save you a lot of time and hassle (imagine forgetting one of your seven web servers when disabling the basic authentication for your website).

## How to do it...

Let's try to execute a few simple commands on multiple servers in parallel:

1. Retrieve the status of the `nginx` processes from all your web servers (assuming you have at least one host up and running, which has the role `web_server`):

   **mma@laptop:~/chef-repo $ knife ssh 'role:web_server' 'sudo sv status nginx'**

   ```
   www1.prod.example.com run: nginx: (pid 12356) 204667s; run:
   log: (pid 1135) 912026s
   www2.prod.example.com run: nginx: (pid 19155) 199923s; run:
   log: (pid 1138) 834124s
   www.test.example.com  run: nginx: (pid 30299) 1332114s;
   run: log: (pid 30271) 1332117s
   ```

2. Display the uptime of all your nodes in your staging environment running on Amazon EC2:

   **mma@laptop:~/chef-repo $ knife ssh 'chef_environment:staging AND ec2:*' uptime**

   ```
   ec2-XXX-XXX-XXX-XXX.eu-west-1.compute.amazonaws.com
   21:58:15 up 23 days, 13:19,  1 user,  load average: 1.32,
   1.88, 2.34
   ec2-XXX-XXX-XXX-XXX.eu-west-1.compute.amazonaws.com
   21:58:15 up 10 days, 13:19,  1 user,  load average: 1.51,
   1.52, 1.54
   ```

## How it works...

First, you have to specify a query to find your nodes. It is usually a good idea to test your queries by running a command such as `uptime` (instead of dangerous commands such as `sudo restart now`). Your query will obviously use the node index and the complete `knife search` query syntax is available.

Knife will run a search and connect to each node found executing the given command on every single one. It will collect and display all outputs received by the nodes.

## There's more...

You can open terminals to all the nodes identified by your query by using either `tmux` or `screen` as commands.

If you don't want to use a search query, you can list the desired nodes using the -m option:

```
mma@laptop:~/chef-repo $ knife ssh -m 'www1.prod.example.com www2.prod.
example.com' uptime
```

```
www1.prod.example.com  22:10:00 up 9 days, 16:00,  1 user,  load
average: 0.44, 0.40, 0.38
www2.prod.example.com    22:10:00 up 15 days, 10:28,  1 user,
load average: 0.02, 0.05, 0.06
```

## See also

▶ The knife search syntax is described at the following location: http://docs.chef.
io/knife_search.html

▶ Find more examples at http://docs.chef.io/knife_ssh.html

# Setting up SNMP for external monitoring services

**Simple Network Management Protocol** (**SNMP**) is the standard way to monitor all your network devices. You can use Chef to install the SNMP service on your node and configure it to match your needs.

## Getting ready

Make sure that you have a cookbook named my_cookbook and that the run_list of your node includes my_cookbook, as described in the *Creating and using cookbooks*, section in *Chapter 1, Chef Infrastructure*.

Create your Berksfile in your Chef repository including my_cookbook:

```
mma@laptop:~/chef-repo $ subl Berksfile
```

```
cookbook 'my_cookbook', path: './cookbooks/my_cookbook'
```

## How to do it...

Let's change some attributes and install SNMP on our node:

1. Add the dependency on the snmp cookbook to your cookbook's metadata.rb:

   ```
   mma@laptop:~/chef-repo $ subl cookbooks/my_cookbook/metadata.rb
   ```

   ```
   depends "snmp"
   ```

2. Install the dependent cookbooks:

   **mma@laptop:~/chef-repo $ berks install**

   ```
   ...TRUNCATED OUTPUT...
   Installing snmp (3.0.1)
   Using my_cookbook (0.1.0) at './cookbooks/my_cookbook'
   ```

3. Edit your cookbook's default recipe:

   **mma@laptop:~/chef-repo $ subl cookbooks/my_cookbook/recipes/**
   **default.rb**

   ```
   node.default['snmp']['syslocationVirtual'] = "Vagrant VirtualBox"
   node.default['snmp']['syslocationPhysical'] = "My laptop"
   node.default['snmp']['full_systemview'] = true
   include_recipe "snmp"
   ```

4. Upload the modified cookbook to the Chef server:

   **mma@laptop:~/chef-repo $ berks upload**

   ```
   ...TRUNCATED OUTPUT...
   Uploaded snmp (3.0.1) to: 'https://api.opscode.com:443/
   organizations/awo'
   ...TRUNCATED OUTPUT...
   ```

5. Run the Chef client on your node:

   **user@server:~$ sudo chef-client**

   ```
   ...TRUNCATED OUTPUT...
      - restart service service[snmpd]
   ...TRUNCATED OUTPUT...
   ```

6. Validate that you can query snmpd:

   **user@server:~$ snmpwalk -v 1 localhost -c public**
   **iso.3.6.1.2.1.1.5.0**

   ```
   iso.3.6.1.2.1.1.5.0 = STRING: "vagrant"
   ```

## How it works...

First, we need to tell our cookbook that we want to use the snmp cookbook by adding a depends call to our metadata file. Then, we modify some of the attributes provided by the snmp cookbook. The attributes are used to fill the /etc/snmp/snmp.conf file, which is based on the template provided by the snmp cookbook.

The last step is to include the snmp cookbook's default recipe in our own recipe. This will instruct the Chef client to install snmpd as a service on our node.

## There's more...

You can override `['snmp']['community']` and `['snmp']['trapcommunity']` as well.

## See also

▶ Find the `snmp` cookbook on GitHub at `https://github.com/atomic-penguin/cookbook-snmp`

# Deploying a Nagios monitoring server

Nagios is one of the most widely spread monitoring packages available. Chef provides you with a cookbook to install a Nagios server, as well as Nagios clients. It provides ways to configure service checks, service groups and so on, using data bags instead of manually editing Nagios configuration files.

## Getting ready

Make sure that you have a cookbook named `my_cookbook` and that the `run_list` of your node includes `my_cookbook`, as described in the *Creating and using cookbooks* recipe in *Chapter 1, Chef Infrastructure*:

1. Create your `Berksfile` in your Chef repository including the nagios cookbook:

   **mma@laptop:~/chef-repo $ subl Berksfile**

   ```
   cookbook 'resource-control'
   cookbook 'nagios'
   ```

2. Install the `nagios` cookbook:

   **mma@laptop:~/chef-repo $ berks install**

   ```
   Using nagios (7.0.2)
   ...TRUNCATED OUTPUT...
   ```

3. Upload the `nagios` cookbook to the Chef server:

   **mma@laptop:~/chef-repo $ berks upload**

   ```
   ...TRUNCATED OUTPUT...
   Uploading nagios (7.0.2) to: 'https://api.chef.io:443/
   organizations/awo'
   ...TRUNCATED OUTPUT...
   ```

## How to do it...

Let's create a user (called mma in the following example) for the Nagios web interface and set up a Nagios server with a check for SSH.

1. Create a password hash for your Nagios user:

   ```
   mma@laptop:~/chef-repo $ htpasswd -n -s mma
   ```

   ```
   New password:
   Re-type new password:
   mma:{SHA}AcrFI+aFqjxDLBKctCtzW/LkVxg=
   ```

    You may want to use an online htpasswd generator such as http://
   www.htaccesstools.com/htpasswd-generator/, if you don't have
   htpasswd installed on your system.

2. Create a data bag for your Nagios user, using the password hash from the preceding step. Further, we use mma as the username and mm@agilweboperations.com as the e-mail address. Please use your username and email address instead of mine:

   ```
   mma@laptop:~/chef-repo $ subl data_bags/users/mma.json
   ```

   ```
   {
     "id": "mma",
     "htpasswd": "{SHA}AcrFI+aFqjxDLBKctCtzW/LkVxg=",
     "groups": "sysadmin",
     "nagios": {
       "email": "mm@agileweboperations.com"
     }
   }
   ```

3. Upload the user data bag to your Chef server:

   ```
   mma@laptop:~/chef-repo $ knife data bag from file users mma.json
   ```

   ```
   Updated data_bag_item[users::mma]
   ```

4. Create a data bag for your service definitions:

   ```
   mma@laptop:~/chef-repo $ knife data bag create nagios_services
   ```

   ```
   Created data_bag_item[nagios_service]
   ```

5. Create a data bag item for your first service:

   ```
   mma@laptop:~/chef-repo $ mkdir -p data_bags/nagios_services
   mma@laptop:~/chef-repo $ subl data_bags/nagios_services/ssh.json
   ```

```
{
  "id": "ssh",
  "hostgroup_name": "linux",
  "command_line": "$USER1$/check_ssh $HOSTADDRESS$"
}
```

6. Upload your service data bag item:

**mma@laptop:~/chef-repo $ knife data bag from file nagios_services ssh.json**

```
Updated data_bag_item[nagios_services::ssh]
```

7. Create a role for your Nagios server node:

**mma@laptop:~/chef-repo $ subl roles/monitoring.rb**

```
name "monitoring"
description "Nagios server"
run_list(
  "recipe[apt]",
  "recipe[nagios::default]"
)

default_attributes(
  "nagios" => {
    "server_auth_method" => "htauth"
  },
  "apache" => {
  "mpm" => "prefork"
  }
)
```

8. Upload your monitoring role to your Chef server:

**mma@laptop:~/chef-repo $ knife role from file monitoring.rb**

```
Updated Role monitoring!
```

9. Apply the monitoring role to your node called server:

**mma@laptop:~/chef-repo $ knife node run_list set server 'role[monitoring]'**

```
server:
  run_list: role[monitoring]
```

10. Run the Chef client on your node:

**user@server:~$ sudo chef-client**

```
...TRUNCATED OUTPUT...
[2015-06-12T22:50:09+00:00] INFO: Processing service[nagios]
action start (nagios::server line 284)
...TRUNCATED OUTPUT...
```

11. Validate the **Nagios** web interface by navigating to your node on `port 80`. Use the user/password combination that you set for your user in the user's data bag:

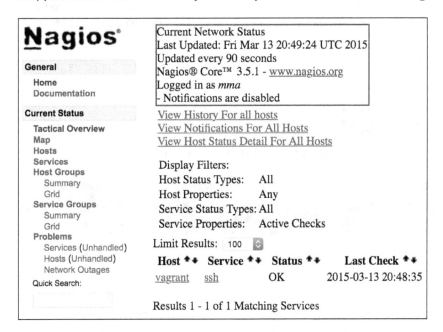

## How it works...

First, we set up a user to manage the Nagios web interface. We create a data bag called `users` and a data bag item for your user (in the preceding example, the user is called `mma`. You will change that to the username you desire).

By default, Nagios will set up web access for every user in the `sysadmins` group, which has a Nagios email address defined in the data bag.

As we want to use HTTP basic authentication for the Nagios web interface, we need to create a password hash to put into our user data bag.

To make Nagios use HTTP basic authentication, we need to set the `server_auth_method` attribute to `htauth` when defining the `monitoring` role, which we assign to our node.

Then, we configure a service check for SSH using a default template for the Nagios configuration file. To do so, we create a data bag and data bag item for our service.

Finally, we run the Chef client on our node and validate that we can log in with our user/password to the Nagios web frontend running on our node, and make sure that the SSH service check is running.

## There's more...

You can change the default group to choose users for the Nagios web interface by modifying the `['nagios']['users_databag_group']` attribute in the role you use to configure your Nagios server.

You can set up your checks using your own templates and you can configure the contact groups and so on.

## See also

▶   Find the `nagios` cookbook on GitHub at: `https://github.com/tas50/nagios`

# Building high-availability services using heartbeat

If you want to offer any IP-based service with automatic failover to provide **high availability (HA)**, you can use heartbeat to create an HA cluster.

Heartbeat will run on two or more nodes and ensure that the IP address you chose to make highly available will switch to a working node, if one of them goes down. This way, you have a failover IP address, which is guaranteed to reach a running host, as long as there is one left.

Let's take a look at how to install heartbeat on your nodes and configure it with a failover IP address.

## Getting ready

Make sure that you have two machines, named `ha1` and `ha2`, up and running. You can use a `Vagrantfile` like this or use Chef Provisioning to set them up. You need to replace `awo` with a short name of your own Chef organization:

```
def define_node(config, node_name, ip_address=nil, the_recipe=nil)
  config.vm.define node_name do |node|
    node.vm.hostname = node_name.to_s
    node.vm.network :private_network, ip: ip_address if ip_address
```

```
      node.vm.provision :chef_client do |chef|
        chef.provisioning_path = "/etc/chef"
        chef.chef_server_url = "https://api.opscode.com/organizations/
awo"
        chef.validation_key_path = ".chef/awo-validator.pem"
        chef.validation_client_name = "awo-validator"
        chef.node_name = node_name.to_s
        chef.add_recipe the_recipe if the_recipe
      end
    end
  end


  Vagrant.configure("2") do |config|
    config.vm.box = "opscode-ubuntu-14.04"
    config.vm.box_url = "https://opscode-vm-bento.s3.amazonaws.com/
vagrant/virtualbox/opscode_ubuntu-14.04_chef-provisionerless.box"
    config.omnibus.chef_version = :latest
    config.berkshelf.enabled = true

    config.vm.provider :virtualbox do |vb|
      vb.customize ['modifyvm', :id, '--natdnshostresolver1', 'on']
    end

    define_node(config, :ha1, "192.168.0.101", 'my_cookbook')
    define_node(config, :ha2, "192.168.0.102", 'my_cookbook')
  end
```

Start both machines by using `vagrant up`.

 You need to have the Vagrant `Berkshelf` plugin installed:

mma@laptop:~/chef-repo $ vagrant plugin install
vagrant-berkshelf

Make sure that you have a cookbook called `my_cookbook` and `run_list` of all the nodes you want to add to your HA cluster, including `my_cookbook`, as described in the *Creating and using cookbooks* recipe in *Chapter 1, Chef Infrastructure*.

Create your `Berksfile` in your Chef repository, including `my_cookbook`:

**mma@laptop:~/chef-repo $ subl Berksfile**

```
    cookbook 'my_cookbook', path: './cookbooks/my_cookbook'
```

## How to do it...

Let's use the community-provided `heartbeat` cookbook and configure it to work with our nodes:

1.  Edit your cookbook's `metadata.rb` to add the dependency to the `heartbeat` cookbook:

    **mma@laptop:~/chef-repo $ subl cookbooks/my_cookbook/metadata.rb**

    ```
    depends 'apt'
    depends "heartbeat"
    Install your cookbook's dependencies:
    mma@laptop:~/chef-repo $ berks install
    Using my_cookbook (0.1.0) at './cookbooks/my_cookbook'
    ...TRUNCATED OUTPUT...
    ```

2.  Edit your cookbook's default recipe, replacing `192.168.0.100` with the IP address, which should be highly available (your failover IP address) and `eth1` with the network interface that you want to use:

    **mma@laptop:~/chef-repo $ subl cookbooks/my_cookbook/recipes/default.rb**

    ```
    include_recipe "apt"
    include_recipe "heartbeat"

    heartbeat "heartbeat" do
      authkeys "MySecrectAuthPassword"
      autojoin "none"
      warntime 5
      deadtime 15
      initdead 60
      keepalive 2
      logfacility "syslog"
      interface "eth1"
      mode "bcast"
      udpport 694
      auto_failback true

      resources "192.168.0.100"

      search "name:ha*"
    end
    ```

3.  Upload the modified cookbook to the Chef server:

    **mma@laptop:~/chef-repo $ berks upload**

    ```
    ...TRUNCATED OUTPUT...
    Uploading my_cookbook (0.1.0) to: 'https://api.chef.io:443/
    organizations/awo'
    ...TRUNCATED OUTPUT...
    ```

4.  Run the Chef client on both nodes:

    **user@server:~$ sudo chef-client**

    ```
    ...TRUNCATED OUTPUT...
    * service[heartbeat] action restart[2015-03-14T22:02:26+00:00]
    INFO: service[heartbeat] restarted

       - restart service service[heartbeat]

    ...TRUNCATED OUTPUT...
    ```

5.  Validate that your first node holds the failover IP address:

    **user@ha1:~$ ifconfig -a**

    ```
    eth1      Link encap:Ethernet   HWaddr 08:00:27:12:7b:fc
    ...TRUNCATED OUTPUT...
    eth1:0    Link encap:Ethernet   HWaddr 08:00:27:12:7b:fc
              inet addr:192.168.0.100  Bcast:192.168.0.255
    Mask:255.255.255.0
              UP BROADCAST RUNNING MULTICAST  MTU:1500  Metric:1
    ...TRUNCATED OUTPUT...
    lo        Link encap:Local Loopback
    ```

6.  Validate that your second node does not hold the failover IP address:

    **user@ha2:~$ ifconfig -a**

    ```
    eth1      Link encap:Ethernet   HWaddr 08:00:27:62:11:58

    lo        Link encap:Local Loopback
    ```

7.  Stop the heartbeat service on your first node and validate that the failover IP address moves to your second node:

    **user@ha1:~$ sudo service heartbeat stop**

    **user@ha2:~$ ifconfig -a**

```
eth1       Link encap:Ethernet  HWaddr 08:00:27:62:11:58
...TRUNCATED OUTPUT...

eth1:0     Link encap:Ethernet  HWaddr 08:00:27:62:11:58
           inet addr:192.168.0.100  Bcast:192.168.0.255
Mask:255.255.255.0
           UP BROADCAST RUNNING MULTICAST  MTU:1500
Metric:1

lo         Link encap:Local Loopback
...TRUNCATED OUTPUT...
```

## How it works...

The `heartbeat` cookbook installs the heartbeat service on all your nodes. In this example, we assume that your hostnames are `ha1`, `ha2`, and so on.

Then, we need to configure our HA cluster. In the preceding example, we do this within our recipe.

First, you need to define a password. The nodes will use this password to authenticate themselves to each other.

Setting `autojoin` to `none` will make it impossible that new nodes get added outside of your Chef client runs.

Next, we set the timeouts to tell heartbeat when to act, if something seems wrong. The timeouts are given in seconds.

In the preceding example, we ask heartbeat to use the broadcast method on the network interface `eth1`.

The `resources` is your failover IP address. This IP address will be highly available in your setup.

The `search` call contains the query to find all the nodes to be included in the heartbeat setup. In our example, we search for nodes with names starting with `ha`.

After uploading all cookbooks and running the Chef client, we can verify our setup by querying the heartbeat status on both the nodes.

By stopping the heartbeat service on the node that currently has the failover IP address assigned to it, the second node will take over automatically.

## There's more...

You can configure the heartbeat by setting attributes in a role as well. In this case, it would make sense to set the search attribute to find all the nodes that have the role.

## See also

- ▸ Find the `heartbeat` cookbook on GitHub at `https://github.com/opscode-cookbooks/heartbeat`

- ▸ Read more about how to configure heartbeat at `http://www.linux-ha.org/doc/users-guide/_creating_an_initial_heartbeat_configuration.html`

- ▸ Find the complete reference of the heartbeat configuration file at `http://linux-ha.org/wiki/Ha.cf`

# Using HAProxy to load-balance multiple web servers

You have a successful website and it is time to scale out to multiple web servers to support it. **HAProxy** is a very fast and reliable load-balancer and proxy for TCP- and HTTP-based applications.

You can put it in front of your web servers and let it distribute the load. If you configure it on an HA cluster by using heartbeat (see the *Building high-availability services using heartbeat* recipe in this chapter), you have a complete high-availability solution available.

## Getting ready

Make sure that you have at least one node registered on your Chef server with the role `web_server` in its run list. The following example will set up HAProxy so that it routes all requests to all your nodes that have the `web_server` role.

Make sure that you have a cookbook called `my_cookbook` and that the `run_list` of your node includes `my_cookbook`, as described in the *Creating and using cookbooks* recipe in *Chapter 1*, Chef Infrastructure.

Create your `Berksfile` in your Chef repository including `my_cookbook`:

**mma@laptop:~/chef-repo $ subl Berksfile**

```
cookbook 'my_cookbook', path: './cookbooks/my_cookbook'
```

## How to do it...

Let's see how to set up a simple HAProxy balancing to all nodes that have the `web_server` role:

1.  Edit your cookbook's `metadata.rb`:

    **mma@laptop:~/chef-repo $ subl cookbooks/my_cookbook/metadata.rb**

    ```
    depends "haproxy"
    ```

2.  Install your cookbook's dependencies:

    **mma@laptop:~/chef-repo $ berks install**

    ```
    Using my_cookbook (0.1.0) at './cookbooks/my_cookbook'
    ...TRUNCATED OUTPUT...
    ```

3.  Edit your cookbook's default recipe:

    **mma@laptop:~/chef-repo $ subl cookbooks/my_cookbook/recipes/
    default.rb**

    ```
    node.default['haproxy']['httpchk'] = true
    node.default['haproxy']['x_forwarded_for'] = true
    node.default['haproxy']['app_server_role'] = "web_server"

    include_recipe "haproxy::app_lb"
    include_recipe "haproxy::default"
    ```

4.  Upload the modified cookbook to the Chef server:

    **mma@laptop:~/chef-repo $ berks upload**

    ```
    ...TRUNCATED OUTPUT...
    Uploading my_cookbook (0.1.0) to: 'https://api.chef.io:443/
    organizations/awo'
    ...TRUNCATED OUTPUT...
    ```

5.  Run the Chef client on your node:

    **user@server:~$ sudo chef-client**

    ```
    ...TRUNCATED OUTPUT...
    [2015-03-15T21:08:42+00:00] INFO: service[haproxy] restarted
    ...TRUNCATED OUTPUT...
    ```

6. Validate that the HAproxy admin interface runs on your node on `port 22002`:

# HAProxy version 1.4.24, released 2013/06/17

## Statistics Report for pid 3537

### > General process information

**pid** = 3537 (process #1, nbproc = 1)
**uptime** = 0d 0h00m41s
**system limits:** memmax = unlimited; ulimit-n = 8206
**maxsock** = 8206; **maxconn** = 4096; **maxpipes** = 0
current conns = 1; current pipes = 0/0
Running tasks: 1/3

| | active UP | | backup UP |
|---|---|---|---|
| | active UP, going down | | backup UP, going down |
| | active DOWN, going up | | backup DOWN, going up |
| | active or backup DOWN | | not checked |
| | active or backup DOWN for maintenance (MAINT) | | |

Note: UP with load-balancing disabled is reported as "NOLB"

### admin

| | Queue | | | Session rate | | | Sessions | | | | Bytes | | Denied | | Errors | | | Warr |
|---|---|---|---|---|---|---|---|---|---|---|---|---|---|---|---|---|---|---|
| | Cur | Max | Limit | Cur | Max | Limit | Cur | Max | Limit | Total | LbTot | In | Out | Req | Resp | Req | Conn | Resp | Retr |
| Frontend | | | | 1 | 1 | - | 1 | 1 | 2 000 | 1 | | 0 | 0 | 0 | 0 | 0 | | | |
| Backend | 0 | 0 | | 0 | 0 | | 0 | 0 | 2 000 | 0 | 0 | 0 | 0 | 0 | 0 | | 0 | 0 | 0 |

### http

| | Queue | | | Session rate | | | Sessions | | | | Bytes | | Denied | | Errors | | | Warr |
|---|---|---|---|---|---|---|---|---|---|---|---|---|---|---|---|---|---|---|
| | Cur | Max | Limit | Cur | Max | Limit | Cur | Max | Limit | Total | LbTot | In | Out | Req | Resp | Req | Conn | Resp | Retr |
| Frontend | | | | 0 | 0 | - | 0 | 0 | 2 000 | 0 | | 0 | 0 | 0 | 0 | 0 | | | |

### servers-http

## How it works...

First, we change some of the default values: setting `httpchk` to `true` makes sure that HAProxy takes backend servers out of the cluster, if they don't respond anymore.

The `x_forwarded_for` attribute tells HAProxy to set the X-Forwarded-For HTTP header. It will contain the client IP address. If you don't set that header, your web servers will only see the IP address of your HAProxy server in their access logs, instead of your client's IP addresses. This will make it very difficult to debug problems with your web applications.

The third attribute that we need to change is `app_server_role`. You can set whatever role your backend application servers have. The `haproxy` cookbook will include every node (using its `ipaddress` node attribute, as returned by Ohai) having this role within its cluster.

After overriding those attributes, we run the `app_lb` recipe from the `haproxy` cookbook. The `app_lb` recipe will install HAProxy from a package and run a search for all nodes having the configured role.

After uploading all cookbooks and running the Chef client, you'll find the HAProxy admin interface on your node at `port 22002`. Hitting your HAProxy node at `port 80` will forward your request to one of your web servers.

## See also

▶ Read about the *Managing Ruby on Rails applications* section in *Chapter 6, Users and Applications*

▶ Learn more about how you can search for nodes in Chef at `https://docs.chef.io/chef_search.html`

▶ Find HAproxy at `http://www.haproxy.org`

▶ Find the `haproxy` cookbook on GitHub at `https://github.com/hw-cookbooks/haproxy`

# Using custom bootstrap scripts

While creating a new node, you need to make sure that it has Chef installed on it. Knife offers the bootstrap subcommand to connect to a node via **Secure Shell** (**SSH**) and run a bootstrap script on the node.

The bootstrap script should install the Chef client on your node and register the node with your Chef server. Chef comes with a few default bootstrap scripts for various platforms. There are options to install the Chef client using the Omnibus installer packages, or Ruby gems.

If you want to modify the way your Chef client gets installed on your nodes, you can create and use custom bootstrap scripts.

Let's take a look at how to do this.

## Getting ready

Make sure that you have a node that is ready to become a Chef client and can SSH into it. In the following example, we'll assume that you have a username and password to log in to your node.

## How to do it...

Let's see how to execute our custom bootstrap script with knife to make our node a Chef client:

1. Create your basic bootstrap script from one of the existing Chef scripts:

   ```
   mma@laptop:~/chef-repo $ mkdir bootstrap
   ```

```
mma@laptop:~/chef-repo $ curl https://raw.githubusercontent.com/
chef/chef/master/lib/chef/knife/bootstrap/templates/chef-full.erb
-o bootstrap/my-chef-full.erb
```

```
  % Total    % Received % Xferd  Average Speed   Time    Time
Time  Current
                                 Dload  Upload   Total   Spent
Left  Speed
100  2352  100  2352    0      0  23106      0 --:--:-- --:--:--
--:--:-- 23287
```

2. Edit your custom bootstrap script:

   **mma@laptop:~/chef-repo $ subl bootstrap/my-chef-full.erb**

   ```
   mkdir -p /etc/chef

   cat > /etc/chef/greeting.txt <<'EOP'
   Ohai, Chef!
   EOP
   ```

3. Bootstrap your node using your modified custom bootstrap script. Replace
   192.168.0.100 with the IP address of your node and user with your SSH username:

   **mma@laptop:~/chef-repo $ knife bootstrap 192.168.0.100 -x user
   --template-file bootstrap/my-chef-full.erb --sudo**

   ```
   192.168.0.100 [2015-03-21T15:30:44+00:00] WARN: Node bootstrapped
   has an empty run list.
   ```

4. Validate the content of the generated file:

   **user@server:~$ cat /etc/chef/greeting.txt**

   ```
   Ohai, Chef!
   ```

## How it works...

The chef-full.erb bootstrap script uses the Omnibus installer to install the Chef client
and all its dependencies onto your node. It comes packaged with all the dependencies so
that you don't need to install a separate Ruby or additional gems on your node.

First, we download the bootstrap script as part of Chef. Then, we customize it as we like. Our
example of putting an additional text file is trivial so feel free to change it to whenever you need.

After changing our custom bootstrap script, we're only one command away from a fully
bootstrapped Chef node.

If you want to bootstrap a virtual machine like Vagrant to test your bootstrap script, you might need to use localhost as the node's IP address, and add -p 2222 to your command line to tell knife to connect through the forwarded SSH port of your VM.

## There's more...

If you already know the role your node should play or which recipes you want to run on your node, you can add a run list to your bootstrapping call:

```
mma@laptop:~/chef-repo $ knife bootstrap 192.168.0.100 -x user
--template-file bootstrap/my-chef-full.erb --sudo -r 'role[web_server]'
```

Here, we added the web_server role to the run the list of the nodes with the -r parameter.

## See also

▶ Read more about bootstrapping nodes with knife at http://docs.chef.io/ knife_bootstrap.html

▶ Find the chef-full bootstrap script here: https://github.com/chef/chef/ blob/master/lib/chef/knife/bootstrap/templates/chef-full.erb

# Managing firewalls with iptables

Securing your servers is very important. One basic way of shutting down quite a few attack vectors is running a firewall on your nodes. The firewall will make sure that only those network connections that hit the services you decide to allow are accepted.

On Ubuntu, iptables is one of the tools available for the job. Let's see how to set it up to make your servers more secure.

## Getting ready

Make sure that you have a cookbook called my_cookbook and that the run_list of your node includes my_cookbook, as described in the *Creating and using cookbooks* recipe in *Chapter 1*, Chef Infrastructure.

Create your Berksfile in your Chef repository including my_cookbook:

```
mma@laptop:~/chef-repo $ subl Berksfile

    cookbook 'my_cookbook', path: './cookbooks/my_cookbook'
```

## How to do it...

Let's set up `iptables` so that it blocks all network connections to your node and only accepts connections to the SSH and HTTP ports:

1. Edit your cookbook's `metadata.rb`:

   **mma@laptop:~/chef-repo $ subl cookbooks/my_cookbook/metadata.rb**

   ```
   depends "iptables"
   ```

2. Install your cookbook's dependencies:

   **mma@laptop:~/chef-repo $ berks install**

   ```
   Using my_cookbook (0.1.0) at './cookbooks/my_cookbook'
   ...TRUNCATED OUTPUT...
   ```

3. Edit your own cookbook's default recipe:

   **mma@laptop:~/chef-repo $ subl cookbooks/my_cookbook/recipes/default.rb**

   ```
   include_recipe "iptables"
   iptables_rule "ssh"
   iptables_rule "http"

   execute "ensure iptables is activated" do
     command "/usr/sbin/rebuild-iptables"
     creates "/etc/iptables/general"
     action :run
   end
   ```

4. Create a template for the SSH rule:

   **mma@laptop:~/chef-repo $ subl cookbooks/my_cookbook/templates/default/ssh.erb**

   ```
   # Allow ssh access to default port
   -A FWR -p tcp -m tcp --dport 22 -j ACCEPT
   ```

5. Create a template for the HTTP rule:

   **mma@laptop:~/chef-repo $ subl cookbooks/my_cookbook/templates/default/http.erb**

   ```
   -A FWR -p tcp -m tcp --dport 80 -j ACCEPT
   ```

6. Upload the modified cookbook to the Chef server:

```
mma@laptop:~/chef-repo $ berks upload
```

```
...TRUNCATED OUTPUT...
Uploading my_cookbook (0.1.0) to: 'https://api.chef.io:443/
organizations/awo'
...TRUNCATED OUTPUT...
```

7. Run the Chef client on your node:

```
user@server:~$ sudo chef-client
```

```
...TRUNCATED OUTPUT...
Recipe: iptables::default
  * execute[rebuild-iptables] action run
    - execute /usr/sbin/rebuild-iptables
...TRUNCATED OUTPUT...
```

8. Validate that the `iptables` rules have been loaded:

```
user@server:~$ sudo iptables -L
```

```
Chain FWR (1 references)
target     prot opt source               destination
ACCEPT     all  --  anywhere             anywhere
ACCEPT     all  --  anywhere             anywhere
state RELATED,ESTABLISHED
ACCEPT     icmp --  anywhere             anywhere
ACCEPT     tcp  --  anywhere             anywhere              tcp
dpt:http
ACCEPT     tcp  --  anywhere             anywhere              tcp
dpt:ssh
REJECT     tcp  --  anywhere             anywhere              tcp
flags:SYN,RST,ACK/SYN reject-with icmp-port-unreachable
REJECT     udp  --  anywhere             anywhere
reject-with icmp-port-unreachable
```

## How it works...

First, we download the `iptables` cookbook from the Chef community site.

Then, we modify our own cookbook to install `iptables`. This will set it up in such a way that all network connections are refused by default.

To be able to access the node via SSH afterwards, we need to open up `port 22`. To do so, we create the `my_cookbook/templates/default/ssh.erb` template and include the required iptables rule.

We do the same for `port 80` to accept HTTP traffic on our node.

The `iptables` cookbook will drop off those templates in `/etc/iptables.d` and configure `iptables` so that it loads all those files on startup. It installs the script `rebuild-iptables` to do this.

Finally, we make sure that `iptables` has been activated. We add this step because I saw that the `iptables` cookbook ran, but did not load all the rules. This is fatal because you deem your box secured, whereas in fact, it is wide open.

After doing all our modifications, we upload all cookbooks and run the Chef client on our node.

We can validate whether `iptables` runs by listing all the active rules with the `-L` parameter to an `iptables` call on our node. You see the `ACCEPT` lines for ports `http` and `ssh`. That's a good sign. The last two lines shut down all other services.

## See also

▶ Find the `iptables` cookbook on GitHub at `https://github.com/opscode-cookbooks/iptables`

# Managing fail2ban to ban malicious IP addresses

Brute-force attacks against any of your password protected services, such as SSH, and break-in attempts against your web server happen frequently for every public-facing system.

The `fail2ban` tool monitors your log files and acts as soon as it discovers malicious behavior in the way you told it to. One common use case is blocking malicious IP addresses by establishing firewall rules on the fly using iptables.

In this section, we'll take a look at how to set up a basic protection for by SSH using `fail2ban` and `iptables`.

## Getting ready

Make sure that you have a cookbook named `my_cookbook` and that the `run_list` of your node includes `my_cookbook`, as described in the *Creating and using cookbooks* recipe in *Chapter 1, Chef Infrastructure*.

Make sure that you have created the `ssh.erb` template for your `iptables` rule as described in the *Managing firewalls with iptables* recipe in this chapter.

Create your `Berksfile` in your Chef repository including `my_cookbook`:

```
mma@laptop:~/chef-repo $ subl Berksfile
```

```
cookbook 'my_cookbook', path: './cookbooks/my_cookbook'
```

## How to do it...

Let's install `fail2ban` and create a local configuration by enabling one additional rule to protect your node against **SSH DDos attacks**. This approach is easily extensible for various additional services.

1. Edit your cookbook's metadata.rb:

   ```
   mma@laptop:~/chef-repo $ subl cookbooks/my_cookbook/metadata.rb
   ```

   ```
   ...
   depends "iptables"
   depends "fail2ban"
   ```

2. Install your cookbook's dependencies:

   ```
   mma@laptop:~/chef-repo $ berks install
   ```

   ```
   Using my_cookbook (0.1.0) at './cookbooks/my_cookbook'
   ...TRUNCATED OUTPUT...
   ```

3. Edit your own cookbook's default recipe:

   ```
   mma@laptop:~/chef-repo $ subl cookbooks/my_cookbook/recipes/
   default.rb
   ```

   ```
   include_recipe "iptables"
   iptables_rule "ssh"

   node.default['fail2ban']['services'] = {
     'ssh-ddos' => {
         "enabled" => "true",
         "port" => "ssh",
         "filter" => "sshd-ddos",
         "logpath" => node['fail2ban']['auth_log'],
         "maxretry" => "6"
     }
   }
   include_recipe "fail2ban"
   ```

4. Upload the modified cookbook to the Chef server:

   ```
   mma@laptop:~/chef-repo $ berks upload
   ```

```
...TRUNCATED OUTPUT...
Uploading my_cookbook (0.1.0) to: 'https://api.chef.io:443/
organizations/awo'
...TRUNCATED OUTPUT...
```

5.  Run the Chef client on your node:

    **`user@server:~$ sudo chef-client`**

    ```
    ...TRUNCATED OUTPUT...
       * service[fail2ban] action restart
         - restart service service[fail2ban]
    ...TRUNCATED OUTPUT...
    ```

6.  Validate that your local fail2ban configuration has been created:

    **`user@server:~$ cat /etc/fail2ban/jail.local`**

    ```
    [ssh-ddos]

    enabled  = true
    ...TRUNCATED OUTPUT...
    ```

## How it works...

First, we need to install `iptables` because we want fail2ban to create iptables rules to block malicious IP addresses. Then, we pull the `fail2ban` cookbook down to our local Chef repository.

In our cookbook's default recipe, we install `iptables`.

Then, we define a custom configuration for fail2ban to enable the ssh-ddos protection. fail2ban requires you to put your customizations into a file called `/etc/fail2ban/jail.local`.

Then, we install fail2ban.

It first loads `/etc/fail2ban/jail.conf` and then loads `jail.local` overriding the `jail.conf` settings. This way, setting `enabled=true` for the ssh-ddos section in `jail.local` will enable that section after restarting the `fail2ban` service.

## There's more...

Usually, you want to add the recipe with the `fail2ban` configuration to a base role, which you apply to all nodes.

You can add more sections to the `['fail2ban']['services']` attribute hash, as needed.

## See also

▶  Read more about the *Managing firewalls with iptables* recipe in this chapter

▶  Find the `fail2ban` manual at the following location: `http://www.fail2ban.org/wiki/index.php/MANUAL_0_8`

▶  Find the `fail2ban` cookbook on GitHub at `https://github.com/opscode-cookbooks/fail2ban`

# Managing Amazon EC2 instances

**Amazon Web Services** (**AWS**) includes the **Amazon Elastic Compute Cloud** (**EC2**), where you can start virtual machines running in the Cloud. In this section, we will use Chef to start a new EC2 instance and bootstrap the Chef client on it.

## Getting ready

Make sure that you have an account at AWS.

To be able to manage EC2 instances with knife, you need security credentials. It's a good idea to create a new user in the **AWS Management Console** using **AWS Identity and Access Management** (**IAM**) as shown in the following document: `http://docs.aws.amazon.com/IAM/latest/UserGuide/Using_SettingUpUser.html`

Note down your new user's **AWS Access Key ID** and **AWS Secret Access Key**.

Additionally, you will need to create a SSH key pair and download the private key to enable knife to access your node via SSH.

To create a key pair, log in to AWS Console and navigate to **EC2 service** (`https://console.aws.amazon.com/ec2/home`). Then, choose **Key Pairs** under the **Network & Security** section in the navigation. Click on the **Create Key Pair** button and enter `aws_knife_key` as the name. Store the downloaded `aws_knife_key.pem` private key in your `~/.ssh` directory.

## How to do it...

Let's use the `knife-ec2` plugin to instantiate and bootstrap an EC2 node with Ubuntu 14.04 in the following way:

1.  Install the `knife-ec2` plugin to be able to use the AWS API via knife:

    ```
    mma@laptop:~/chef-repo $ chef gem install knife-ec2

    Fetching: knife-ec2-0.10.0.gem (100%)
    Successfully installed knife-ec2-0.10.0
    1 gem installed
    ```

2. Create your EC2 instance:

```
mma@laptop:~/chef-repo $ knife ec2 server create -d 'chef-full'
-r 'recipe[apt]' -S 'aws_knife_key' -x ubuntu -i ~/.ssh/aws_knife_
key.pem -I 'ami-fc99c294' -f 'm1.small' -A 'Your AWS Access Key
ID' -K 'Your AWS Secret Access Key'

Instance ID: i-01e227fd
Flavor: m1.small
Image: ami-fc99c294
Region: us-east-1
Availability Zone: us-east-1c
Security Groups: default
Tags: Name: i-01e227fd
SSH Key: aws_knife_key

Waiting for EC2 to create the instance.......................
Public DNS Name: ec2-54-161-86-119.compute-1.amazonaws.com
Public IP Address: 54.161.86.119
Private DNS Name: ip-10-145-212-110.ec2.internal
Private IP Address: 10.145.212.110

Waiting for sshd access to become available......done
Connecting to ec2-54-161-86-119.compute-1.amazonaws.com
ec2-54-161-86-119.compute-1.amazonaws.com Installing Chef
Client...
...TRUNCATED OUTPUT...
ec2-54-161-86-119.compute-1.amazonaws.com Chef Client finished,
3/4 resources updated in 26.807762127 seconds
...TRUNCATED OUTPUT...
```

 You need to look up the most current AMI ID for your node at http://cloud-images.ubuntu.com/locator/ec2/ and use it in your knife call, instead of ami-fc99c294. See the following How it works... section for more details about how to identify the correct AMI.

3. Log in to your new EC2 instance:

```
mma@laptop:~/chef-repo $ ssh -i ~/.ssh/aws_knife_key.pem ubuntu@
ec2-54-161-86-119.compute-1.amazonaws.com

Welcome to Ubuntu 14.04.2 LTS (GNU/Linux 3.13.0-46-generic x86_64)
...TRUNCATED OUTPUT...
ubuntu@ip-10-145-212-110:~$
```

## How it works...

First, we need to install the EC2 plugin for knife. It comes as a Ruby gem.

Then, we need to make a few decisions on which type of EC2 instance we want to launch and where it should run:

1.  Decide on the node size. You'll find a complete list of all the available instance types at the following location: `http://aws.amazon.com/ec2/instance-types/`. In this example, we'll just spin up a small instance (`m1.small`).

2.  Choose the **Region** to run your node in. We use the AWS default region US East (Northern Virginia) in this example. The shorthand name for it is `us-east-1`.

3.  Find the correct **Amazon Machine Image** (**AMI**) by navigating to `http://cloud-images.ubuntu.com/locator/ec2/` and selecting the desired one based on the Availability Zone, the Ubuntu version, the CPU architecture, and the desired storage mode. In this example, we'll use the 64-bit version of Ubuntu 14.04 LTS code named trusty, using instance-store. At the time of writing this, the most current version was `ami-fc99c294`.

As soon as you know what you want to achieve, it's time to construct the launch command. It consists of the following parts:

The `knife-ec2` plugin adds a few subcommands to knife. We use the `ec2 server create` subcommand to start a new EC2 instance.

The initial parameters we will use to deal with the desired Chef client setup are as follows:

▶  `-d 'chef-full'`: This asks knife to use the bootstrap script for the Omnibus installer. It is described in more detail in the *Using custom bootstrap scripts* recipe in this chapter.

▶  `-r 'recipe[apt]'`: It defines the run list. In this case, we install and run the `apt` cookbook to automatically update the package cache during the first Chef client run.

The second group of parameters deals with SSH access to the newly created instance:

▶  `-S 'aws_knife_key'`: This lists the name of the SSH key pair you want to use to access the new node. This is the name you defined in the AWS console while creating the SSH key pair.

▶  `-x ubuntu`: This is the SSH username. If you use a default Ubuntu AMI, it is usually `ubuntu`

▶  `-i ~/.ssh/aws_knife_key.pem`: This is your private SSH key, which you downloaded after creating your SSH key pair in the AWS console

The third set of parameters deals with the AWS API:

- ► `-I 'ami-fc99c294'`: This names the AMI ID. You need to take the latest one, as described in the preceding paragraph.

- ► `-f 'm1.small'`: This is the instance type, as described in the preceding point

- ► `-A 'Your AWS Access Key ID'`: This is the ID of your IAM user's AWS Access Key

- ► `-K 'Your AWS Secret Access Key'`: This is the secret part of your IAM user's AWS Access Key

> The AWS Access Key ID and AWS Secret Access Key are the security credentials of a user, who is allowed to use the AWS API. You create such users in the IAM section of the AWS management console.
>
> The SSH key pair is there to secure the access to your nodes. By defining the name of the key pair in the knife command, the public key of your SSH key pair will be installed for the SSH user on your new node. You create such SSH key pairs in the EC2 section of the AWS management console.

The command will now start a new EC2 instance via the AWS API using your AWS credentials. Then, it will log in using the given SSH user and key and run the given bootstrap script on your new node to make it a working Chef client and register it with your Chef server.

## There's more...

Instead of adding your AWS credentials to the command line (which is unsafe as they will end up in your shell history), you can put them into your `knife.rb`:

```
knife[:aws_access_key_id]   = "Your AWS Access Key ID"
knife[:aws_secret_access_key] = "Your AWS Secret Access Key"
```

Instead of hard coding it there, you can even use environment variables to configure `knife`:

```
knife[:aws_access_key_id] = ENV['AWS_ACCESS_KEY_ID']
knife[:aws_secret_access_key] = ENV['AWS_SECRET_ACCESS_KEY']
```

> Never expose your `knife.rb` file to a public Git repository!

The `knife-ec2` plugin offers additional subcommands. You can list them by just typing the following command line:

```
mma@laptop:~/chef-repo $ knife ec2

    ** EC2 COMMANDS **
    knife ec2 flavor list (options)
    knife ec2 instance data (options)
    knife ec2 server create (options)
    knife ec2 server delete SERVER [SERVER] (options)
    knife ec2 server list (options)
```

## See also

 ▸ Read more about the *Using custom bootstrap scripts* recipe in this chapter

 ▸ Find the `knife-ec2` plugin on GitHub at `https://github.com/chef/knife-ec2`

# Loading your Chef infrastructure from a file with spiceweasel and knife

Having all your cookbooks, roles, and data bags as code under version control is great, but having your repository alone is not enough to be able to spin up your complete environment from scratch again. Starting from the repository alone, you will need to spin up nodes, upload cookbooks to your Chef server, and recreate data bags there.

Especially when you use a Cloud provider to spin up your nodes, it would be great if you could spin up your nodes automatically and hook them up to your freshly created and filled Chef server.

The spiceweasel tool lets you define all your cookbooks, data bags, and nodes, and generates all the necessary knife commands to recreate your complete environment, including spinning up nodes and populating your empty Chef server or organization on the hosted Chef.

Let's see how to dump our current repository to spiceweasel and how to recreate our infrastructure with it.

## Getting ready

Make sure that you are able to spin up Amazon EC2 instances using knife, as described in the *Managing Amazon EC2 instances* section in this chapter.

## How to do it...

Let's use `spiceweasel` to dump our current configuration, add some EC2 nodes and recreate our complete environment:

1.  Install the `spiceweasel` Ruby gem:

    **`mma@laptop:~/chef-repo $ chef gem install spiceweasel`**

    ```
    Fetching: spiceweasel-2.8.0.gem (100%)
    Successfully installed spiceweasel-2.8.0
    1 gem installed
    ```

2.  Let `spiceweasel` dump your current repository into a `infrastructure.yml` file:

    **`mma@laptop:~/chef-repo $ spiceweasel --extractyaml > infrastructure.yml`**

3.  Look into your new `infrastructure.yml` file (the contents depend on the current state of your Chef repository):

    **`mma@laptop:~/chef-repo $ cat infrastructure.yml`**

    ```
    ---
    berksfile:
    cookbooks:
    - apt:
        version: 2.6.1
    - heartbeat:
        version: 1.0.0
    roles:
    - monitoring:
    - web_server:
    ...TRUNCATED OUTPUT...
    ```

4.  Print all the knife commands and `spiceweasel` will run:

    **`mma@laptop:~/chef-repo $ spiceweasel infrastructure.yml`**

    ```
    berks upload -b ./Berksfile
    knife cookbook upload apt heartbeat
    knife role from file monitoring.rb web_server.json
    knife data bag create accounts
    knife data bag from file accounts google.json
    knife data bag create hooks
    knife data bag from file hooks request_bin.json
    knife data bag create nagios_services
    ```

```
knife data bag from file nagios_services ssh.json
knife data bag create users
knife data bag from file users mma.json
```

5. Let `spiceweasel` run the knife commands, as follows:

   **mma@laptop:~/chef-repo $ spiceweasel -e infrastructure.yml**

   ```
   ...TRUNCATED OUTPUT...
   Data bag users already exists
   Updated data_bag_item[users::mma]
   ```

## How it works...

The spiceweasel tool scans your local Chef repository and notes down everything as a YAML file.

When reading a YAML file, it generates knife commands to make the contents of the Chef repository available on the Chef server.

## There's more...

You can define nodes in your `infrastructure.yml` file either as local nodes, which spiceweasel will then bootstrap, or nodes for cloud providers. spiceweasel will then create `knife <provider> server create` commands for each specified node.

Using nodes in your `infrastructure.yml` file enables you to recreate a complete environment, including all the necessary VMs using spiceweasel.

You can use spiceweasel to delete your setup from your Chef server by using the `--delete` flag when running spiceweasel:

**mma@laptop:~/chef-repo $ spiceweasel --delete infrastructure.yml**

## See also

▶ You can find the source code of spiceweasel on GitHub at `https://github.com/mattray/spiceweasel`

# Index

**Thank you for buying**
**Chef Infrastructure**
**Automation Cookbook**
*Second Edition*

# About Packt Publishing

Packt, pronounced 'packed', published its first book, *Mastering phpMyAdmin for Effective MySQL Management*, in April 2004, and subsequently continued to specialize in publishing highly focused books on specific technologies and solutions.

Our books and publications share the experiences of your fellow IT professionals in adapting and customizing today's systems, applications, and frameworks. Our solution-based books give you the knowledge and power to customize the software and technologies you're using to get the job done. Packt books are more specific and less general than the IT books you have seen in the past. Our unique business model allows us to bring you more focused information, giving you more of what you need to know, and less of what you don't.

Packt is a modern yet unique publishing company that focuses on producing quality, cutting-edge books for communities of developers, administrators, and newbies alike. For more information, please visit our website at www.packtpub.com.

# Writing for Packt

We welcome all inquiries from people who are interested in authoring. Book proposals should be sent to author@packtpub.com. If your book idea is still at an early stage and you would like to discuss it first before writing a formal book proposal, then please contact us; one of our commissioning editors will get in touch with you.

We're not just looking for published authors; if you have strong technical skills but no writing experience, our experienced editors can help you develop a writing career, or simply get some additional reward for your expertise.

## Chef Essentials

ISBN: 978-1-78398-304-9        Paperback: 218 pages

Discover how to deploy software, manage hosts, and scale your infrastructure with Chef

1. Learn how to use Chef in a concise manner.

2. Learn ways to use Chef to integrate with cloud service such as EC2 and Rackspace Cloud.

3. See advanced ways to integrate Chef into your environment, develop tests, and even extend Chef's core functionality.

## Instant Chef Starter

ISBN: 978-1-78216-346-6        Paperback: 70 pages

A practical guide to getting started with Chef, an indispensable tool for provisioning and managing your system's infrastructure

1. Learn something new in an Instant! A short, fast, focused guide delivering immediate results.

2. Learn the core capabilities of Chef and how it integrates with your infrastructure.

3. Set up your own Chef server for managing your infrastructure.

Please check **www.PacktPub.com** for information on our titles

# Chef Infrastructure Automation Cookbook

ISBN: 978-1-84951-922-9        Paperback: 276 pages

Over 80 delicious recipes to automate your cloud and server infrastructure with Chef

1. Configure, deploy, and scale your applications.

2. Automate error prone and tedious manual tasks.

3. Manage your servers on-site or in the cloud.

4. Solve real world automation challenges with task-based recipes.

# Managing Windows Servers with Chef

ISBN: 978-1-78398-242-4        Paperback: 110 pages

Harness the power of Chef to automate management of Windows-based systems using hands-on examples

1. Discover how Chef can be used to manage a heterogeneous network of Windows and Linux systems with ease.

2. Configure an entire .NET application stack, deploy it, and scale in the cloud.

3. Employ a step-by-step and practical approach to automate provisioning and configuration of Windows hosts with Chef.

Please check **www.PacktPub.com** for information on our titles

www.ingramcontent.com/pod-product-compliance
Lightning Source LLC
Chambersburg PA
CBHW060528060326
40690CB00017B/3417